Art Photography

David Bate

ART PHOTOGRAPHY

Tate Publishing

First published 2015 by order of the Tate Trustees by Tate Publishing, a division of Tate Enterprises Ltd, Millbank, London SW1P 4RG www.tate.org.uk

A catalogue record for this book is available from the British Library

ISBN 978 1 84976 224 3

Distributed in the United States and Canada by ABRAMS, New York

Designed by Micha Weidmann Studio
Colour reproduction by DL Imaging, London
Printed in Hong Kong by Printing Express

Front cover:
John Hilliard, *Sixty Seconds of Light* 1970 (detail of fig.60)

Back cover:
Tom Hunter, *Woman Reading Possession Order* 1998 (detail of fig.7)

Measurements of artworks are given in centimetres, height before width and depth

CONTENTS

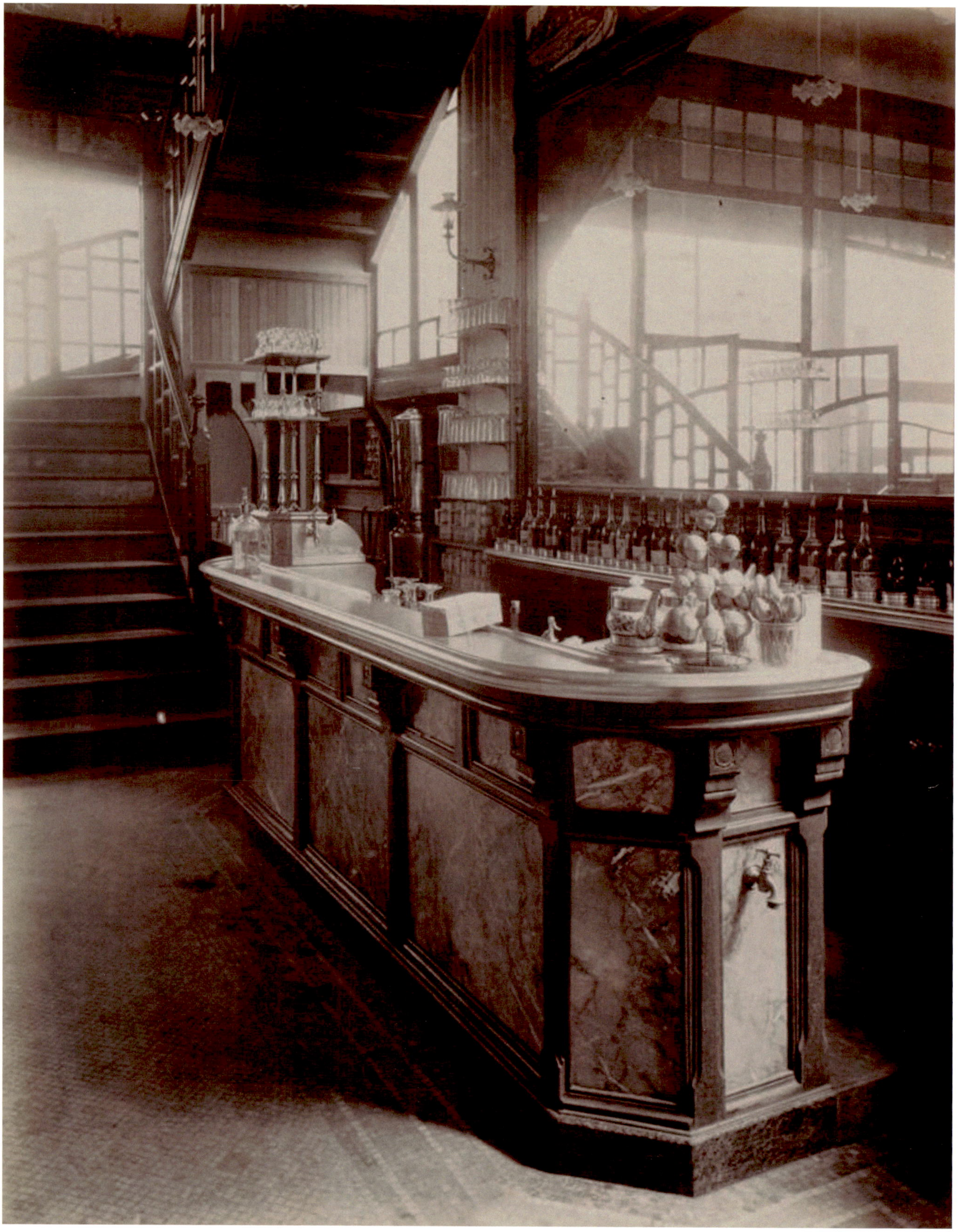

INTRODUCTION

Recent books on art photography have tended to focus on the last few decades. With good reason they have acknowledged, showcased and celebrated the interest in the new expanding world of contemporary art photography.[1] In this book I have taken a longer view though, partly due to preference, but also because the question of what makes photography 'art' today demands a different historical outlook and approach. Where photography was once considered the second cousin of art, relegated to the margins, today it is firmly at the centre of contemporary art discourses. With the spatial arts on one side (painting, sculpture and installation) and the temporal arts on the other (video, digital media and performance), photography is pivotal to the mutability of these practices. The photographic image is central in both the dark-box technology of the cinema and the white walls of the gallery. Photography is as implicated in the layout of magazines and book pages as the illuminated screen of the computer. In analogue and digital forms, the photographic image has mutated the assumed relations between different media. These changes speak not only to the history of media technology, but to alterations in culture, which also have their impact on art practice. The new centrality of photography in art belongs to this history and set of circumstances, but is caught in a time lag within art history, trailing behind in these accounts. So the aim of this book is not to show the 'latest thing' in photography, but to show how and why photography is so central in art.

The photographic image remains a central and most dominant form of visual image across contemporary culture. For this reason, many may find the distinction between art and non-art photography hard to sustain. Indeed, long ago, John Berger showed how art, reproduced through photography, had already permeated throughout everyday culture.[2] Images of art could be found used or quoted in advertising, fashion, and reproduced on the walls of our homes to make claims for specific cultural values. So can 'art photography' be justified as a separate category? If there were no contextual information available, would it be possible to say whether a photographic image was from art or advertising? Photography is so prolific and central to almost all domains of everyday life that such distinctions may appear to have become completely dissolved, and only further diffused by the way websites also mix all kinds of pictures together, making it hard to know what is what. Yet art and advertising are clearly separate institutions with different functions, even if their use of art images overlaps.

Equally, the photojournalist or passionate amateur photographer has developed distinct sets of visual practices, which, despite any commonality as digital images, are not entirely interchangeable or compatible. Photography, in fact, is a plural term in the same way that 'writing' and 'painting' refer to a host of different practices – writing a letter is clearly

1 Anglophone examples here would be Susan Bright, *Art Photography Now* London 2005; David Campany, *Art and Photography*, London 2003; Charlotte Cotton, *The Photograph as Contemporary Art*, London 2004; Demos 2006, and Soutter 2013.

2 Berger 1972.

Figure 1
Eugène Atget, *Marchand du vin, rue Boyer* 1910–11
From the album *Métiers, boutiques et étalages de Paris* (1912)

not the same as writing a report, a novel or a shopping list. Photography is similarly polymorphous. Yet there is something specific to the function of art that photography is involved in. Changes in contemporary art and aesthetics are very much linked to the rise of photography in art, but also across all cultural spheres. Photography is hard to ignore as an established, if not dominant, practice, and its extensive worldly presence means that art is almost obliged to interrogate its uses, even while it stole the clothes of these other practices in the process. We are no longer faced with the same attitudes towards photography as art of even two or three decades ago, and so it is possible to embark on a slightly different project.

This book introduces art photography via a series of different 'frames'. The first chapter frame is explicitly historical and pursues the idea of the 'photographic' as an image value that precedes the actual invention of photography. Only a positivist historian would claim that the idea of photography arrived with the technical invention of photographic chemistry. As the curious interaction between Dutch seventeenth-century painting, specifically Rembrandt and Vermeer, and pictorial ideas in early photography demonstrates, there is a remarkable homology between them, with questions about the link recurring ever since. The subsequent aesthetics of nineteenth-century photographic pictorialism (and new-pictorialism in the 1990s) were always various and frayed, becoming more so as it devolved into formalist modernism. Modernist photography was a kind of compromise, made up on the one hand of an aesthetic belief in the descriptive realism found in Dutch painting, and the compositional abstractions invoked by cubist art of the early twentieth century on the other. Twentieth century modernism settled on the 'straight' photograph as aesthetic truth, embodying a set of photographic ideas derived from Eugène Atget in Europe. The third chapter shows how, even though Atget did not consider himself an artist, his work became a pivotal model for avant-garde and modernist photography movements in Europe in the 1920s and 1930s, and for the new modernist art photography established in the USA after his canonisation.

The role played by a younger generation of post-World War II artists emergent in the 1950s, defined now as 'conceptual' art brought another function to bear on photography in art. Conceptual uses of photography were, to put it mildly, ambiguous or hostile toward any claim that it was 'artistic'. Deeply suspicious of the sentimental values of humanism involved in Cold War and imperialist politics, such art rejected the traditional aesthetics of beauty that pictorial and modernist photography had fought to achieve. In this sense conceptual art was 'anti-aesthetic', since its pleasures came through routes other than optical pleasure. Conceptual artists began to absorb, interrogate and respond to the modern media society that now saturated modern social, cultural and private lives. Some of these issues were inherited by postmodernism, the fashionable term introduced in the late 1970s and 1980s, first in New York and then elsewhere, to recognise the intrusion and mixing of popular culture into art, the appropriation of mass media and confusions of historical style and content. Although some features of conceptualism were retained in postmodernism, even weakly, these strategies were situated in a new and different way, as indicated below.

3 Lessing 1984.

4 It is only really with the legacy of modernist art photography discourse that critics retrospectively assume pictorialism had tried to abolish social content too.

5 See Eklund 2009.

Each of the key categories used in chapters here – pictorialism, documentary, conceptualism – all feature in art today. They are separated into chapters for clarity, but they overlap in significant ways in practice. Contemporary art photography continues to mutate or hybridise as it negotiates itself, its social environment and histories. The categories of art photography are certainly not mutually exclusive, as their repeated historical shifts have shown. Notwithstanding this, I try to lay out the conditions that inform them, while also beginning to broaden their international scope beyond the usual confines of a European-North American axis. The final two chapters, on the archive and geographic imagination, examine these different fields of practice in terms of time and space respectively.

Time and space, the two categories that Gotthold Lessing separated the arts into in his 1766 essay The Laocoön, has continued to haunt the visual arts ever since.[3] The influential US art critic Clement Greenberg, in his 1940 essay 'Towards a Newer Laocoön', revised the distinction, turning it into a dogmatic rejection of literature and time in visual art altogether. In Greenberg's view, photography had to be purified, not of representation, which was essentially the character of photography for him, but of narrative implication or story, as in photojournalism. For Greenberg such work belonged to mass culture and thus kitsch. This distinction declined during 1980s postmodernism. While photography initially inherited much of the aesthetic baggage of painting, these were rejected under the ideology of early twentieth-century modernism. The modernist aim was initially to develop 'pure' art photography, uncontaminated by commercial or industrial photography. The capacity of photographic art to exorcise any social purpose was severely limited in this model without resorting to abstraction.[4] Social meanings had to be turned into formal attributes, in effect making a cul-de-sac argument. This model collapsed under the strain of its own attempts to abstract photography (painting and sculpture too) from social reference, and the competing discourse of conceptualist art re-established it. Conceptualist art since the 1950s called up references to everyday life, politics, mass-media images and visual culture and metamorphosed them into art. Andy Warhol's pop art – coloured screen-print versions of iconic American images: Coca-Cola, Marilyn Monroe, Elvis Presley – serves as an early obvious example, in stark contrast to painting's drift from representation into abstraction. Even though pre-war art of the European avant-gardes (dada and surrealism) had already appropriated news and magazine pictures to show a different way in art by engaging directly with the orthodox, consensual values of popular culture to dismantle them, it was to be almost fifty years before the programme of modernist photography was officially challenged. This challenge came in the 1980s. Postmodernism and the success of the so-called pictures generation artists like Cindy Sherman, Richard Prince, Louise Lawler, Sherrie Levine and others who used photography, which notably included far more women artists than ever before.[5]

In postmodernism, artists drew freely on imagery from popular media culture, from advertising and fashion images, cinema and news photography, not only as a source of material but also of style. Slick and glossy colour photography made the gallery walls glow with vibrant effects, rich with a new and exciting ambivalence. Was art photography now just another form of popular culture, a complicit celebration of popular ideology? Or did postmodernist art open up a visual space to examine or critique this popular culture? Some consider this very ambiguity to be a postmodern tactic to place spectators in the position of having to ask questions and infer meanings for themselves. This was decidedly different from modernist art, which was supposed to instil awe in the spectator as the technical and aesthetic skill of the artist, a signifier of their inherent genius. The preponderance of photography in postmodern art also had another effect: photography re-entered the art world via the commercial 'kitsch' culture that Greenberg had rejected, distorting the aesthetic values that art discourse had come to assume. This postmodern art could thus be understood as in implicit opposition to the dominant economic values of modernist high art, which - unlike earlier conceptualist ambitions - were distorted into the wild commercial success of later shock-effect art.

Modernist ideas of aesthetic autonomy and purism had already been challenged through the critical frame of conceptual art and theory, most notably in writings by conceptual artists that developed the critical art uses of photography: Victor Burgin, Martha Rosler and Allan Sekula.[6] Postmodernism, however, had made optical pleasure acceptable again, aligning it with the 'base' visual pleasures of popular imagery in advertising and media images, albeit conditioned with an ironic wink to a knowing viewer. The overt theatricality in much of this work made it clear this was social criticism by other means: irony, parody and pastiche. By the 1990s a panoply of new 'neo-pictorial' realist photography was being developed in new forms of spectacle, returning with a vengeance. Most clearly articulated by the Canadian artist Jeff Wall and European photographers like Andreas Gursky and Thomas Struth, these new varieties of large-scale pictorial image turned photography away from ironic quotation of media images towards the representation of an 'everyday life' aesthetic. The large-scale photographs competed with painting for equal space on the wall. Dubbed as a 'return of the real', the pictorial paradigm has itself mutated, like the earlier pictorialism before it, into various strands of photo-collage, critical realism and new forms of (digital) abstraction.[7]

Yet perhaps such a narrative places too much emphasis on a singular story, one of which we have become suspicious. Wary of grand narratives that tend to exclude alternative or oppositional discourses and their practices, there is a growing consciousness that art photography is multiple, diverse and global. Perhaps it is true that art history is indeed no longer linear and we can recognise that art in one place may be addressing questions that are not asked in another. Globalism means recognising localism, yet does this mean we should give up on grand narratives altogether, an excuse to drop attempts to understand history?

It is striking how far pictorialism, documentary and conceptualist practices have been central to the international developments of photography in art, even if they have been overlooked as world or global movements. Early pictorialism, for example, emergent in late nineteenth-century Britain, quickly became international and is surely the first world art movement in photography. By the time of its demise in the 1920s and 1930s, pictorialist aesthetics had been taken up globally, not only across Europe and the USA, but also in Australia, Canada, New Zealand, Japan Africa and South America. Equal global arguments can be made for

6 See Burgin 2009; Sekula 2003; Rosler 2004.

7 See Squiers 2014.

8 Rancière 2007, pp.22–9.

9 The term 'dissensus' is opposed to 'consensus' in Rancière 2010.

documentary and conceptualist art too. Any account of these movements requires nuance, recognising local practices and rules and parameters of discourse, even if they later became hybridised with local variant aesthetics mutating over time. The relation between art and non-art photography has been crucial to these developments.

Accustomed to thinking that photography is about showing the world as it is, it may come as a surprise to hear that art photography has not followed this idea. In a 2002 lecture at the National Centre of Photography in Paris, the French philosopher Jacques Rancière argued that the aim of contemporary art is not to produce resemblances, but dissemblances. The claim may seem counter-intuitive to the many devotees of art photography who consider the function of the medium to be to show things 'as they are' in mimesis. This book aims to explore these artistic operations of dissemblance as they have specifically operated through photography in art, and to explore some of the many ways that photography and art have intersected since the invention of the medium.

In his lecture Rancière introduced three different categories of interaction between what he calls the 'aesthetic regime of art' with non-art images: the naked image, the ostensive image and the metamorphic image.[8] A naked image is one not intended as art, but which ends up in art because of its document-like qualities – an aspect that applies to specific types of document photograph. The ostensive image is one that refers to something that is not itself, as often in conceptual art. The metamorphic image is one that refers to commercial or media imagery, filtered back into art with difference. These categories, which we could clearly name as document, conceptual and postmodern (or allegory), are taken up where relevant, their associated strategies noted as a means to open up a space for visual dissensus (not consensus).[9] The new centrality of the photographic image in art recognises the necessity of such engagements of art outside itself. Photography is a pervasive social practice linked to all social types of image use and thus porous to changing definitions and practices. Such interactions are now crucial to what we consider art to be and what photography performs within it.

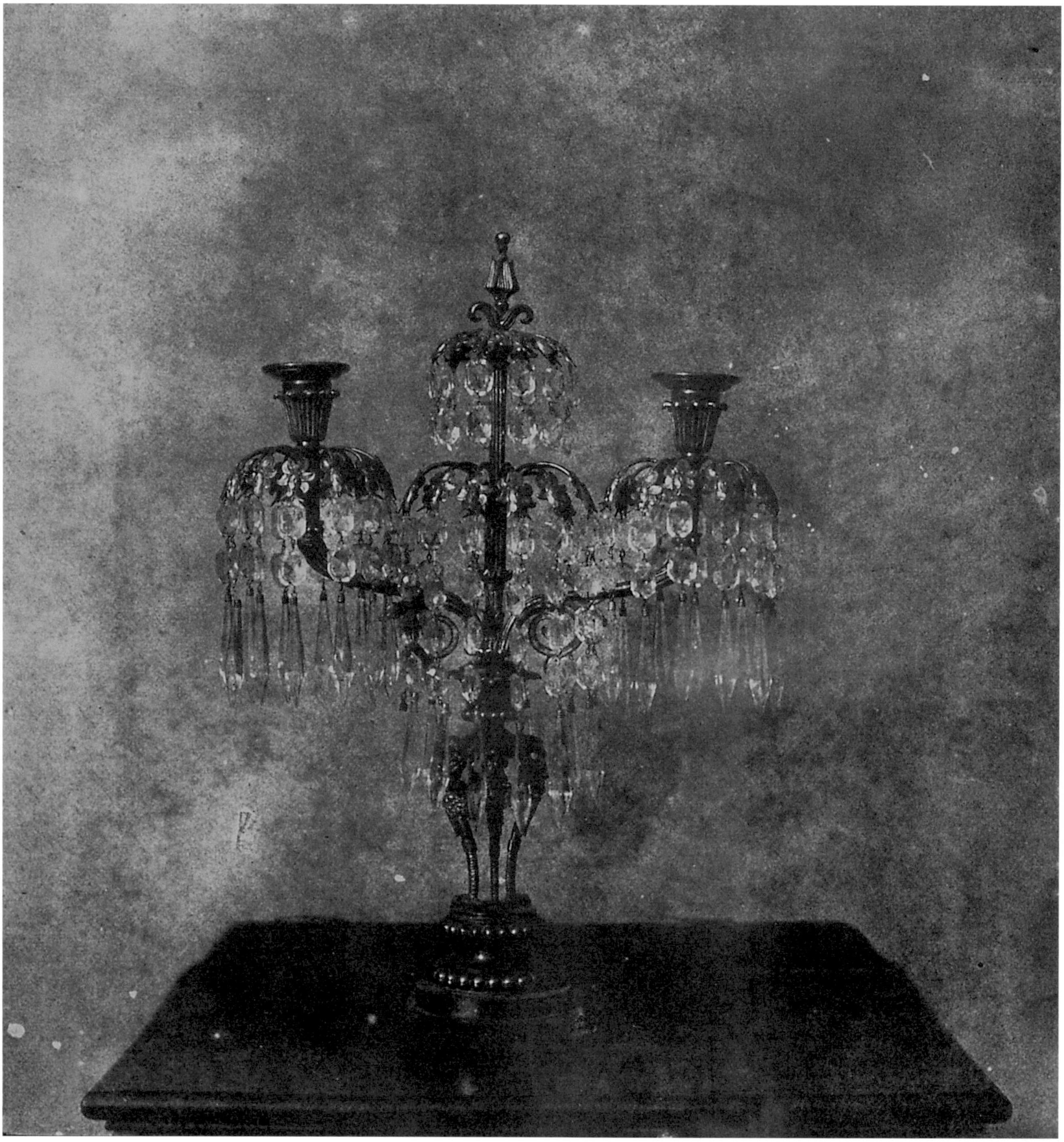

THE IDEA OF PHOTOGRAPHY

Can you imagine a world without photography? Given that photographic images are so abundant today, it is worth considering what the idea of photography meant before such a thing existed materially. In this way we can reflect on some of the foundational issues that photography raises, not only for art – and painting particularly, which it was considered to rival – but for the role of visual images in culture ever since. The historical idea of 'photography' involves an archaeology of the present and the photographic image today.

Even though the discovery of photography seems a long time ago, its invention belongs to a set of wider industrial transformations, which turned manual crafts into mechanical arts. Today the cultural origins of photography seem even further away, with the ubiquity of digital photography and the computer system that has replaced older analogue systems. It may also be worth noting here that declarations about the 'end of photography', with the advent of digital imagery, have long been premature. Rather like the old phrase 'The King is dead. Long Live the King!', used to anoint a new king upon the death of the old one, it is as though this has been adopted for photography: 'Photography is dead. Long live photography!' Digital photography has not denied photography an existence; rather, it has not only inherited the clothes and estates of the analogue forms of photography, albeit in mutated forms – it has also rapidly expanded them.

Ideas and Origins

As is common with many inventions, the *idea* of photography began long before it was actually discovered. The story of how the three main ingredients of photography – light, chemistry and the camera obscura – were organised and combined is much longer than that of the discovery of photography itself. Some may even argue that only one of these three components really constitutes the idea of photography: the chemical action of light registered on a material surface.[1] This is because the other key ingredients – the use of light to produce perspectival images via the camera obscura and optics – were already familiar before the invention of photography. But this would be to misrepresent the origin of photography, since the wish to fix permanently the fugitive images appearing on the screen of the camera obscura was already an earlier ambition.

Thus the invention of photography is part of a longer and more complex history of picture construction. While the development of optical lenses and theories of light had long since been sources of speculation in mathematics and science, they only later developed in the visual arts when geometry and perspective became central to Renaissance European art during the 1400s. Notably this begins with the practical architectural

1 'Chemistry' has of course now mostly been replaced by electronic sensors in cameras, along with the computer technics that control them, the main effect of which has been to speed up and automate the process of integrating images into the computer networks that cameras are now usually linked to.

Figure 2
William Henry Fox Talbot, *Ornate candelabra* 1843
Salt print from calotype negative, 22.6 × 18.6

Talbot invented the first negative/positive process for producing photographs between 1835 and 1839. This meant that for the first time any number of prints could be made from the same scene by transferring the negative image on to special paper to make a positive print. Talbot's process for achieving this is known as the calotype process.

experiments of Filippo Brunelleschi and the *Della Pictura* treatises of Leon Battista Alberti, in which he claimed painting as a 'window on the world'.[2]

The separate pre-photographic histories of perspective, geometry, the camera obscura and lenses, which are often confused, are important because they indicate the specific interests in knowledge acquired through vision as a system, an idea that both precedes and informs the later development of photography.

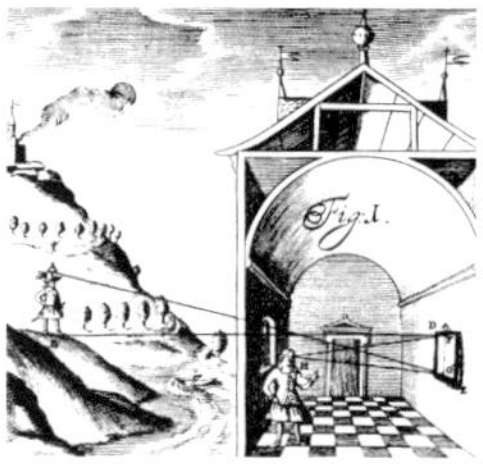

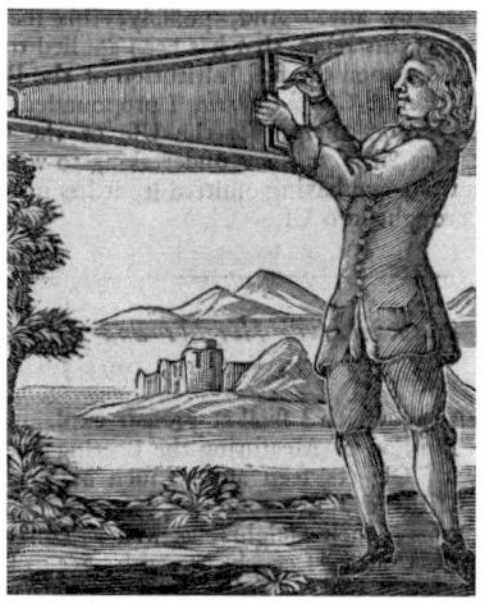

Figure 3
A camera obscura from *Magia Universalis* (1657) by German physicist Gaspar Schott.

A camera obscura is a box or darkened room with a lens or hole through which an image of an external object is projected onto the opposite internal wall. The camera obscura was known to the ancient Chinese and Greeks, and was used by Arab astronomers in the tenth century to observe the sun and by Renaissance artists to help them draw 'accurately'.

Figure 4
A small, portable camera obscura designed by Robert Hooke (1694)

From *Philosophical Experiments and Observations* (1726)

The Picture Box

The camera obscura or 'dark room' is essentially a box or room with a small aperture on one side. The light that is cast on the opposite wall creates an upside down image of the view outside. The popular thrill derived from seeing any camera obscura image is that it appears 'automatically', producing as if by magic the upside-down view of what is opposite the pinhole lens. Interest in light and the effect of the camera obscura can be traced back to antiquity, or even earlier. In the fifth century BCE the Chinese philosopher Mo Ti had already identified this optical effect of light to form an image.[3] In the thirteenth and fourteenth centuries there is evidence of the camera obscura being used as a technical aid by astronomers, enabling them to look at the sun indirectly. The image cast on the wall of a dark room was far from blinding, and an added lens produced a better, sharper image for study. In the fifteenth century, when European Renaissance painting took up the geometry of perspective, Leonardo da Vinci compared the anatomy of the human eye to a camera obscura, although it does not appear to have been used by artists in the study of perspective or to make pictures.[4] A century later a popular book by Giovanni Battista della Porto, a nobleman and scientist from Naples, is credited with popularising the camera obscura as a device for entertainment. *Magia Naturalis*, first published in 1558 and expanded in 1589, was widely translated and included a range of subjects about natural elements, animals, food, tips on everyday life, health and living, in addition to later sections on optics and the camera obscura.[5]

Porto, like many others in Europe after him, drew on the works of the Arab mathematician and scholar Abū ʿAlī al-Ḥasan or Alhazen as he had become known in medieval Europe.[6] Alhazen was born in Basra about 965 and worked in Egypt, where his important texts on optics, light and perspective were written. He died in Cairo in 1039. His numerous treaties included commentaries on ancient Greek texts by Aristotle, Euclid, Ptolemy and many others. His works, like *De aspectibus* or *Perspectiva* c.1015, developed the foundation for modern theories of vision, and became highly influential in Europe following their retranslation in the sixteenth century.[7] Like da Vinci, Porto considered the human eye to be a miniature camera obscura, despite the curvature of the human retina, and this analogy would play a key role in subsequent arguments about art and perception. After the invention of photography the details of these issues would inform the development of new lenses, as well as questions about subjective and objective vision.

It was the German astronomer and optics specialist Johannes Kepler who finally gave the modern name 'camera obscura' to the device, which he had learnt of from Porto's book.[8] Kepler made his own camera obscura with a lens in 1620 for the purpose of observing solar activity, and noted

2 See White 1987, pp.113-4; also Edgerton 1976.

3 Hammond 1981, p.1.

4 The first published illustration of a camera obscura is said to be in 1544 by the Dutch mathematician and astronomer, Reinerus Gemma Frisius. See Steadman 2001, p.5.

5 Lindberg 1976, p.184.

6 Other versions of his name are Ibn-Hasan or Ibn al-Haytham. See Lindberg 1976, p.58.

7 Lindberg 1976, p.86.

8 Steadman 2001, pp.4-5.

9 Lindberg 1976, p.24.

10 Ibid., pp.185–205.

11 Hammond 1981, p.82.

the advantage of a convex lens to invert the image, making it the correct way up for the human eye.[9] Of course, we now know that the image on the back of the human eye is also received upside down. It is Kepler's study and improvements in optical devices that should really be credited with founding modern optics.[10] The role of optics and lens design is often a neglected dimension in the history of photography and the camera obscura, but it is of central importance to the formation of visual images. Lenses are used to organise and reorganise the light that is refracted through them, for example to help to sharpen the overall image or to convert the perspectival shape to better suit human vision.

Figure 5
Abelardo Morell,
Camera Obscura, View of Central Park. Looking North – Fall 2008 2008

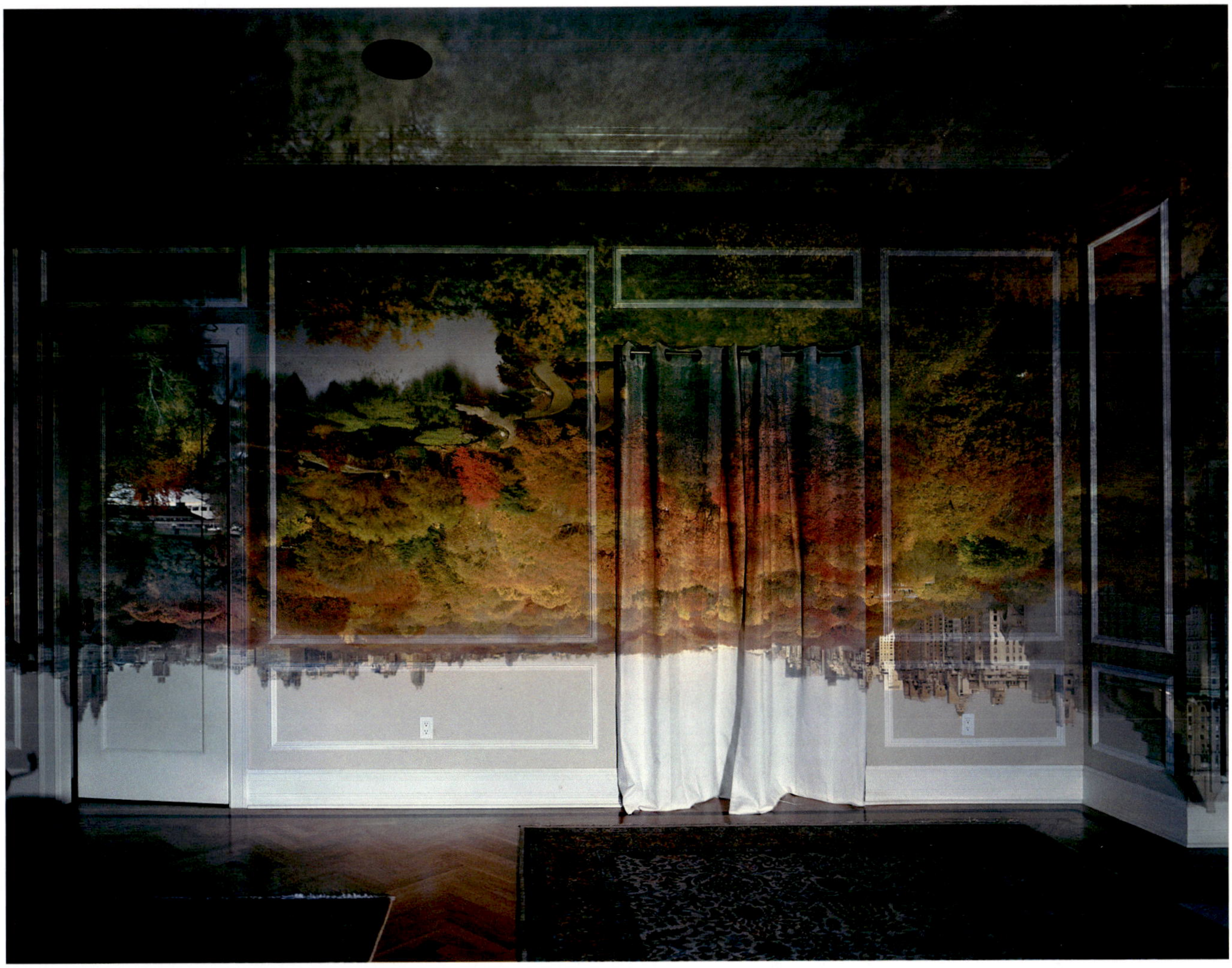

Representation

By the eighteenth century the notion of the camera obscura image as 'nature writing a picture' was already a well-established idea.[11] Portable models of the camera obscura were commercially available, made of wood, sometimes with canvas and lenses attached to improve the clarity and definition of their images. These cameras had an opaque glass screen, used for tracing the projected scene onto paper or another material. Robert Hooke (fig.4) had demonstrated his portable version to the Royal Society as early as 1694 and published an illustration of his 'picture-box',

Figure 6
Johannes Vermeer, *Girl Reading a Letter at an Open Window* 1657–9
Oil paint on canvas, 83 × 64.5
Gemäldegalerie Alte Meister, Dresden

Figure 7
Tom Hunter, *Woman Reading Possession Order* 1998
Ilfochrome print, 150 × 120. From the series *Persons Unknown*

which he suggested would be of use to 'curious navigators and travellers'.[12] This novel use, he argued, would help travellers on land or sea in 'procuring the pictures, draughts, or true forms and shapes of such things as are, or may be taken notice of by them'.[13] In other words, the device could help the untrained person to produce picture representations of the places they visited, the shores, plants, people and insects there, and as illustrations for travel books. Thus the impulse of the operator to fix an image produced by the camera obscura was already evident long before chemical photography was ever conceived.

A qualification is required here, though. While the camera obscura is often linked to use by artists as a tool for composing pictures, this should not be immediately linked to the emergence of perspective in Renaissance art. It is argued that Alberti, for example, makes no reference to the camera obscura in his famous 1435 treatise on perspective and drawing.[14] His theories were constructed through mathematics and geometry, with models of perspectival vision and pictorial space that were not necessarily consistent with images produced by the camera obscura, as can be seen in early Italian art of the period. While the effect of the camera obscura was known at this time, it is not explicitly linked to painting and pictorial space until later in the sixteenth century, and only then as an aid to drawing.[15] In Hooke's 1694 presentation to the Royal Society, the camera obscura was seen as a tool for scientific knowledge, for the observation of nature and not in relation to art. Furthermore, even once the camera obscura was widely known and available in the eighteenth century, some artists, such as William Hogarth, still wanted nothing to do with it. Even

12 Hooke 1930, pp.753–6.

13 Hooke 1930, pp.753–6.

14 See Hammond 1981, p.40; also Edgerton 1976, pp.89–90.

15 Leonardo da Vinci, for example, links the effect of the camera obscura to the human eye, but not to painting or perspective directly. Hammond 1981, p.40.

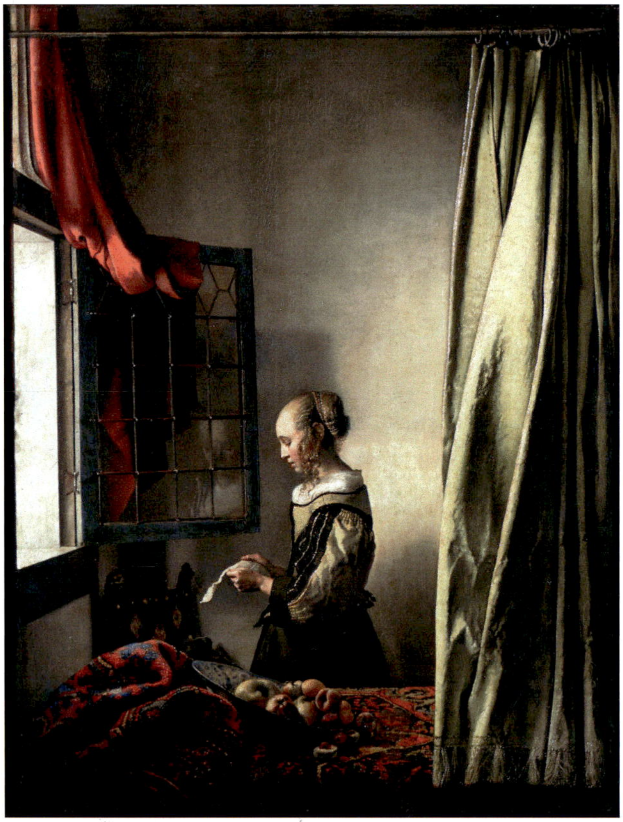

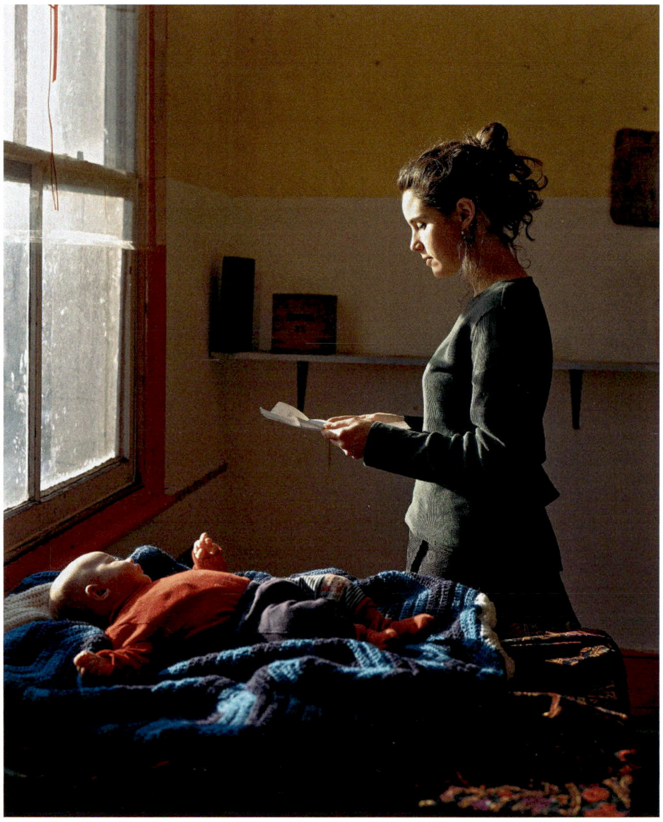

Hunter photographs the people and places of his immediate community. In this photograph he makes explicit reference to the composition and colours from Vermeer's *Girl Reading a Letter at an Open Window* to address a modern issue.

Joshua Reynolds, who owned one, did not use it or advocate its employment to make paintings.[16] The common assumption that art has been wholly driven by the desire to 'perfect' perspective is not true, since the visual aims of art have varied from era to era and from society to society.

The Photographic Effect

However, the question of the historical relation between the camera obscura and perspectival painting has preoccupied art historians for decades. The usual case study is the work of Dutch painter Jan Vermeer, whose paintings are credited, in hindsight, with being highly 'photographic' in appearance (fig.6).[17] These European paintings are modern in another sense, in that they are secular, having little or nothing to do with religious stories. Instead, they construct a view of the everyday domestic space and lives of ordinary people, much as a photograph might today. The Dutch art of this period is descriptive of the human habitat, with paintings of scenes that, as Roland Barthes once put it, aim 'to accumulate the secondary vibrations of appearance'.[18] In these paintings it is at though we are really there inside the scene. It is this type of illusion of three-dimensional space and perspectival verisimilitude that is identified with photographic realism.

Because the seventeenth-century Dutch tradition of 'descriptive' painting has a distinct quality of 'photographic' space, some art historians have speculated that Vermeer's paintings were made with or were indeed derived from the visuality of a camera obscura.[19] A recent case study of his work by Philip Steadman marshals extensive circumstantial evidence in an attempt to prove that Vermeer knew and used the camera obscura in his work, even though the evidence does not lead directly to Vermeer's door.[20] In *Vermeer's Camera* (2001) Steadman conducts a detailed iconographic analysis of the rooms in Vermeer's paintings, concluding that he did in fact use a camera obscura. However, he notes: 'The truth is that Vermeer manages to achieve "photographic" results while painting in a way which is often locally imprecise, where focus is sometimes lost, where areas of colour may be simplified and flattened, texture obliterated.'[21] Steadman thus concedes 'that to copy or work from an image of a camera obscura is distinctly not like taking a photograph. The process is not instantaneous but protracted.'[22] The difference between painting and photography is indicated here as a question of time and mechanical precision of representation.

Quite what all these comparisons of photography and painting prove in the end is not really very much at all, beyond the recognition that if painters did use a camera obscura, the interaction led to a different style of painting than that produced in Italy, for example, by way of other models of geometry and perspective.[23] It also has to be said that such technical discussions are less interesting than they seem, and tend to ignore the substance of the pictures. After all, exactly what is the significance of all these scenes of young women trapped in domestic spaces - despite the bright daylight shining in through the windows that illuminates them - usually remains beyond the realms of such discussion. Certainly, the verisimilitude of these spaces enables human relations to be addressed in a place no longer as sacred as in Renaissance art. Dutch art is tangibly human, and constructs primarily a visual space for the viewer to inhabit that is

16 Ibid., p.47. Samuel Edgerton reinforces this point: 'Human beings generally, even those born with so-called artistic talent, are never automatically inclined to draw images in the same way we perceived them perspectivally - that is, according to the geometric-optical laws of vision.' See Edgerton 2009, p.3.

17 Canaletto is the other common example cited in art history. See Hammond 1981, pp.42-6.

18 Barthes 2000, p.64.

19 Erwin Panofsky, for example, notes that Northern or Dutch perspective varies from Italian Renaissance perspective, due to the 'peculiarly Northern ideal of an impression of a quite specifically interior space, that is, an impression of including the beholder within the represented space'. See Panofsky 1997, p.81.

20 Steadman 2001.

21 Ibid., p.156.

22 Ibid., p.161. In a more recent book Svetlana Alpers hints that the studio itself is used like a camera obscura, especially in the Dutch tradition. See her essay 'The View from the Studio' in Alpers 2005.

23 This is really the main argument of David Hockney's book, *Secret Knowledge: Rediscovering the Lost Techniques of the Old Masters*, London 2001.

recognised as 'natural', human and realistic. It is this verisimilitude of what can be called the photographic effect that would become the defining aspiration for the later industrial developments of photography. In summary, then, the fascination of the camera obscura in the pre-history of photography had already touched a variety of social fields of visual interest, and was put to work in different contexts, from entertainment to science and eventually art. This multiple and complex history is, of course, exactly what photography also inherited.

With the invention of photography in the nineteenth century, the relations of pictures to vision, art and society are transformed by the reproducible image that has served industrial culture so well in so many areas. Yet more than this, the analogy between camera and human vision also begins to dominate different intellectual fields of thought, with seeing as believing at the centre of the idea of 'photographic vision'. This new privilege given to human vision – named as the scopic drive – was extended into photographic images and is developed further through computerised versions of photography. Art remains a key realm in which the aims of this representational vision is still directly addressed or contested.

The Photographic Apparatus

Two different historical drives can be seen to have informed the invention of photography: on the one side, the desire for illusion and imagination; on the other, to capture the transient real world in an image. Both drives coalesced in the need to fix an image and the pursuit of the means to do this. The invention of photography was motivated by the need to fix the evasive images registered by light onto a chemically based material, whether from the camera obscura screen image or directly onto paper, copper, etc. For the sake of convenience more than of historical accuracy, these two drives can be personified by the two key developers of the photographic apparatus: Louis Jacques Mandé Daguerre and William Henry Fox Talbot.[24] These figures serve to show the respective tendencies of the desire to fix images in the service of the imagination and the reproduction of reality. The locations of these two historical inventors of photography were England and France. Let's start with Daguerre in France.

Louis Daguerre, the inventor of the first useable system for making photographic images, was a trained painter. He was apprenticed at seventeen to the Italian chief theatre set designer Ignace E.M. Degotti at the Paris Opera in 1804.[25] With a demonstrated ability in drawing, Daguerre was also something of an acrobat – he could walk a tightrope and cross the studio on his hands – and showed a precocious propensity for spectacle and illusion. After three years he became an assistant to the prominent painter Pierre Prévost, whose panorama paintings of famous battle scenes, picturesque harbours, landscapes and views of famous cities (Amsterdam, London, Paris and Rome) were hugely popular pre-cinema entertainment attractions. It was in this context of theatre sceneography and panorama painting that Daguerre invented his own new commercial enterprise, the Diorama, with architectural painter Charles Marie Bouton in 1821. The Diorama was a huge panorama, with scenes that dissolved into one another, from night to day or day to night, and across different scenes altogether. This animated effect of time on landscapes was achieved with transparent paints and carefully

24 For a recent re-evaluation of Daguerre and his career see Pinson, 2012.

25 Gernsheim 1968, p.4.

placed lights, back and front, transforming what the audience saw. The Diorama was so successful that Daguerre opened another one in London. He clearly knew how to put on a good public show, and his work can be situated in a long line of public visual entertainments, from ancient forms of firework displays and theatre to the contemporaneous popular entertainments of the panorama, diaphanorama and cosmorama. Since these inventions were intended as a spectacle to amaze or mystify their audiences and to lose them in reverie, it is curious, then, that Daguerre's photographic invention should spark a similar craze with the daguerreotype by transforming it into a highly personal and private experience. This silver and iodine-based photographic technology enabled people to carry around miniature pictures of themselves and their loved ones, to cherish or to show friends, just as we might still do with a small mobile screen device today.[26]

The history of photography often assumes that Daguerre invented the photographic process. However, this was, as far as we know, another Frenchman, Joseph Nicéphore Nièpce, who had already fixed an image photographically on pewter plates in 1826.[27] Daguerre agreed a contract with Nièpce in 1829 to improve the formula, but Nièpce died in 1833 before success was achieved. Daguerre continued the work somewhat obsessively and developed a better process to achieve the stability required to claim the invention. Thus, we should really, as Helmut and Alison Gernsheim suggested in 1955 in their magisterial *The History of Photography*, credit Nièpce with the invention of photography in 1826, and Daguerre as the inventor of the first practical process in 1838.[28] Daguerre then famously sold the invention to the French government, who announced it in August 1839 – the date often cited as the official birth of photography – and in effect gave it to the world free, without copyright. The significance of that moment can be considered as important as the transformation of communications and visual media heralded by the invention of the World Wide Web in 1992.

26 Cinema returned the favour; and the public spectacle returned, of course, with the invention of cinema.

27 Gernsheim 1968, p.51.

28 Ibid., p.103.

29 Ibid., p.164.

30 Bann 2001, p.108.

Daguerreotype

The daguerreotype, so named by the painter Antoine F.J. Claudet,[29] one of its early fans, was crisp, sharp and amazingly detailed. Printed on a silver-coated copper sheet, its disadvantage was that only one copy was possible. Nevertheless, soon after its invention, shops selling the apparatus were besieged and Paris was suddenly full of the black box cameras on three-legged tripods, planted in front of famous buildings. Curiously, it does seem to be buildings that attracted early photographers, perhaps due to the process's long exposure times, and despite the swell of portraiture that soon followed and became the dominant early commercial application. The first artist to take up the new practice, landscape painter Horace Vernet, embarked on a trip to Egypt with daguerreotype equipment within months of its public release.[30]

The daguerreotype was taken up very quickly in the USA, with portraiture studios opening all over the country after improvements to the process made it more efficient to use and faster for mass production. One jewel-case maker called Matthew Brady started making cases for daguerreotypes, but soon turned to making daguerreotypes themselves. He opened his own daguerreotype studios: one on Broadway, New York,

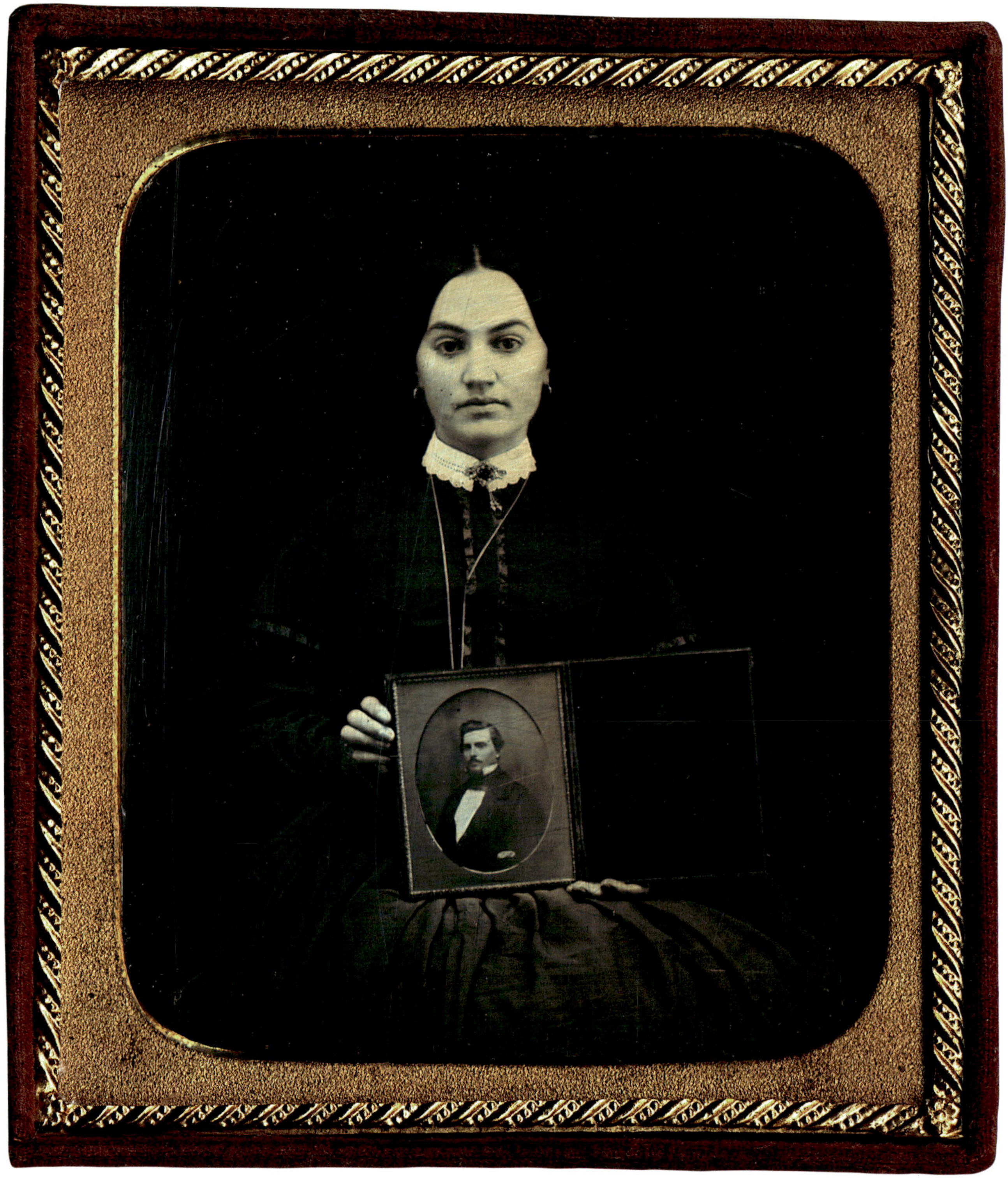

in 1844, another in Washington DC in 1847 and another at the other end of Broadway in 1853, a particularly lucrative location due to the celebrities and society people who promenaded nearby.[31] Brady's, as it was called, accrued a fortune before the company finally folded in the 1870s with the commercial failure of his US Civil War photography, for which he had employed twenty photographers. The portrait studio craze had already spread to other cities too: to Boston in 1841, with the establishment of Southworth and Hawes' studio, and to Philadelphia in 1842 with Frederick and William Langenheim. The Langenheim brothers also tried to import the English calotype invented by Talbot, but this did not displace the supreme popularity of the daguerreotype, which boomed in USA until the late 1850s.[32]

As soon as Daguerre's process was declared public, others who had already been working on their own processes speeded up attempts to conclude them. In February 1839 Friedrich Gerber, at Berne University, Germany, announced that he had already fixed images from a camera obscura onto paper.[33] Albrecht Beyer, a medical student in Liège, Belgium, produced heliographic pictures in March 1839, while another Frenchman, Hippolyte Bayard, had independently fixed a positive image directly onto paper by May 1839.[34] There were others too, in one place or another before and after this, who would make similar claims, but the real international success of Daguerre's process, and its official announcement by the French government, overshadowed them all.

Calotype

In England, William Henry Fox Talbot had also been experimenting for several years, and on hearing of Daguerre's invention in early January 1839, accelerated his own work to hastily present an outline of his quite different process to the Royal Institution by the end of that month.[35] Talbot was a busy man of science, a typical if eminent English gentleman scholar with a prolific interest in a wide range of fields, including mathematics, linguistics (specifically philology and translation), astronomy, a life-long passion for botany and, as it would turn out, the chemistry of photography.[36] In 1832 he was briefly elected as a Member of Parliament; he published numerous papers on mathematics, was a member of the Royal Astronomical Society, the Royal Society and the Royal Institution, and in 1839 alone he published four books and twenty-seven scientific papers.[37] In 1841 Talbot patented his improved photographic process, the calotype (derived from the Greek word for beauty), which proved to be the first viable negative-positive process. As many prints as desired could be made from a single negative, thereby overcoming a drawback of the singular daguerreotype process.[38] Whereas Talbot's negatives were on paper, and later on glass,[39] and could be used to make multiple prints on paper, Daguerre's images were on metal and one-off. Although the daguerreotype had better detail, which could be explored even with a magnifying glass, Talbot's system lent itself to making multiple copies of prints, for example as illustrations in books. Talbot's assistant Nicholas Henneman set up the first photographic establishment to mass-produce prints in Reading, England, in 1843, and it was here that the plates of Talbot's publication *The Pencil of Nature*, issued in parts between 1844 and 1846, was produced – the first ever photography book.

31 See Beaumont Newhall, 'The Broadway Galleries', in Newhall 1976.

32 See Newhall 1976, pp.49–51. The Langenheim brothers also became agents for Voigtländer's metal camera with a Joseph Petzval designed special portrait lens.

33 Gernsheim 1969, p.88.

34 Eder 1978, pp.334–6.

35 Schaaf 2000, p.16.

36 Schaaf 1992, p.12.

37 Schaaf 2000, p.11.

38 The first person to be granted a license to practice Talbot's calotype process was Henry Collen, who established the first calotype studio in London. See Gernsheim 1969, pp.163–4.

39 According to the Gernsheims, the earliest extant photograph on glass was taken by John F. Herschel in September 1839 and shows the scaffolding of his father's telescope. Gernsheim 1969, p.110, pl.39.

Figure 8
Woman seated, holding full plate daguerreotype portrait of a man c.1850
Daguerreotype, 8 × 6

There is an obvious parallel with today's hand-held portable computer devices, which also store images for display.

What is evident from these independent forays into photography is that it was a dispersed but simultaneous project right from the start. There is no single origin. The forerunners in this – England and France – while traditional rivals, had much in common as countries undergoing industrialisation, and in this respect the development of photography is intertwined with the history of the industrial revolution.[40] The new photographic process developed into the industrial mass-production of pictures, with work undertaken to achieve improvement in the quality of image production to make it faster, simpler and cheaper. And so began mass-produced photography.

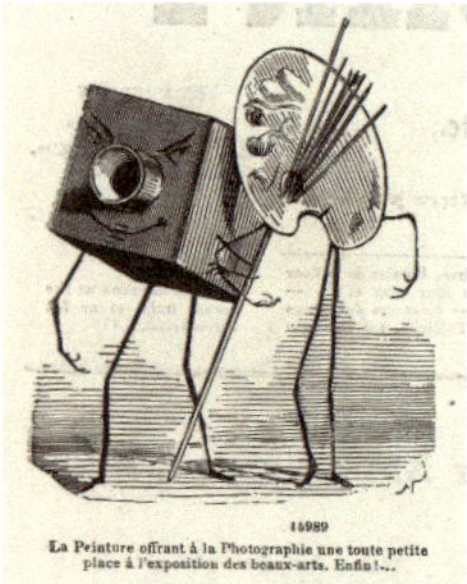

Figure 9
Nadar, *The ingratitude of Painting. Refusing the Smallest Place in its Exhibition, to Photography to whom it Owes so much* 1857
Cartoon from *Le Journal Amusant* (17 January 1857)

This old history of the mechanisation of pictures has moved into another stage since the late twentieth century, with the 'electronicisation' of pictures. The photographic image is now integrated within computer digital systems and data networks, and globally introduced to all cultures, whether industrialised or not. This transformation has played a profound role in understandings of the world, also raising the awkward issue of the relation between art and non-art photography. We might again consider this issue by returning to the origin of photography, precisely because this was a question already faced then too. The mechanisation of image-making through photography created as many questions about the idea of art as electronic developments do today. So I now turn this question into a historical matter: what did art mean for photography and photography for art?

Photography and Art

Some qualification of the term 'art' is required. Although there are many instances of the new invention of photography being referred to as an art, this was often in the context of technical discussions. 'Art' was used in recognition of the skill and knowledge involved, just as we might speak of the 'art of cooking' or the 'art of writing'. This use of the term is exemplified in the title of John Herschel's paper 'On the Art of Photography; or the application of the chemical rays of light for the purpose of pictorial representation' delivered at the Royal Society, London, in March 1839.[41] Herschel was also the first to use the term 'photography' in public (although others had used the term privately before), as well as the adjective 'photographic', as opposed to 'photogram' or Talbot's term 'photogenic'.[42] Herschel, like Talbot, was a scientist, and although he had an interest in art, and sketched travel scenes, he could hardly be described as an artist. Like many others, he collected images as a means to advance scientific knowledge. The camera obscura, camera lucida, telescope, microscope and photography were all aids to this extension of the scope of human vision with prosthetic devices aiming to improve macro and micro vision, or to fix the images produced by them.[43] This expansion of human vision, the 'optical unconscious' as Walter Benjamin would later call these magnifications of things the human eye cannot see, could thus also be argued as extending into art too.[44] This historical dichotomy between art and science has not gone away. While none of the art academies in France or England acknowledged photography when it was first invented, artists themselves would have a different view.[45]

When Daguerre submitted his invention to the French government, a committee of artists, led by the painter Paul Delaroche, were asked to report

40 By the 1840s Britain, Germany and the USA were all in the process of industrialisation; France was slower, with the upheavals of the 1848 revolution. See Eric Hobsbawm, 'Towards an Industrial World', in Hobsbawm 1997.

41 Gernsheim 1969, p.96.

42 Eder 1978, pp.258–9.

43 The camera lucida had a split mirror that enabled the user to look both at the scene they wished to draw and the drawing. It was slightly tricky to use and many found it frustrating, including Talbot. Herschel's camera lucida drawings can only be described as 'elementary'. For examples, see Schaaf, 1989.

44 Walter Benjamin, 'The Short History of Photography', in Trachtenberg 1980, p.203.

45 See Aaron Scharf, *Art and Photography*, Harmondsworth 1979, p.34.

on its potential uses, including its artistic value. Several painters – Thomas Couture, Jean-François Millet and Charles Daubigny – then students with Delaroche, immediately took up photography, although their fame is now for their contributions to painting.[46] Delaroche concluded that photography 'has rendered an immense service to the arts', although it has never been very clear exactly what this service was.[47] Some imagined – and perhaps still do – that photography would be simply an aid to art, for artists to reproduce paintings and record exhibitions, or to help make preliminary preparations for artworks. Later many others had the more radical vision that art would be usurped by photography because of its speed and veracity, and for its apparent democratic accessibility.

Yet the debates around photography were more complex than merely placing it in a simple dichotomy of art versus science. Louis Daguerre and Henry Fox Talbot are again useful cases in point. Daguerre, an artist and entrepreneur, was orientated towards visual spectacle and popular public entertainment; although as one of the new French artists interested in landscape, his paintings are still in many art collections today, including the Louvre in Paris.[48] He was particularly fond of picturesque sceneography with gothic overtones, bleak interiors and ruins, and his landscape

46 Ibid., p.36.

47 It should be noted that the famous phrase 'from today painting is dead' is wrongly attributed to Delaroche, who certainly did not give up painting. See Bann 2001, pp.91–2

48 For a comprehensive review of Daguerre's work in painting see the 'Catalogue of Works' in Pinson 2012, pp.151–220.

49 Bann 2001, p.102.

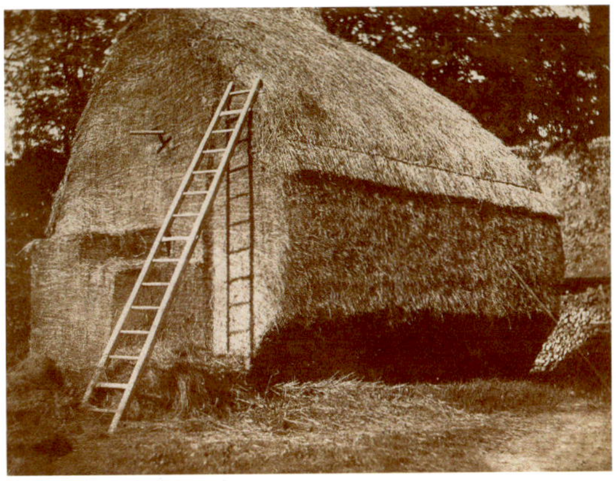

Figure 10
William Henry Fox Talbot, *The Haystack* April 1844
Plate X from *The Pencil of Nature* (1844–5)
Salt print from calotype negative, 16.4 × 21

paintings also feature the same chiaroscuro light as his diorama scenes. Talbot, meanwhile, was a widely read 'amateur' scholar and man of science, less familiar with the art world of London or Paris than Daguerre. Curiously, though, in retrospect it is Talbot who is often considered to be a better photographic artist, more attuned to modern ideas, freed from the academic artistic conventions of his time and seemingly more motivated to experiment with photography. Daguerre seems not to have grasped the potential for this new technology to make different kinds of pictures, or at least he left that to others to pursue. In his later years, for example, he turned to pastels and watercolour pictures.[49] Talbot, on the other hand, relished all kinds of subject matter. While he had developed a traditional gentleman's passion for collecting paintings in the 1820s, albeit in an amateur capacity, this did not seem to inhibit his visual taste. Talbot's self-proclaimed frustrations at his inability to draw, and his reputed desire to 'preserve' the sight of the lakes of Northern Italy, were nevertheless what had spurred him on to invent photography.

Talbot was quick to point out the advantages of photography for artists with his picture *The Haystack* 1844 (fig.10), published in *The Pencil of*

Nature. Pointing to the future, Talbot wrote, alongside the photograph: 'one advantage of the discovery of the Photographic Art will be, that it enables us to introduce into our pictures a multitude of minute details which add to the truth and reality of the representation, but which no artist would take the trouble to copy faithfully from nature. Contenting himself with a general effect, he would probably deem it beneath his genius to copy every accident of light and shade, nor could he do so indeed, without a disproportionate expenditure of time and trouble which might be otherwise made better employed.'[50]

The texture of the haystack and strong sunlight in his composition lend themselves well to this delight in mass detail. Talbot, already speaking the language of industrial labour efficiency (the 'expenditure of time and trouble'), nevertheless displays a familiarity with the art discourse of the day. For Talbot, the artist would 'deem it beneath his genius to copy every accident of light and shade'. In fact, with this remark Talbot shows that he understands the aim of art to be different from the mere reproduction or 'copying' of nature. No doubt the term 'pencil' in *The Pencil of Nature* had a double meaning, at once a metaphor for the way light in photography traces the contours of an object, and also the early calotype's rendering of subjects in shades of grey. The difference between a pencil and a camera in this metaphor also cleverly evades the issue of copying, with its implications of accuracy and detail, although, interestingly, Talbot did actually use a pencil sometimes to retouch his prints.

The copying of nature, or the mimetic reproduction of the objects in front of the camera, does not necessarily turn a picture into art. On the other hand, of course, Talbot is quite aware that the automatic recording of detail by the photographic image is one of the virtues of the process. The camera is 'the pencil of nature' held in the hand of the photographer, but whether this hand belonged to an artist or copyist was another issue. Even though photography could automate the process of recording any scene in detail, this did not by itself constitute photography as an aesthetic or an art. Thus one question was, what exactly did photography bring to art? Yet conversely, as Talbot saw it, there was another question about the much wider social potential for photography, and he in many ways anticipated its numerous subsequent other uses. However, it is Talbot's views on art that are often highlighted in his text.

Talbot again alludes to art in *The Pencil of Nature* when he refers to his picture *The Open Door* 1844 (fig.11), suggesting that an image may become art if the artist has the necessary sensibility to perceive it as such:

'We have sufficient authority in the Dutch school of art, taking as subjects of representation scenes of daily and familiar occurrence. A painter's eye will often be arrested where ordinary people see nothing remarkable. A casual gleam of sunshine, or a shadow thrown across his path, a time-withered oak, or a moss-covered stone may awaken a train of thought and feelings, and picturesque imaginings.'[51]

The Open Door is the first picture in the second part of *The Pencil of Nature*, and has generated much speculation about what Talbot's imaginings were, whether there are deeper meanings to this simple scene of a broom, stable yard door and dark interior.[52] Like many of his pictures, this one has a modest but elegant composition. The broom across the door offers a ready metaphor for photography 'sweeping away' the darkness

50 Quoted in Schaaf 2000, p.198.

51 Ibid., p.196.

52 Talbot made the picture *Garden implements in front of a hedge* in 1840, and *The Soliloquy of the Broom* in January 1841. See Schaaf 1992, p.99; Schaaf 2000, pp.106–7;

53 See Green 1990, p.99.

54 Williams 1979, p.48.

55 For a discussion of picturesque composition and the beautiful see David Bate, 'Notes on Beauty and Landscape', *Shifting Horizons*, Liz Wells (ed.), London 2000.

within, the lantern hanging on the right side of the door offering another clue. Yet Talbot was also keen at this time to show how his process could produce a finely detailed image, qualities enhanced here in the bright sunlight and contrasting shadow. It is worth remembering that at this time the daguerreotype process had better definition and astonishingly sharp detail in comparison to Talbot's calotype. This is why Talbot's reference to the Dutch school of painters is so significant, as he hints that the 'painter's eye' is brought to photography via Dutch art, through Vermeer's descriptive impulse and Rembrandt's chiaroscuro light.

Talbot was probably the first to propose a relation between photography and the photographic style of Dutch art. Many have since returned to this pictorial genre convention as a reference point for photography (see figs.6 and 7), and this line of thinking became, within a few years, translated into theories and practices of pictorialism. As it happens, those same Dutch paintings of everyday life genre scenes were also very popular at that time, and were frequently taken up by collectors of art as a form of secure financial investment.[53] Talbot finds a double authority in the Dutch school, first as a historical precedent for the aesthetics of photography in the detailed representation of everyday secular life, and

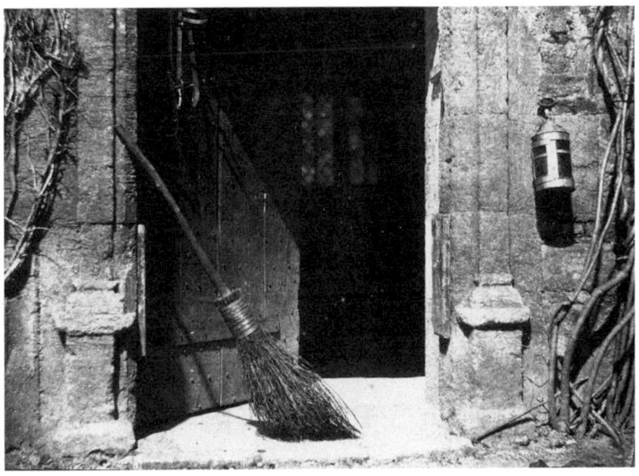

Figure 11
William Henry Fox Talbot, *The Open Door* April 1844
Plate VI from *The Pencil of Nature* (1844–5)
Salt print from calotype negative, 14.3 × 19.4

secondly as a visual style, the value of which was already established in the social taste of the period.

The 'picturesque imaginings' that Talbot invokes in his text are embodied by the romantic artist, more concerned, as the cultural historian Raymond Williams once put it, with 'natural beauty and personal feelings' than with social or politics affairs.[54] These expressive feelings are to be brought to photography through a harmonious and detailed picturesque composition, such as Talbot saw in Dutch painting. Talbot thus brings a conventional idea of the beautiful or 'picturesque' into photography as art. The beautiful image is a scene that aims to abolish any tension or conflict, whether social, political or compositional, and to subdue it with positive feelings of aesthetic harmony.[55] The picturesque is intended to cathartically rejuvenate the spirits of viewers, especially those embroiled in the turmoil of daily life. The vast audiences who paid to swoon before Daguerre's landscape dioramas in the cities of Paris and London, for example, are also a testimony to this desire for the cathartic process of 'picturesque imagining', taking the viewers 'somewhere else'. Talbot's ideas on art in photography have this much in common with Daguerre's paintings and diorama scenes, although there is far more gothic tension suggested in Daguerre's work than in Talbot's placid musings on descriptive pictorial ideals. As mentioned above, Talbot was driven by scientific interests, and yet his observational studies of botanical and other specimens are also beautiful, inflected with ideals of harmony in nature. Photography offered a new type of visual space in which these apparently contradictory impulses of scientific interest and aesthetic beauty could co-exist or merge, the phrase 'the pencil of nature' being the encapsulation of just such a fusion.

Beauty in Nature

Just as with the term 'art', we should not take the term 'nature' too literally in these early discourses on photography, or imagine that it is a singular object or concept. While nature referred to things that were not industrial or cultural, it also had inconsistent meanings. For natural scientists, for example, nature reflected that which God had made, although Charles Darwin's theories would soon challenge this theological view. For the time being, though, natural scientists like Talbot considered themselves to be recording the details of a pre-given nature with a photographic process. In art, however, there was a different modern discourse on nature, exemplified by the writings of critic and poet Charles Baudelaire. Nature 'teaches us nothing', Baudelaire argued, 'being none other than the voice of our own self-interest'.[56] The idea of nature invoked here is a fully human nature. Baudelaire continues: 'Evil happens without effort, naturally, fatally; Good is always the product of some art'.[57] In this conception, nature is not the botanist's harmless insect specimens or leaves pressed against a glass plate to show off their prettiness, but the wild, uncivilised contradictory vices of humankind, of which Baudelaire apparently had first-hand experience. For him, art was urbane, a civilising virtue intended to tame human nature, a definition closer to what today we would call an aesthetic pleasure. Such were the terms of modern art, a nineteenth-century discourse that was already different from the scholarly science of Talbot and the sentimental Victorian ideal of nature-as-beautiful. While it might have been claimed that such discourses of beauty and aesthetics expired in the late twentieth century, and were finally dead with the emergence of postmodernism in the 1980s, they certainly seem to still be alive today, revived even with the demise of analogue photography.

In his influential 1863 essay, 'The Painter of Modern Life', Baudelaire's understanding of nature as something hostile to be tamed is extended to everything, including women. Cosmetics, he argued, were part of this civilising endeavour. For him, art was not about truth or the ugliness of the world, as brought forth by photography, but beauty and the imagination. His writings and poetry mobilised new ideas and images of art. While his views on nature and beauty were undoubtedly problematic, they also chimed with his views on photography. His essay 'The Salon of 1859' was a review of the art salon in the year when photography was first included (albeit in a separate space to the fine art exhibition). It is worth quoting at length, for it is crucial in situating attitudes to the 'progress' of photography: 'Poetry and progress are like two ambitious men who hate one another with an instinctive hatred, and when they meet upon the same road, one of them has to give place. If photography

56 Baudelaire 2012, p.32.

57 Ibid., p.32.

58 Charles Baudelaire, 'The Salon of 1859', extracts reprinted in Frascina and Harrison 1982, p.20.

59 'The shortcomings of Edward Weston's art ... His camera defines everything, but it defines everything in the same way...' Greenberg 1986, p.61.

60 Other daguerreotypes by Daguerre in 1839 also show high viewpoints. See *View of the Pont Neuf* (pl.26) and *View of the Pavilion de Flore* (pl.28) in Pinson 2012.

is allowed to supplant art in some of its functions, it will soon have supplanted or corrupted it altogether, thanks to the stupidity of the multitude which is its natural ally. It is time, then, for it to return to its true duty, which is to be the servant of the sciences and arts - but the very humble servant, like printing or shorthand, which have neither created nor supplanted literature. Let it hasten to enrich the tourist's album and restore to his eye the precision which his memory may lack; let it adorn the naturalist's library, and enlarge microscopic animals; let it even provide information to corroborate the astronomer's hypotheses; in short, let it be the secretary and clerk of whatever needs an absolute factual exactitude in his profession - up to that point nothing could be better. Let it rescue from oblivion those tumbling ruins, those books, prints and manuscripts which time is devouring, precious things whose form is dissolving and which demand a place in the archive of our memory - it will be thanked and applauded. But if it be allowed to encroach upon the domain of the impalpable and the imaginary, upon anything whose value depends solely upon the addition of something of a man's soul, then it will be so much the worse for us!'[58]

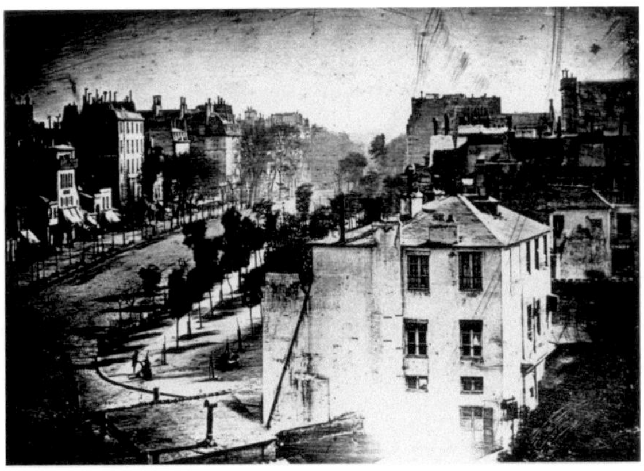

Figure 12
Louis Daguerre, *View of Boulevard du Temple, (8am)* 1838/9
Daguerreotype
Bavarian Museum, Munich

This is claimed as the first photograph with a human presence recorded in it.

For Baudelaire, the problem with photography was that it was too close to nature and not close enough to the human imagination: there was no art in the detail of photography. The influential twentieth-century art critic Clement Greenberg would say something similar in the 1960s, complaining, for example, about the excess of detail in Edward Weston's photographs.[59] But although for Baudelaire photography should know and keep its place, its 'scientific vision' did affect the thinking of artists in many different ways. There is no doubt that photography was usefully employed to 'sketch' figures or find poses for paintings, but the singularity of the lens also offered a model for new and different subject viewpoints that had not been imagined before. In this way, photography had already begun to dislocate the idea of art and painting in many subtle ways, even though it took decades to be registered.

Representation and Dissemblance

Daguerre's early photograph, *View of Boulevard de Temple* 1838/9 (fig.12), is thought to be the first photograph to include a human accidentally registered by a camera. Its high vantage point is also significant as a new and original departure.[60]

Locals called the street 'boulevard de crimes' because of the nature of the plays staged in its theatres. Here it is empty save for a solitary commercial transaction on the street corner: a man's boots are being cleaned. The standing figure is only registered on the plate because he was more or less stationary during the minutes-long exposure, the slight movements of his body creating a smudgy, 'blurred' presence. Indeed, this is probably the first photograph ever to introduce the effect of blur. Historians of photography thus frequently cite this image as an example of the failure of early photography to 'capture' instantaneous movement, with the usual street traffic absented from the picture; but its unusual point of view is also part of its historical significance.

It is instructive to compare Daguerre's boulevard with Claude Monet's later painting, *Boulevard des Capucines* 1873 (fig.13). It has the same high vantage point and angle of view onto the boulevard below, albeit slightly zoomed in and with smudged figures blended into the street. The sunlight of Daguerre's photograph contrasts with the flatter winter light of

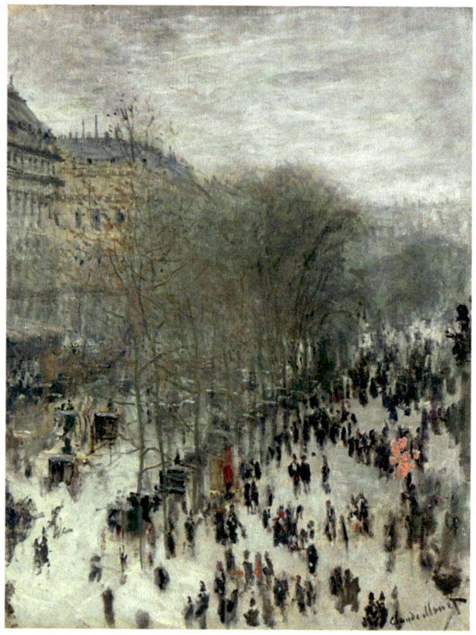

Figure 13
Claude Monet, *Boulevard des Capucines*, 1873–4
Oil paint on canvas
80.3 × 60.3
Nelson-Atkins Museum of Art, Kansas City

The painting was made from the window of Nadar's photography studio, also the location of the first Impressionist exhibition where this picture was first shown.

Monet's painting, yet how is it possible to imagine such a view down onto the street from this angle without recourse to the earlier photographic visual experiments and the concurrent mass appeal of aerial balloon photography, for example by Gaspard-Félix Tournachon Nadar? Monet's painting was in fact made directly from Nadar's photography studio windows – the same studio space that hosted the first impressionist exhibition, and where this painting was also exhibited. It is surely hard to imagine a painter's invention of these blur effects to signify movement without the invention of photography. The point here is not to suggest that Monet simply 'copied' Daguerre's picture, nor to claim that photography precipitated impressionism, but to show the mutual and inseparable historical interactions between photography and painting as representations of the world. These interactions and exchanges are so interwoven that it is futile to try to establish origins or the influence of one over the other, even though the connections are clearly there. Monet's impressionist painting introduces a subjective and fleeting moment, a glance, the enjoyment of which lies in the painterly quality of the scene: the busy boulevard, famous for hosting the promenades of Parisians. That some photographers would then take this painterly quality as an inspirational model for their own pictorialist way of seeing photographically only shows how photographers and artists were trying to rethink ways of seeing the world.

Modern Art

The aim of art to produce a dissemblance, rather than a resemblance, of the world is nowhere more clearly manifest than in the dialogue between the codes of photography and the values of painting. When the invention of photography brought a new sense of literal factuality to the visual, Baudelaire was quick to counter that art required more than fact. Art required something of the 'impalpable and the imaginary' to operate effectively. Art must offer the spectator something more than the already known and the already seen. However, it seems that Baudelaire could not quite imagine how the idea of fact itself might bring something new to the human imagination. This factual aspect of photography would come to dominate twentieth-century renewals in art, where realism and the imaginary realm of idealism would interact in new ways, by responding to the impact of the photographic apparatus.

The significant point then is that modern art tried to change the way we see the world and experience it. The idea of photographic vision that was first explored with the camera obscura has been industrialised and computerised, and through these processes has also become normalised. With the real world increasingly mediated via photographic images, it inevitably becomes harder to avoid their gravitational pull. As older forms of photography are eclipsed by computational forms of image, it is impossible to exclude these expanded forms of photographic image from the domain of art, as the early modern art period had once tried to do. Art today needs to address how the visual world beyond art comes to shape any resemblances of the world, and photographic images are central to this, active across every sphere of contemporary life. Through strategies of dissemblance, art photography questions these resemblances and sometimes turns them inside out, using the very same apparatus that created them. Photographic interventions in art are multiple and diverse, eclectic even, and art is unthinkable now without them. The following chapters build a picture of just such an understanding of art, not only through analysis of the interchange between art and non-art photography, but within the different social and aesthetic values of photography that they articulate.

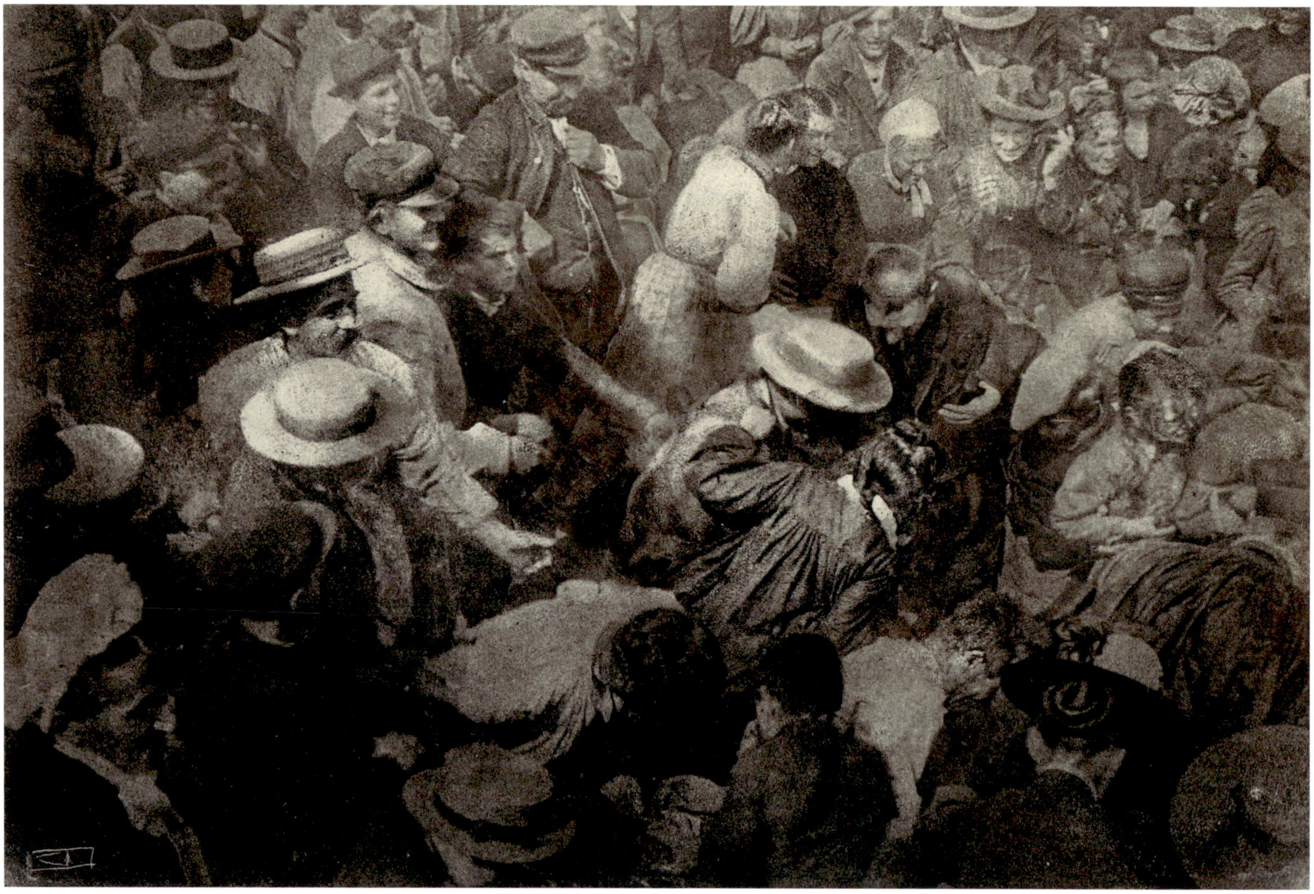

THE PICTORIAL TURN

1 Galassi 1995, pp.14–15.

Figure 14
Robert Demachy,
The Crowd 1910
Oil print photograph,
15.8 × 22.8
Alfred Stieglitz
Collection, 1949.
The Metropolitan
Museum of Art,
New York

Pictorialism is a rather loose assembly of ideas about what makes a good art photograph. Historically, it belongs to a longer-established theory of the tableau in painting and to ideas about composition and pictorial space. The pictorial image aims to render the real as an ideal; composition should have an ideal meaning. There have been at least two turns towards pictorialism in photography. The first was in the 1870s, when the term was coined to refer to art photography, and the second emerged in the late 1970s, although it only really became popular in the 1990s. While this later work cannot be called 'pictorialist' in the same way, and did not have the same international coherence of the earlier movement, there are definite continuities across them. The new or neo-pictorial photography, as it might be called, borrowed the historical clothing of the older pictorialism, but was sharpened up and modernised in full-colour and larger-scale photographs; meaning, too, was renovated.

Pictorialism

Early pictorialist photographers operated through international competitions, exhibitions and publications. These forums for exhibition and exchange were modelled on the art salon system, which often included painters among the judges. Successful pictures selected for inclusion or a prize were circulated through the many pictorialist photography magazines and annual publications, which also served as a forum for debate about what made good art photography. Although initially centred in Britain, pictorialism spread worldwide to become the first truly international art movement in photography. It began to fade in the 1910s within key metropolitan centres of art, displaced by new avant-garde ideas, but it lingered elsewhere for decades.

Despite its massive popularity and important role in the history of art photography, pictorialism is still generally viewed in negative terms, attracting little or no contemporary critical discussion. This attitude was effectively summed up by Peter Galassi, when, as curator of photography at the Museum of Modern Art in New York, he wrote:

'Dominated by themes of nature (including the nude) and domestic leisure (again including the nude, as well as the ubiquitous portrait of the fellow aesthete), pictorialist imagery is heavy with pious sentiment and romantic metaphor. The prints favoured chiaroscuro over precise detail and were executed on platinum paper, prized for the intervention of the artist's hand.'[1]

Galassi is certainly right in his summary of the themes typical in pictorialism: nature, nudes, portraits and domestic leisure are repeated frequently. However, it is important to recognise that these subjects were also common in painting at that time too. Since pictorialism was pursued in relation to painting – the dominant form of art movements such as

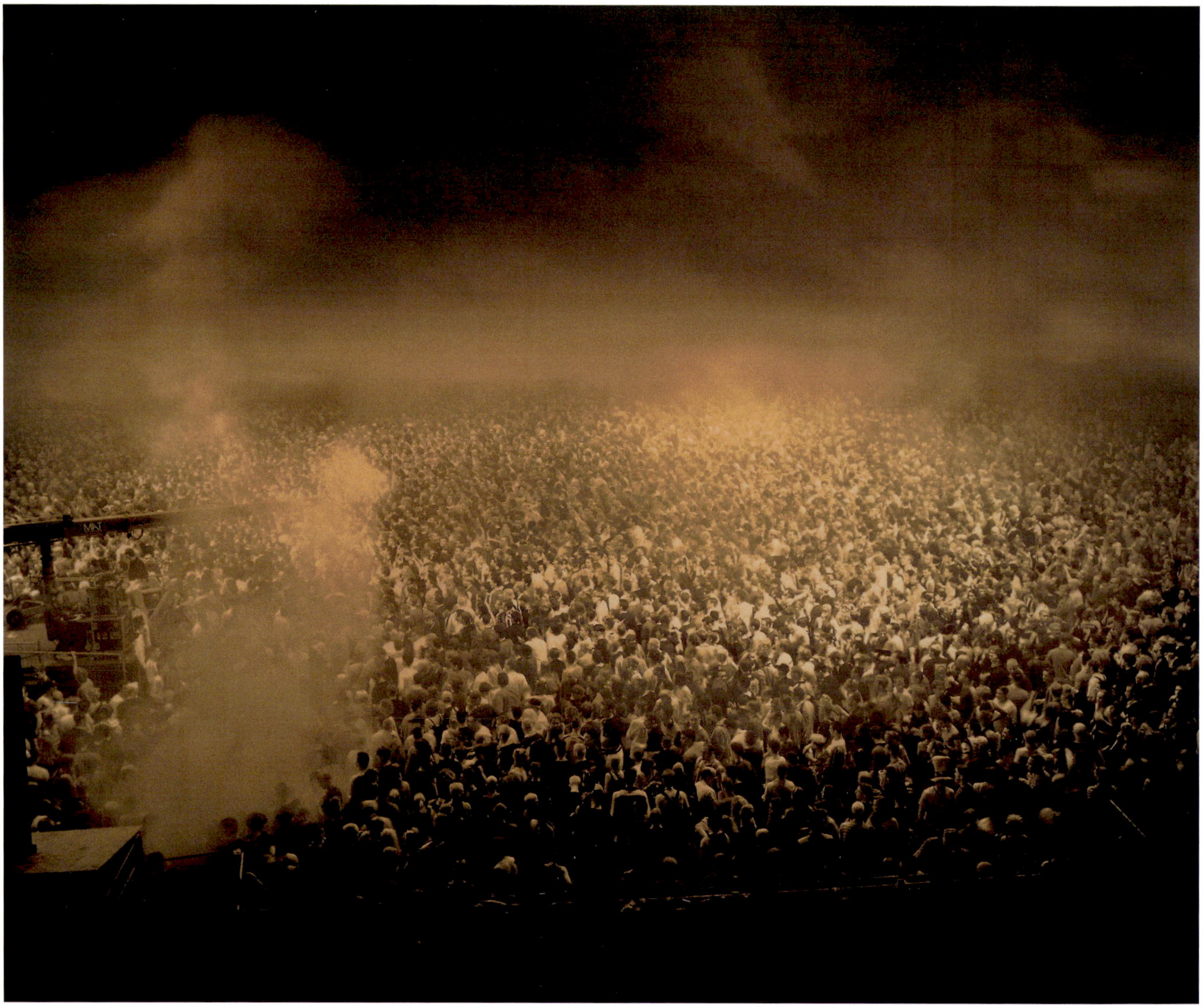

2 Robinson 1869. For a history of Robinson's work and life see Harker 1988.

3 Nochlin 1978.

realism, impressionism, tonalism and post-impressionism – it is not surprising that these themes were echoed in photography that aspired to art. Rather than simply aiming to be 'painterly', pictorialist photographers also shared subject matter with the impressionists in France, the Pre-Raphaelites in Britain and, later, the Secessionists in Vienna. And internationally, its reach was even broader and more popular, developing preoccupations with nature, domestic life and the body through different ways of representing local life. For all the problems that it involved, the issues at work in historical pictorialism are wider than Galassi's cursory view admits, since it began to generate new themes and interpretations of art that varied across different places, making it worth examining further.

Figure 15
Andreas Gursky,
May III 1998
C-print, 132 × 167

Figure 16
Henry Peach Robinson,
Fading Away 1858
Albumen silver print from glass negatives, 23.8 × 37.2

In this picture, five separate images were shot and combined into one seamless assemblage: much the same technique is used today in 'Photoshop' and other image manipulation software. 'Fading away' refers to death from tuberculosis, common at the time of the image.

The Pictorial Effect

Photographic pictorialism was developed in the nineteenth century after the English photographer Henry Peach Robinson argued for a set of techniques that would render photography as art. Robinson announced these techniques, after fifteen years of work as a photographer, in his book *Pictorial Effect in Photography: Being Hints on Composition and Chiaroscuro for Photographers*, first published in 1869.[2] His early picture *Fading*

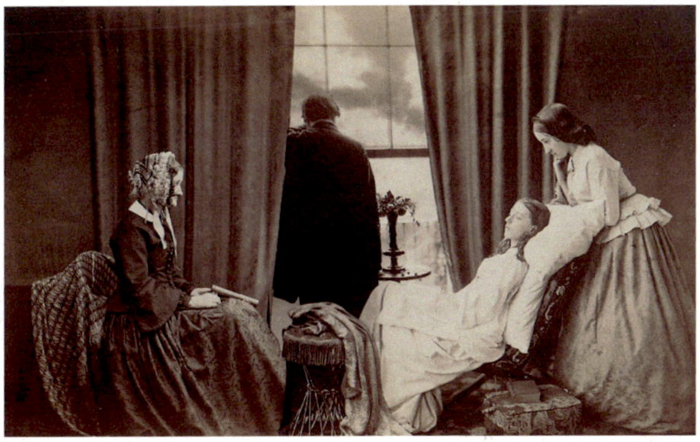

Away 1858 (fig.16), showing a young woman dying of consumption, or tuberculosis, as we know it today, had been highly successful and gave strong critical credentials to his working method.

Early death was a commonplace in nineteenth-century European life, with high infant mortality rates and tuberculosis rife even among wealthy or middle class families. But besides this, *Fading Away* also tells us something about Victorian family values and social roles. The photograph shows an angelic death watched over by the girl's mother and sister. The father turns away towards the outside world, his arm signifying that he hides his grief from them, and us. The women are facing towards this death, a domestic event inside a room that is thus defined as a feminine space. The models are posed to create a harmonious composition, implying a good and beautiful death. This, the picture suggests, is a spiritual event, a saintly sleep, which was often how tuberculosis was viewed in art and literature – far from the reality of bodies ravaged by disease.[3] One version of Robinson's print is accompanied by a lyric verse of the English romantic poet Shelley, which reinforces the idea that one might die well. This sentiment adhered to the aesthetic belief that art must be beautiful to be true, which is the basic argument advanced by H.P. Robinson:

Shelley's verse

Must then that peerless form,

Which love and admiration cannot view

Without a beating heart, those azure veins

Which steal like streams along a field of snow,

That lovely outline which is fair
As breathing marble, perish!

that the beauty of pictorial composition is necessary for any photograph to be art. This involved montaging ideal parts together into one coherent pictorial composition. *Fading Away* is composed of five separate negatives, the final picture creating a coherent composition and an idealised depiction of death. The fact that death was of course a real preoccupation in everyday life was not new, but this 'staged' photographic interpretation was. To some, even today, such fabricated staging of a scene defies and betrays the realist depiction that photography is capable of by using artifice to create a 'fake' photographic reality. Yet this is to misunderstand the ideals of beauty that inform such a practice.

Robinson, for example, drew on the theory of the picturesque, already prevalent at that time. He was well educated in art and admired the landscape paintings of John Constable and J.M.W. Turner. Curiously, he even advised students of photography to go and study Turner's paintings –

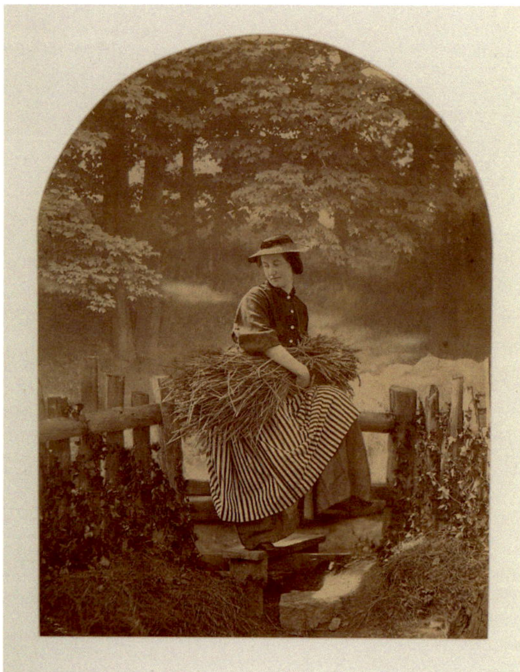

Figure 17
Henry Peach Robinson,
A Gleaner 1872
Albumen print from two negatives, 55.9 × 40.6

an acquired taste for some people even then.[4] Such works were part of a re-evaluation of rural life in the wake of the industrial revolution, and it is worth remembering that romantic aesthetics began initially as a critique of new developments in societal values introduced by industrialism.

Robinson was also familiar with the influential aesthetic writings of the English art critic John Ruskin, and often referred directly to his volumes of *Modern Painters*.[5] In Ruskin's view, beauty was truth and the role of the artist was to reveal it. Robinson argued that the way to achieve this was through combining whatever components needed to be used in their ideal form. With nature and landscape a new tendency in painting, partly in response to industrialisation, Robinson subscribed to this new romantic attitude towards rural life, and applied it in his staged pictorialist photography. However, in this early photographic technology different exposures were required to achieve the effect of the combined picture. The correct sky might have to be photographed separately from the land

4 Harker 1988, pp.44–5.

5 Robinson 1902, p.64.

and combined in the darkroom. This procedure generated not only the acceptability of image manipulation, but also its necessity in attaining the ideal 'pictorial effect', as Robinson called it. His ideas about landscape and everyday rural life resonated with themes emerging in modern art movements elsewhere, especially in France.

Figure 18
Jean-François Millet,
The Gleaners 1857
Oil paint on canvas
83.8 × 111.8
Musée d'Orsay, Paris

Millet's painting shows three peasant women 'gleaning': having been authorised at sunset to pick up quickly the ears of corn left over by the harvesters in the fields. The austerity of the gleaners' work is contrasted with the abundant harvest in the background distance, the three figures echoed by the three huge haystacks.

Impression of Life

In Paris, the acknowledged centre for avant-garde art at the time, the realists and impressionists were discussing new ideas about landscape and nature, particularly the effects of new urban and rural ways of life. Often handled critically and sometimes sentimentally in painting, these new and different attitudes towards country and city life can also be found in pictorialist photography. Robinson's later photographs act out rural scenes according to a romantic view of rural life. In *Wayside Gossip* 1882 and *A Merry Tale* 1882, for example, he drew on themes popular in French painting.

Robinson's *A Gleaner* 1872 (fig.17) unmistakably takes the theme of Jean-François Millet's painting *The Gleaners* 1857 (fig.18), but he treats it very differently, bringing a new interpretation to its subject. Unlike the

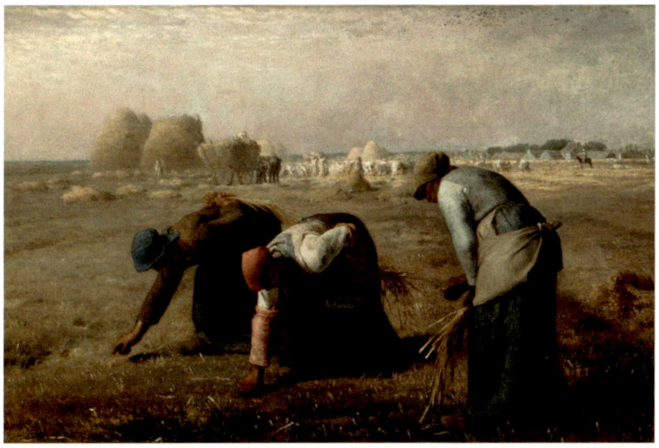

moral dignity of the three toiling figures in Millet's picture, Robinson places a single woman centrally, as if it were a portrait. She poses on a stile between two spaces and we suppose she has gleaned the twigs she is holding from the forest behind her. Robinson offers an allegorical reading of the position of the woman, hovering between the forest and the garden: she is pivotal in the 'natural' order of things. Her manual work is situated just on 'one side of the fence', between the wild nature of the forest and the nurtured garden. Unlike Millet's earthy and strong working women, Robinson's cheerful rustic models often do look rather fake today. The pictures seem artificial and theatrical, not just because we can see that the models are acting the characters, but because they also look as if they are posing for the photograph. Robinson's gleaners seem to mock Millet's women, their manual work and their toil to survive, domesticating the issue of rural poverty by turning it into a picturesque cliché. But Robinson was also articulating the new potentials of leisure for his class, which the burgeoning railway network was making possible. His pictures portray an idealised version of what a middle-class family might enjoy on a daytrip to the country: gathering twigs for a cosy fire.

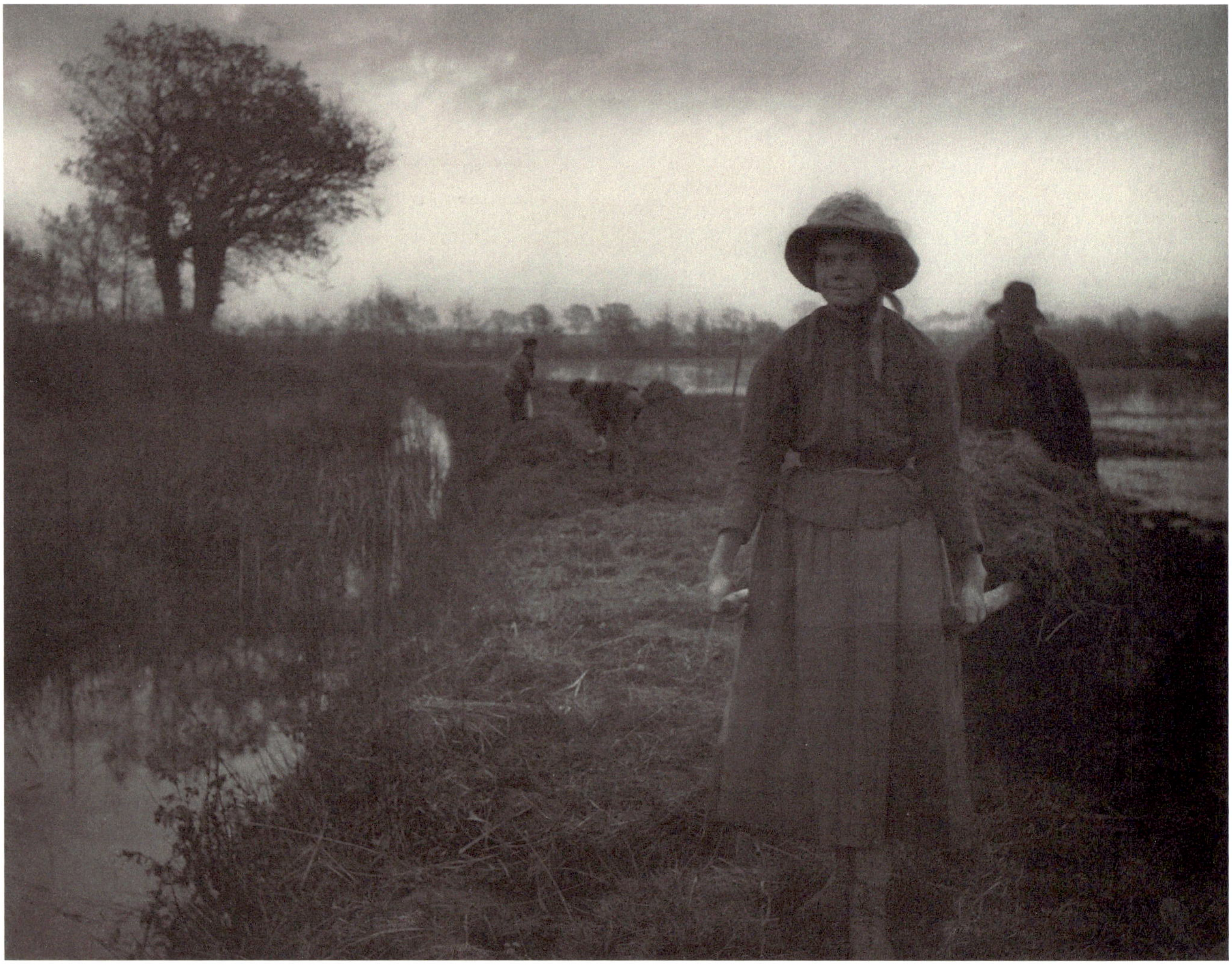

6 Robinson 1902, p.57.

7 Emerson 1890.

8 Robinson 1896, p 81.

9 Harker 1988, p.42.

Figure 19 Henry Peter Emerson, *Poling the Marsh Hay* 1886 Platinum print from glass negative, 23.2 × 29

Robinson explained his method, describing how a subject would 'arise before my mind's eye in a most inexplicable manner, and remain there till I lay the ghosts by making sketches of them'.[6] These sketches then became the basis for his photographs, with each part photographed as a separate element and composited together in the darkroom during the printing stage. This was the best way, Robinson argued, to achieve harmony of composition and beauty as the pictorial effect. Robinson's method of merging separate elements to create a whole – like that of Oscar Rejlander, also working at this time – prefigures the later techniques of photomontage developed in the early twentieth century. Today, Robinson's method is of course a common basis for the production of commercial images, with idealised elements seamlessly montaged through the widespread use of Photoshop and other digital software.

In 1889 Peter Henry Emerson, Robinson's famous rival, published *Naturalistic Photography*, in which he made hostile comments about Robinson's 'academic' allegorical scenes.[7] Emerson argued that photographs should employ selective focus, as the human eye does, to reflect the subjective vision of an individual. So whereas Robinson's pictures tended to be sharper all over, Emerson's employed differential focus and soft tones. Emerson also departed from Robinson's montage method and use of models, instead photographing the people who actually worked the land directly, and the difference in effect is clearly visible.

Subjective and Objective Composition

The arguments between Robinson and Emerson echoed the discussions in Paris on painting, in which studio-based art was seen as artificial, and the new plein-air painters, such as Claude Monet, argued that art must be derived directly from nature. This dichotomy between studio and street is still common today, albeit in a technically modified form, with studio-based photography distinguished as 'manipulated' or constructed, as opposed to the 'real observation from nature' of land, street and documentary-orientated photography. Another historical debate around painting concerned the overall effect of the picture, positing that this should be more important than its constituent details. Emerson's use of partial focus adhered to this idea too, as seen in his naturalistic views of rural life on England's Norfolk Broads (fig.19). Even though he eventually renounced his assertion that photography could be art, his ideas stuck, and other pictorialists developed the notion of a diffused focus replicating human subjective vision. However, some introduced Robinson's techniques of studio manipulation to emphasise this, even explicitly orientating their pictures towards an impressionistic, painterly effect.

The differences between these pictorial tendencies of Robinson and Emerson are sometimes exaggerated though. Robinson, for instance, stated that if the artist copied nature faithfully, there was no art.[8] He worked with lens maker J.H. Dallmeyer, who had developed the Portrait Triple Lens, which softened focus by diffusing the hard focus of the lens, except in one plane.[9] The aim was beauty, a pictorial effect, rather than any putative truth to nature, for which Emerson had argued. These different strategies produced various understandings of the value of photography as art: was it the construction of an ideal meaning or the reporting of an optical fact? Pictorialism never resolved these issues, tending instead to

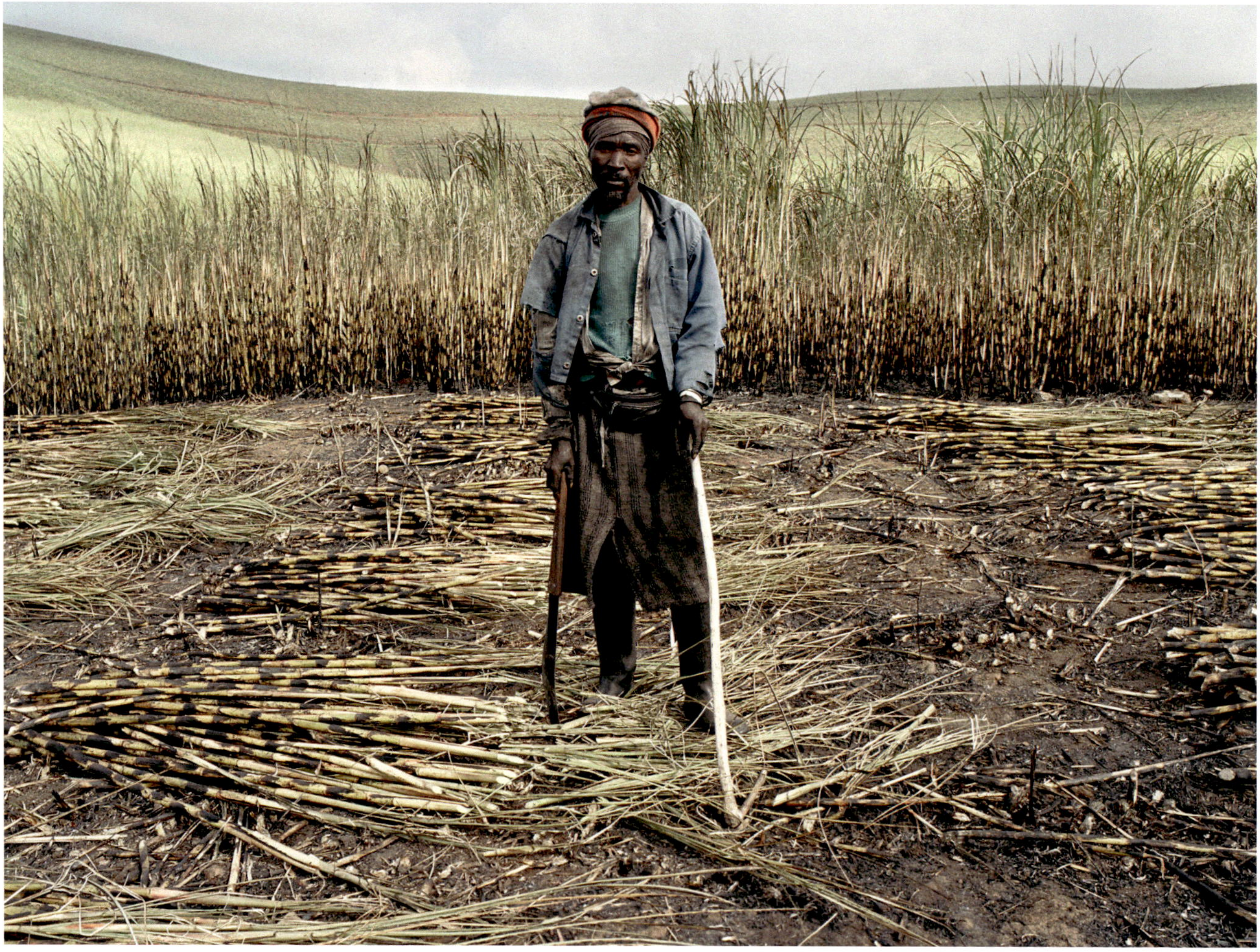

10 Caillebotte's pictures are thought to be based on camera views, from which he then made sketches that altered the perspectival dynamics of the scene. See Kirk, Varnedoe and Lee 1976.

merge and mix them gradually together in different ways. Perhaps what made the aesthetic dispute between Robinson and Emerson more acute is their position at opposing ends of the political spectrum: Robinson was a conservative while Emerson expressed concern for the conditions of the working people he photographed and their ways of life. We should remember that the awful conditions of rural workers in France had made them important subject matter for Millet and other painters. Pictorialists were sometimes in dialogue with these same themes, but were developing their own approaches to them, opposed or similar, and sometimes alongside concurrent painting movements.

Figure 20
Zwelethu Mthethwa, *Untitled* 2003
From the series *Sugar Cane*
Digital c-print, 63.6 × 85.6

In this series Mthethwa photographs the contemporary rural sugar cane workers in his native South Africa.

As others have already noted, pictorialists such as Emerson and Robinson always seemed to be squabbling, with factions splitting off, appropriating, evolving and mixing techniques from all the various technical tendencies and aesthetic values available. In this way, pictorialism evolved differently across the international landscape of pictorialist activity. Technological developments eventually rendered Robinson's lengthy composite technique less relevant, but his painterly manipulations in the darkroom remained a legitimate process in the pictorialist's repertoire. Selective focus and composite techniques could be used together or applied individually to areas of a print, which would then be re-photographed to enhance and emphasise the dark and light tones of the image. Such artistic reworking of negatives and prints was common. Some even made their own photographic paper to mimic the texture of canvas. Just as the techniques evolved, so did new themes and attitudes towards nature, leisure, work and the human body. The city and the industrial landscape also began to provide a new photographic subject matter, which differed strikingly from the mythical rural leisure of Robinson and the working life themes of Emerson, while having much in common with the copious impressionist paintings of city life and leisure.

While debates about painting and photography have often sought to identify them as radically different media, the historical links between impressionism and pictorialism are clear, not only because they were simultaneously developed alongside each other, but also because their practitioners shared an aesthetic of the imagination, that is, a common aim to invoke the perceptual impression of a scene, with the image as the view of a subjective instant. As with the new painting of this period, pictorialist photography constructed an optical experience of seeing something 'directly' but infused with an imagined human experience of looking. This aesthetic invites the viewer to imagine what it is like to be in the scene, and to identify with its subject as a pictorial composition and scheme.

Photography of Modern Life

Just as the ideas of the impressionists provided a clear reference point for pictorialist photographers, so too did photography for painters. This is visible in Gustave Caillebotte's impressionist painting *Rue de Paris, temps de pluie* 1877 (see the painting in fig.22). Caillebotte's painting is striking in many ways, not only for its apparent photographic quality – the wide-angle lens view (an angle approximately equivalent to a 24mm lens on a 35mm film camera) associated with photographic vision[10] – but also the casualness of the moment depicted. The painter seems to have chosen

Figure 21
Alfred Stieglitz,
Snapshot 1911
Photogravure
printed in 1912,
13.8 × 17.4

an instant like a snapshot photograph, with no significant event, only the passing by of anonymous figures in the rain. We see the people go about the damp streets, promenading in the rain, perhaps unwillingly from necessity, their spatial isolation evoking both the charm and the desolation of modern life.[11] The painting exudes a 'photographic' quality in its form and through the apparent non-specific frozenness of the moment. Painting and photography exchanged these aesthetic codes and themes of representation back and forth between one another.

11 See Clark 1990, p.15

Now compare Caillebotte's painting with Alfred Stieglitz's pictorialist photograph (fig.21), made three decades later, also on a damp day in Paris. The rain softens the feel of the photograph and the atmosphere of the scene. Stieglitz was brilliant at using the weather to achieve plein air impressionist effects and developed these with great effect, especially in his later photographs of New York in snowy winter. He would let the impact of rain, snow, steam and heat generate an atmospheric effect when the photograph was being taken, and enhance this afterwards during processing and printing.

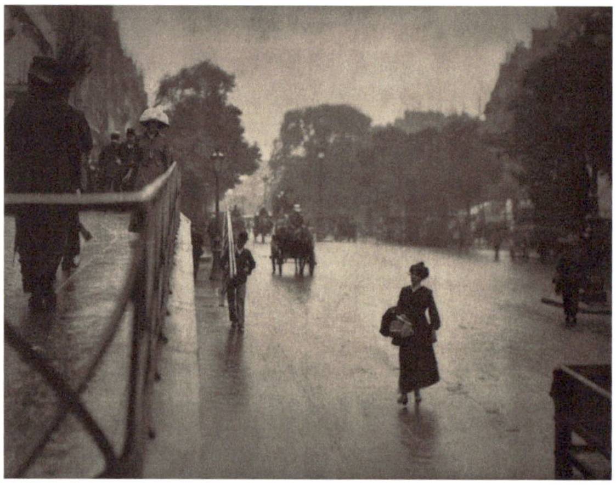

However, Stieglitz would eventually drop the pictorialist mood and techniques altogether, favouring photographs that were bold in their sharpness, with clean, stark compositions. He would claim the 'straight photograph' as a modern art form with a new confidence, and on its own terms rather than those of painting. We can gain an understanding of this relation between impressionism and pictorialism by considering a more recent photographic work by the contemporary German photographer Thomas Struth.

Struth's series of museum photographs re-examines the theme of modern leisure in city life, but in a completely new way and through a very different treatment. Struth centres his photograph on Caillebotte's painting housed in its museum setting, incorporating it into the pictorial space as a spectacle for the viewer. This viewing space is doubled. Struth's image shows how museum visitors, as strolling spectators, become an extension of the space in Caillebotte's painting and thus in the museum too. The life-sized tableau is integrated within the contemporary art museum, which is shown to be a site of leisure and spectacle, and presented to us through the form of modern pictorial photography. The leisure space of the contemporary urban museum is quite literally in this

12 This media image is what Jacques Rancière calls the *metamorphic* images. See Rancière 2007, pp.23-4.

photograph the space of a history of art remediated via contemporary art photography. This mediation renews art photography as a large-scale pictorial form, absorbing impressionist painting and its audience into a tableau photography based on its descriptive capacity. It is photography that has revived and revised the old function of the classical pictorial tableau, which had been left behind by the turn towards abstraction in modern art.

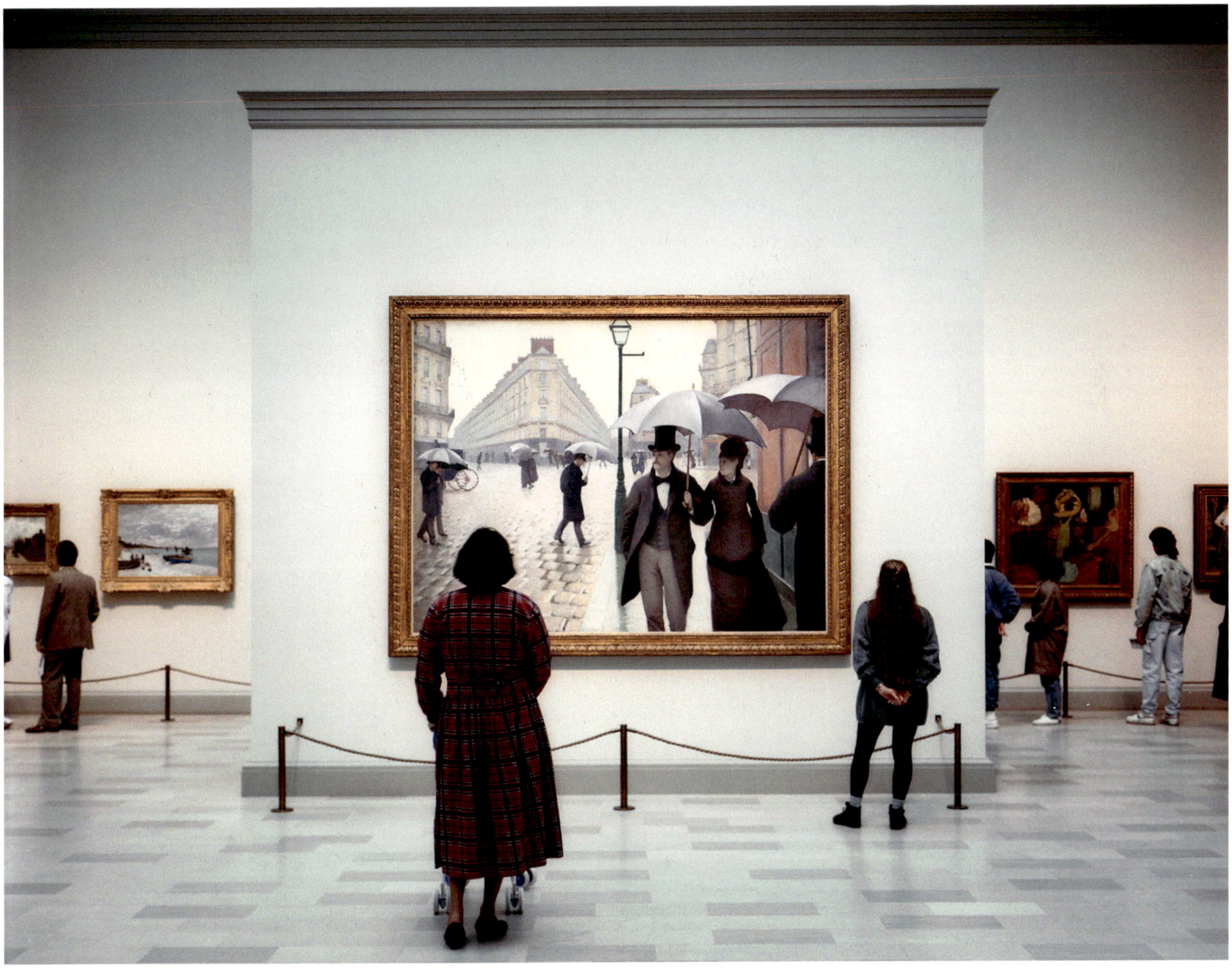

Figure 22
Thomas Struth,
Art Institute of Chicago 2, Chicago 1990 1990
Chromogenic print,
184 × 219
© Thomas Struth

New Pictorial Photography

Nineteenth-century pictorialist photography was heavily intertwined with the values, themes and trends of modern painting. The new pictorial art photography of the late twentieth century took its metamorphic values from an admixture of other visual arts and media, painting, cinema and television, alongside techniques from other types of photography, such as photojournalism, documentary and advertising.[12] Unlike pictorialism, which was primarily monochrome and handmade, most contemporary pictorial art photography is colour and printed on a large industrial scale that rivals painting, and sometimes even advertising billboard images. The result is a new pictorial photography, contemporary in appearance and with subject matter remediated into

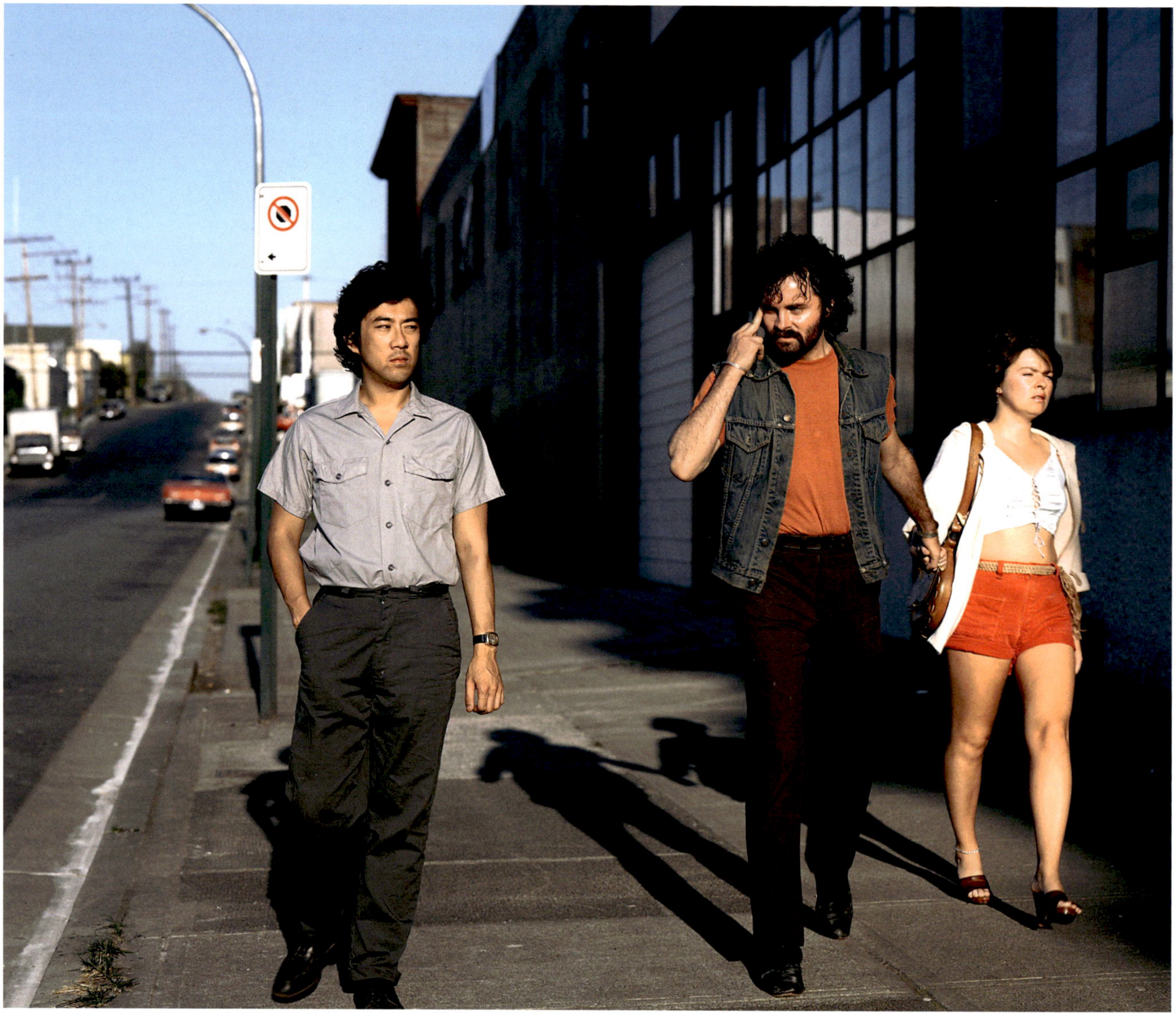

13 See Wall 2005.

14 Baudelaire 2012.

different forms, flanked on one side by the moving cinema image, and by painting, sculpture and art history on the other. This hybrid form sometimes brings together the compositional strategies of 'low' popular culture and 'high' art, embodying aspects of each but belonging to neither. The pictorial aspect of this new photography recognises that artists are immersed in and influenced by the complex contemporary media environment, which the new pictorial practice filters and remediates through individual experience.

It should be stressed that whereas nineteenth-century pictorialism was a coherent movement with its own independently organised events, exhibitions and international competitions held in parallel with established art salons and exhibitions, new or neo-pictorial photography work exists and operates as an international visual art integrated within the contemporary art market. It is not a movement as such, but a set of identifiable ideas and attitudes that has emerged through artists working in similar ways, in different places and under disparate conditions. In some ways these pictorial images may be considered as an international

Figure 23 (Opposite)
Jeff Wall, *Mimic* 1982
Transparency in lightbox, 198 × 228.5
Photographed in Vancouver on 8 × 10-inch film

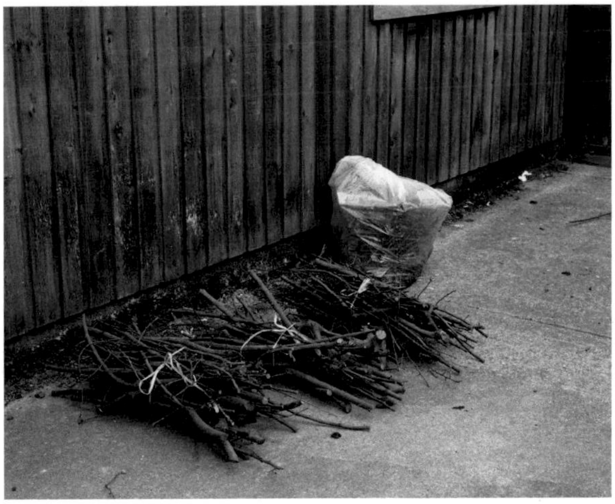

Figure 24
Jeff Wall, *Cuttings* 2001
Transparency in lightbox, 115 × 143
Photographed in Vancouver

photographic 'language', using the basic conventions of photographic apparatus to produce large pictorial images, which are legible to anyone familiar with perspectival images and photographic vision.

Jeff Wall, a key figure in this type of photographic art practice, is explicit about his art historical training, particularly in nineteenth-century art. Based in Canada, he is well known for his long-held fascination with the decisive instant in photojournalism and documentary photography, which he combines with an interest in the aesthetics of the cinematic image.[13] Wall's different-sized tableau pictures usually draw on incidents, events or things he has seen but, like H.P. Robinson, he also re-stages them, using locations, props, actors and models to idealise the photographic meaning through composition. The look and feel of his pictures have something in common with nineteenth-century painting or even, to some extent, with Robinson's pictorialist genre scenes. A sense of frozenness pervades some of the image, so that its artifice may be hinted at but not revealed. Wall's concern and interest in these contemporary scenes from everyday life also recalls Charles Baudelaire's idea of the modern artist as a 'painter of modern life'.[14] The contemporary artist or painter, Baudelaire proposed, is like a *flâneur* who wanders the streets of a city with the detached gaze of an outsider and constructs certain views of 'modern' life from this experience.[15] The ordinary scenes that result offer the viewer a set of quasi-philosophical arguments or framing of ethical problems and questions about how we live. The camera obviously has a similar potential to occupy this role of *flâneur*, with the photographer as a philosopher of modern life.

15 See Griselda Pollock's critique of the male flâneur in her book, *Vision and Difference*, London 1988, pp.70–1.

As in earlier pictorialism and tableau painting, Wall's photographs are usually conceived as single pictures, rather than as a series – the most common mode of modernist photography. However, themes recur and overlap, pointing to three key pictorial genres in Wall's work: still lifes, landscapes and social tableaux.

Mimic 1982 (fig.23) is a tableau that depicts a specific social instant: a racist insult from one man to another as he passes him on the street. Wall's *A Sudden Gust of Wind (after Hokusai)* 1993 is a complex composite image of an instant that makes explicit reference to Hokusai's woodblock print *The Great Wave* c.1830. The water is substituted for sheets of paper blowing in the wind from a businessman's open brief-

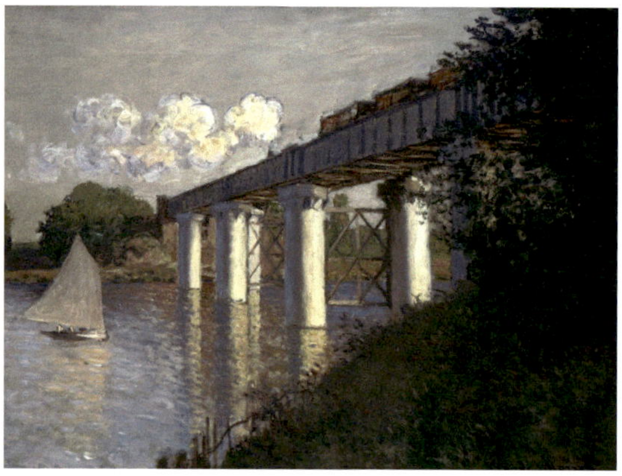

Figure 25
Claude Monet, *Railway Bridge, Argenteuil* 1873
Oil paint on canvas, 54.3 × 73.3
Philadelphia Museum of Art

Monet lived in Argenteuil when he painted this picture, giving the river Seine and railway crossing the impression of a calm and tranquil space.

case. In *Cuttings* (fig.24), neat bundles of freshly cut twigs are stacked before a neat wooden fence in a Canadian suburb, showing two uses of the same natural material, wood. The scene is so banal and literal that we lift it into allegorical meaning. Everything is so neat and clean that, surely, something must be wrong here? All of Wall's pictures speak directly and obliquely about concepts and conflicts in everyday life: social discontent between ethnic groups; a business transaction going wrong; the ephemeral character of contracts, and the cyclical reuse of wood in the suburban battle for tidiness. Wall's motifs are distinctly contemporary, but they also draw on the modes and themes of classic nineteenth-century tableau painting, seeking ideal meanings through composition and a sophisticated description of actual experience. Some of his more recent monochrome pictures also explicitly use the heavy formal qualities of mid- and dark tones so often characteristic of pictorialist photography. While the critical social content of Wall's work might generally seem at odds with this, it is in fact this critical dimension of earlier pictorialism and impressionism that is often obscured by the retrospective 'postcard' ideals attributed to them.

Tableau

16 The French anthropologist Marc Augé coined the term 'non-place' in his popular book, *Non-Places: Introduction to an Anthropology of SuperModernity*, London 1995.

Look at Claude Monet's *Railway Bridge at Argenteuil* 1873 (fig.25), composed in pretty, soft colours. Today it might seem like an ordinary, banal scene, but it explicitly addresses the impact of the industrial revolution on landscape. Wall's photograph *The Storyteller* 1986 (fig.26) has a similar formal composition, although its content and the epoch depicted are clearly different. Monet's painting describes the industrial railway's presence at a natural river scene. The painting itself does not condemn or praise the railway crossing over the river, but it draws attention to it, integrating it as a central element of the picture. Set in the suburban outskirts of Paris, the only apparent movement is the train, signified by its billowing smoke, as it carries people across the river and through the calm, depopulated scene. Indeed, one can imagine that all the local people might be on this train. The painting provokes contemplation on the

Figure 26
Jeff Wall,
The Storyteller 1986
Transparency in lightbox, 229 × 437
Photographed in Vancouver

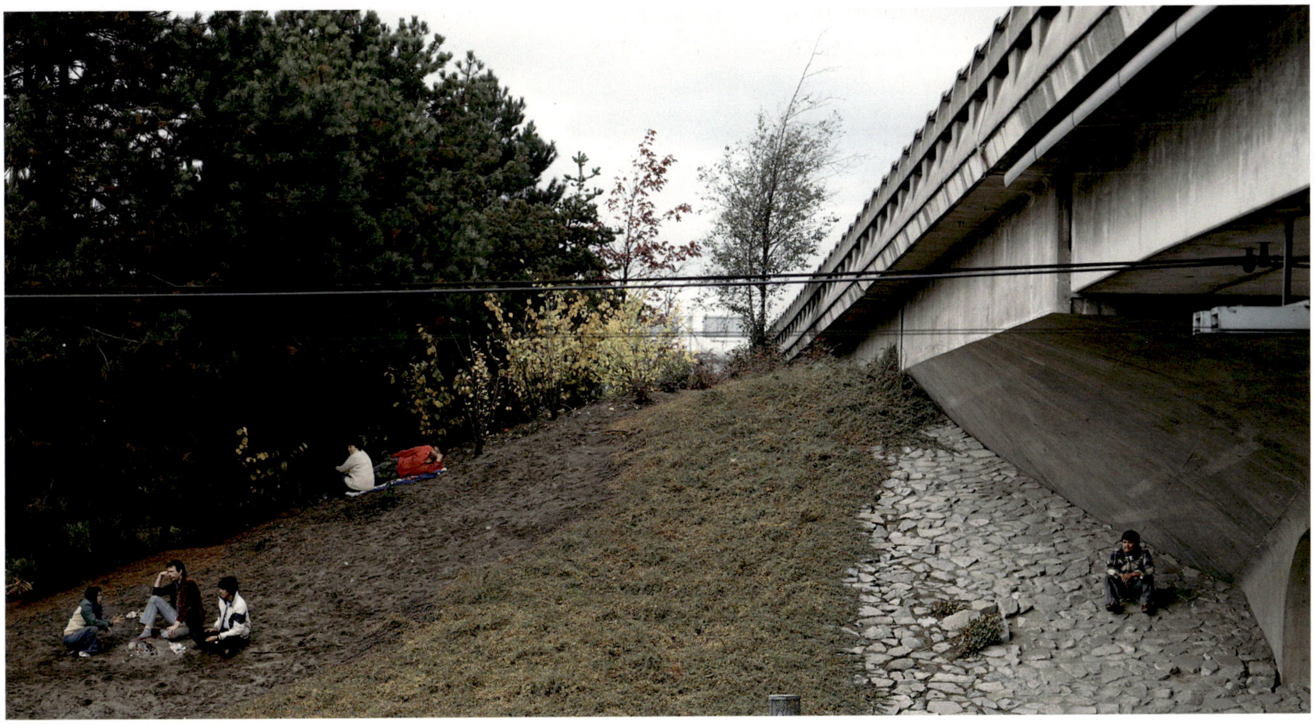

impact of technological progress at this intersection of river and railway and transit of passengers. The historical viewer would have recognised that trains improved transport to the outskirts of Paris or enabled a faster commute to work, which changed the relationship between country and city. The picture does not seem to judge whether this change was good or bad, it merely depicts a contemporary condition for consideration, as reflected in the picture's factual title.

Now look at Wall's photograph *The Storyteller* 1986, where a highway supplants the railway. Monet's flowery river embankment and pretty, mottled sky have been exchanged for the stark bank and a drab concrete bridge. In this modern 'non-place' there is no idyllic nature.[16] The picturesque has vacated Wall's desolate scene, which is charged with a different factual tension. The only sign of movement is what may be construed or imagined from the gestures, poses and expressions of the people sitting alone or in small groups, all scattered throughout a space that has been landscaped only as a by-product of the highway. We might imagine these characters also to be by-products of this modern transport society, social outcasts who, like the space itself, appear to be doing nothing in particular. Like Monet's painting, the picture does not really seem to judge its subject, but merely creates a compositional form and pictorial space in which a viewer may contemplate and consider these meanings.

Yet such bridges are also familiar to any modern road traveller, loaded with meaning through their ubiquitous use in cinema too – a connection that is suggested by Wall's choice of aspect ratio (the frame shape of the photograph), which itself produces implications of narrative. Usually located near the edge of a city, such movie scenes are typically linked to urban crime; they are a hangout for drug users and adolescents; or used by those on the margins, felt to be outsiders. In short, the underpass signifies a space where those with nowhere to go can congregate, a place

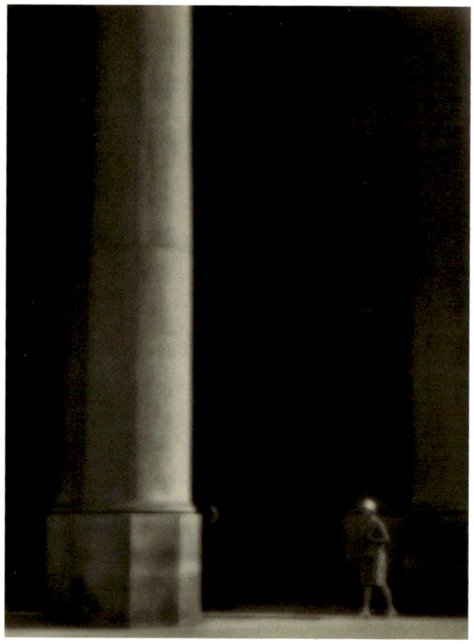

Figure 27 John Vanderpant, *Untitled (Union Station II)* 1930 Silver gelatin print, 35.3 × 27.8 Vancouver Art Gallery

for the homeless. However, Wall's title, *The Storyteller*, also suggests that something is going on here, that there is some form of dialogue, exchange or community fostered through one of the figures, who seems to be narrating a story. Thus Wall proposes a positive event in the scene, drawing our attention to the individuals and prompting the question: how and why did they arrive in this space? The picture does not offer us any answer. Wall leaves us to ponder these people, neither knowing their stories nor their destiny, yet perhaps recognising something of our own alienation in modern life.

On further inspection, a horizontal cable stretches across the foreground of the picture, interrupting this whole scene and hinting at the presence of an electric railway passing across the frontal axis of the pictorial space. This cable suggests, metonymically, that the tableau we see here is not private, but is also visible to passengers on passing trains. We find ourselves positioned alongside these transient voyeurs, who witness a fleeting impression of lives not investigated further, never really

17 Hill 1976, p.3.

18 Cited from the *Photographic Journal*, Volume LXVIII, Nov 1928, p.449, quoted in Hill 1976, p.19.

knowing what any of this 'means'. In this sense, Wall points to our own isolation – as spectators – from such marginalised groups.

Both Monet and Wall's pictures are pictorial studies of modern life, of the 'something' in their respective modernities that makes them particular to their times. For Monet it is the calm, picturesque river and rail embankment disturbed by the train and the smoke of industrial traffic; for Wall it is the makeshift population on a motorway embankment. Despite the historical differences and varying methods of pictorial construction, a suburban reality shapes both artists' constructions. The scenes, while apparently innocent in appearance, both present images for reflection on contemporary existence and life in different subtle ways. They both ask spectators to imagine themselves at these scenes, and to consider the meaning of the events they portray, which is what constitutes their common pictorial effect.

The Pictorialist World

We can also start to see in the internationalism of the early pictorialist movement something of the growing diversity of attitudes towards modern life. Wall's critical sensibility is prefigured in work by pictorialists

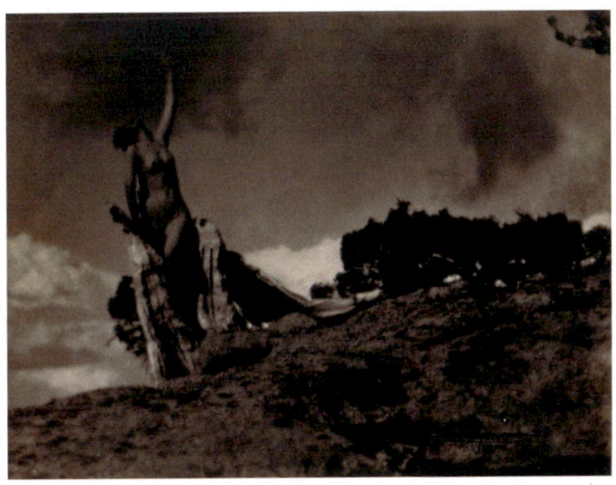

Figure 28
Anne Brigman, *Soul of the Blasted Pine* 1907
Photogravure, 15.4 × 20.8

Published in *Camera Work*, no.25 (1909)

like John Vanderpant, who moved to Canada from Holland in 1910.[17] Vanderpant later aligned himself with Edward Weston's pictorial project and f/64 group in California, with the aim of developing a west coast aesthetic. His series of grain elevator pictures, however, exemplify a different taste. Avoiding the sentimental clichés of rural myths, these dark, soft-focus pictures locate tiny figures and human-scale objects alongside vast concrete grain elevators, the individual diminished beside the industrial architecture. The images belie an ambivalence: they are at once beautiful in their formal poetry, and austere and bleak in their social connotations. Curiously, despite this apparent criticality, Vanderpant's photographs were highly successful in the later established international pictorialist movement, not known for its radicalism. He even had a solo exhibition at the Royal Photographic Society in London in 1928, which was a generosity not afforded to merely anyone.

Vanderpant countered European criticism that his work was drab by saying he was 'looking for the forms, contrasts, proportions and designs which belong to Canada and to no other country'.[18] Similar stories can be found elsewhere, with pictorialism expressing new broader pioneering views on modern culture. Harold Cazneaux, a New Zealand-born studio photographer based in Australia, also contributed to the international exhibitions of pictorialist photography with his iconic images that identified emerging modes of Australian lifestyle. His pictures *Razzle Dazzle* 1910 and *Sydney Surfing* 1929, for instance, show something of the coast's dynamic modern leisure activities. Cazneaux later became renowned for his new landscape visions of the Australian bush and habitat.

Even in Soviet Russia, with the 1917 Russian Revolution and the appearance of radical avant-garde constructivist photography by Alexander Rodchenko and others, pictorialism continued to have a currency, despite the later official imposition of socialist realism as an orthodoxy.[19] Indeed, pictorialism could be seen internationally as a community that offered an alternative space to those who rejected both modern avant-garde and commercial photography. Pictorialism was proud of its 'amateur' status, since this released it from commercial or professional burdens, in favour of aesthetic autonomy. In Soviet Russia pictorialist scenes such as Sergei Lobovikov's *Wandering Across Russia* 1909-10 or Sergei Ivanov-Alliluev's *Vagrant Russia* 1922 could be interpreted along the lines of earlier critical realist painting

Figure 29 Laura Gilpin, *A Visiting Nurse* 1924 Platinum print, 19.5 × 24.7 © 1979 Amon Carter Museum of American Art, Fort Worth, Texas

Gilpin studied photography in New York before returning to her native Colorado, where she alsophotographed American natives of the Navajo.

19 See Sviblova and Misalandi 2005.

20 See Pyne 2007, p.63.

21 Sandweiss 1986.

22 See the crucial work on women impressionists by Linda Nochlin, 'Mary Cassatt's Modernity', *Representing Women*, London 1999; Linda Nochlin, 'Morisot's Wet Nurse: The Construction of Work and Leisure in Impressionist Painting', in Nochlin 1989; and Griselda Pollock 'Modernity and the spaces of femininity', in Pollock 1988.

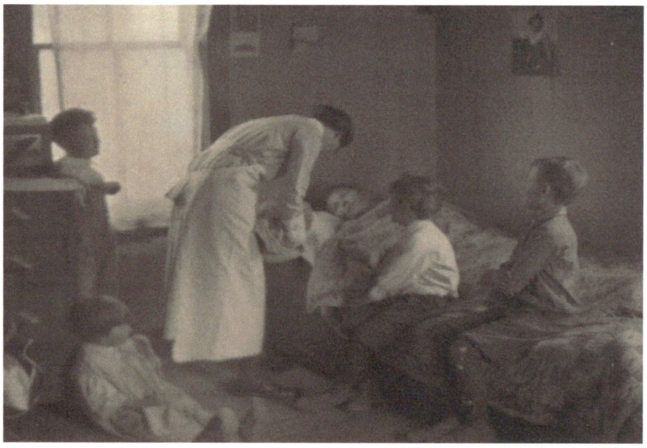

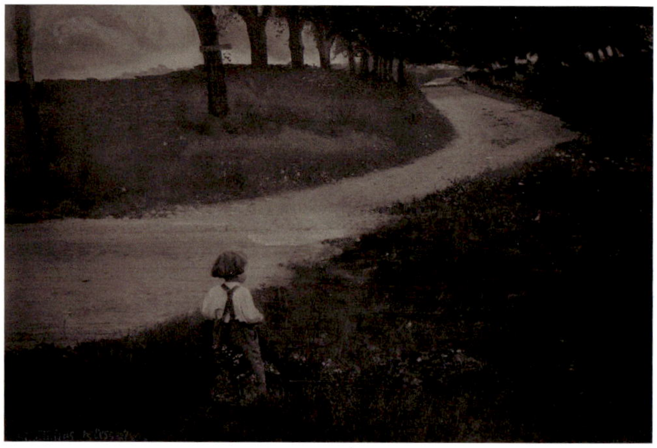

Figure 30 Gertrude Käsebier, *The Road to Rome* 1902 Platinum print, 23.8 × 34 Museum of Modern Art, New York

by Millet, Jules Breton or Gustave Courbet as showing the harsh reality of rural life in the previous regime, which new Soviet ideology claimed it would transform.

Although male photographers tend to dominate the history of early pictorialism, there were also many women photographers, who introduced new subject matter too. One of these was Anne Brigman from Oakland, California.[20] Championed by Alfred Stieglitz and a member of his Photo-Secessionists group, her work with nudes appeared in *Camera Work* magazine and suggested a highly independent attitude to the female figure. Situating the female body within nature and natural forms, her work began to envision an allegorical feminine sublime, where the time of nature was linked to the time of the female body. Brigman's work prefigures the use of the body in performance art, as an element within the pictorial scene, as seen in her famous picture, *Soul of the Blasted Pine* (fig.28).

Laura Gilpin was a younger generation pictorialist, who studied photography for a year in New York and went on to produce stunning pictures of her native Colorado.[21] Already a successful turkey farmer, Gilpin's photography explored the different situations of a woman's life on

23 Michaels 1992

the prairie. Like the women artists among the impressionists in Paris, such as Mary Cassatt and Berthe Morisot,[22] Gilpin depicted domestic scenes peopled not by fanciful erotic nudes, as was common among the male pictorialists, but considered from the social position of a mother. In *A Visiting Nurse* 1924 (fig.29), a nurse tends a boy in bed while other children, presumably siblings, look on with concern, the camera's low vantage point positioning us among them. Gilpin had little interest in city life, addressing instead her own immediate environment. As such, her work offers a critical alternative to Robinson's earlier sentimental views of women and rural life.

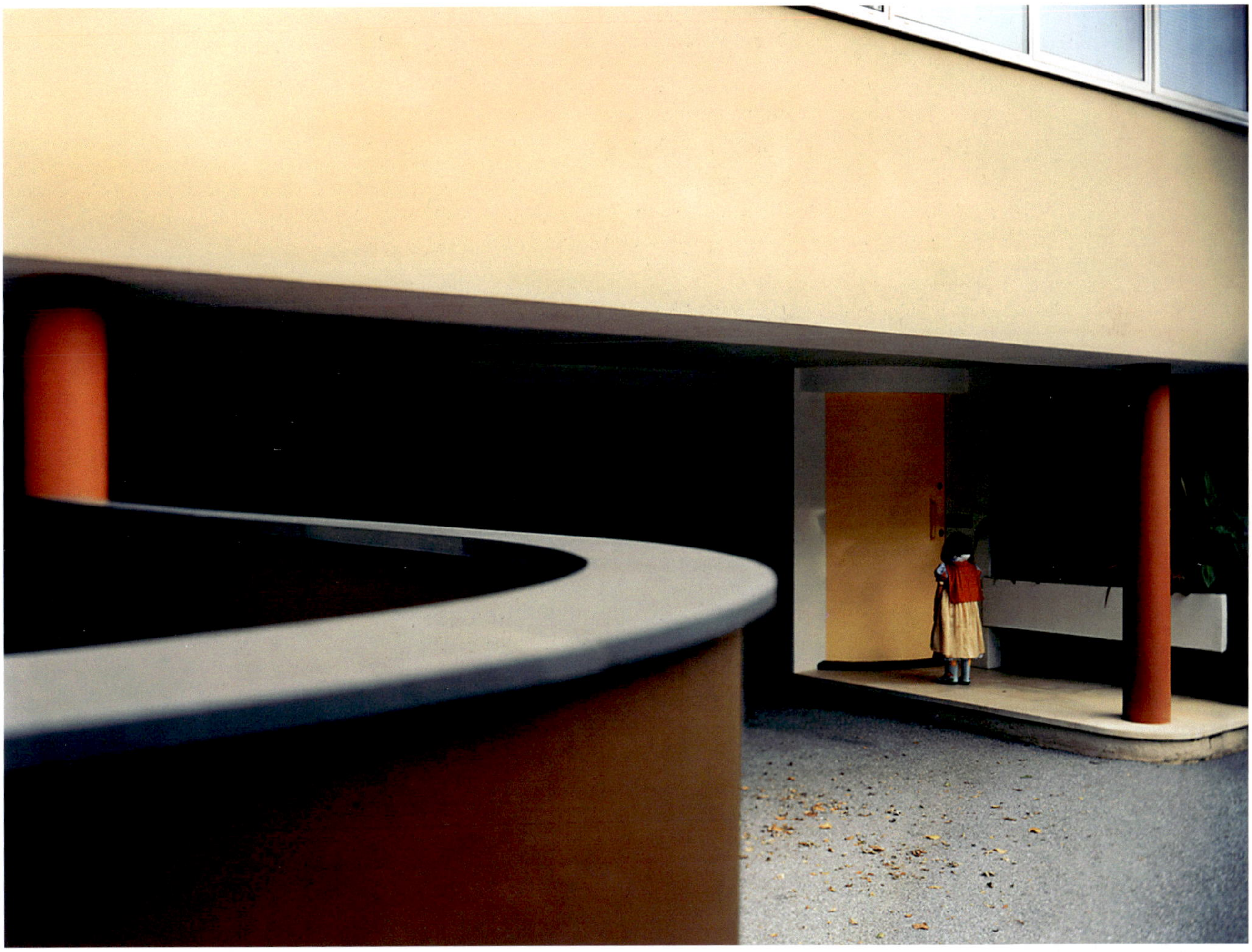

Figure 31
Hannah Starkey, *Untitled*, October 2004
Framed c-type print, 122 × 152

Gertrude Käsebier's photographs were featured in the first issue of Stieglitz's *Camera Work* magazine, although she and others later broke away from him because of his didactic values, setting up the Pictorial Photographers of America group in 1910.[23] Käsebier was familiar with Cassatt's impressionist works and also addressed the viewpoint of children in her work. *The Road to Rome* 1903 (fig.30), featuring her grandson, was painted over and the print rephotographed to achieve a tonal effect that focuses the viewer on the road that winds away into the distance – a metaphor for the twists and turns of life that lie ahead of every child.

We might contrast this poetic pictorialist image of a child's future with Hannah Starkey's contemporary urban tableau image of a child (fig.31). The poignancy of Käsebier's singular figure is still relevant, but here there is a quite different emphasis or attitude. A good deal of Starkey's work pictures young women circumscribed by social spaces. In *October* 2004, a solitary young girl stands at the threshold of a home, but instead of facing an open space with a horizon, as in Käsebier's *The Road to Rome*, she inhabits a claustrophobic urbanism, cluttered with modernist architecture. Whether the door that she contemplates brings respite and comfort from those external forms or not is unknown, but the pathos of her future is hinted at in the pose of her peripatetic hesitation.

There are many other international examples of historical pictorialism that could be discussed here, but the point is that the pictorialist paradigm of photography enabled a different kind of art image to emerge.[24] Since photography was less cumbersome to learn and practice, the camera became a symbol of democratic art, a tool that could be used by those who had little or no skill in drawing or draughtsmanship, but who had a way of seeing, nonetheless. The camera could be used to picture things and places that others had not yet visited, that artists had not yet thought of picturing or that were difficult to access. In this way, pictorialism lent a common, if broad, aesthetic framework to the project of visioning the modern world. If today we can find some of the same themes as this older pictorialism in modern neo-pictorial art photography, it is nevertheless inflected and judged in comparison with other visual representations in circulation. The functions of the pictorial image have been not to contest these media images directly, nor to mimic them, but to reposition art photography and create a distance in relation to them.

Critical Distance

Gregory Crewdson's tableau images relate directly to cinematic and televisual expectations of narrative and drama, often suspending the moment at strange in-between instants (fig.32). The faces and bodies of the characters in his 'Twilight' series seem to be lit by the very objects that preoccupy them, as if they are drawn to some lurking hypnotic 'thing' that we can only imagine.

This overt theatricality is roundly condemned by some, such as the formalist art critic Michael Fried, whose pictorial taste is informed by principles from eighteenth-century pictorial tableau painting, although the uncanny effects of Crewdson's lighting is more modern.[25] Fried prefers naturalistic imagery (he uses the term 'anti-theatrical') over staged and visibly artificial-looking scenarios, arguing that theatricality interferes with the viewer's ability to identify and empathise with characters in the scene. Although the terms of the argument are different, there is an echo of the debate between Robinson's theatrical aesthetics and Emerson's 'naturalistic' subject matter, of idealism versus realism.

Attitudes towards the aesthetic value of these staged scenes have fluctuated over time. For Bertolt Brecht, writing in the 1930s, artifice and theatricality was essential to any critical drama or image, since it distanced and disrupted the illusion of reality. The spectator is forced to ask questions about what it is they are being shown.[26] We should be reminded that images are constructions, he argued, that they are ideologically motivated and purposefully charged with specific meanings produced for our consumption.[27] Jeff Wall employs this type of critical

24 See, for example, the section on Japanese photography in Padon and Nordström 2008.

25 There is no reference at all to Gregory Crewdson's work in Michael Fried's extensive book on pictorial art photography. The arguments by Fried about the theatrical and anti-theatrical relate back to the eighteenth-century writings on painting by Denis Diderot. See Fried 2008.

26 Brecht's writings relate to aesthetic strategies of acting in the theatre, but have been widely adopted for cinema and photography. See Willett 1964.

27 See, for example, the reading of Brecht's theories by Elizabeth Wright in Wright 1989.

28 For a summary of the late 1970s New York-based group see Eklund 2009.

artifice, or Brechtian device of distanciation, in his work to stage scenes that seem to freeze the action, like a film still or photojournalist picture. Given the high-quality definition in the images, their sharpness and frozenness makes them look staged, but they leave room for uncertainty, a hesitation, which the spectator can explore.

It is curious that these historical arguments about theatricality repeat themselves in different epochs with positive and negative values attached to them. The mode of photography developed by Robinson and others in the mid-nineteenth century re-emerged among the photo-artists of the 1930s, whose Brechtian, explicitly theatrical aesthetic was intended to

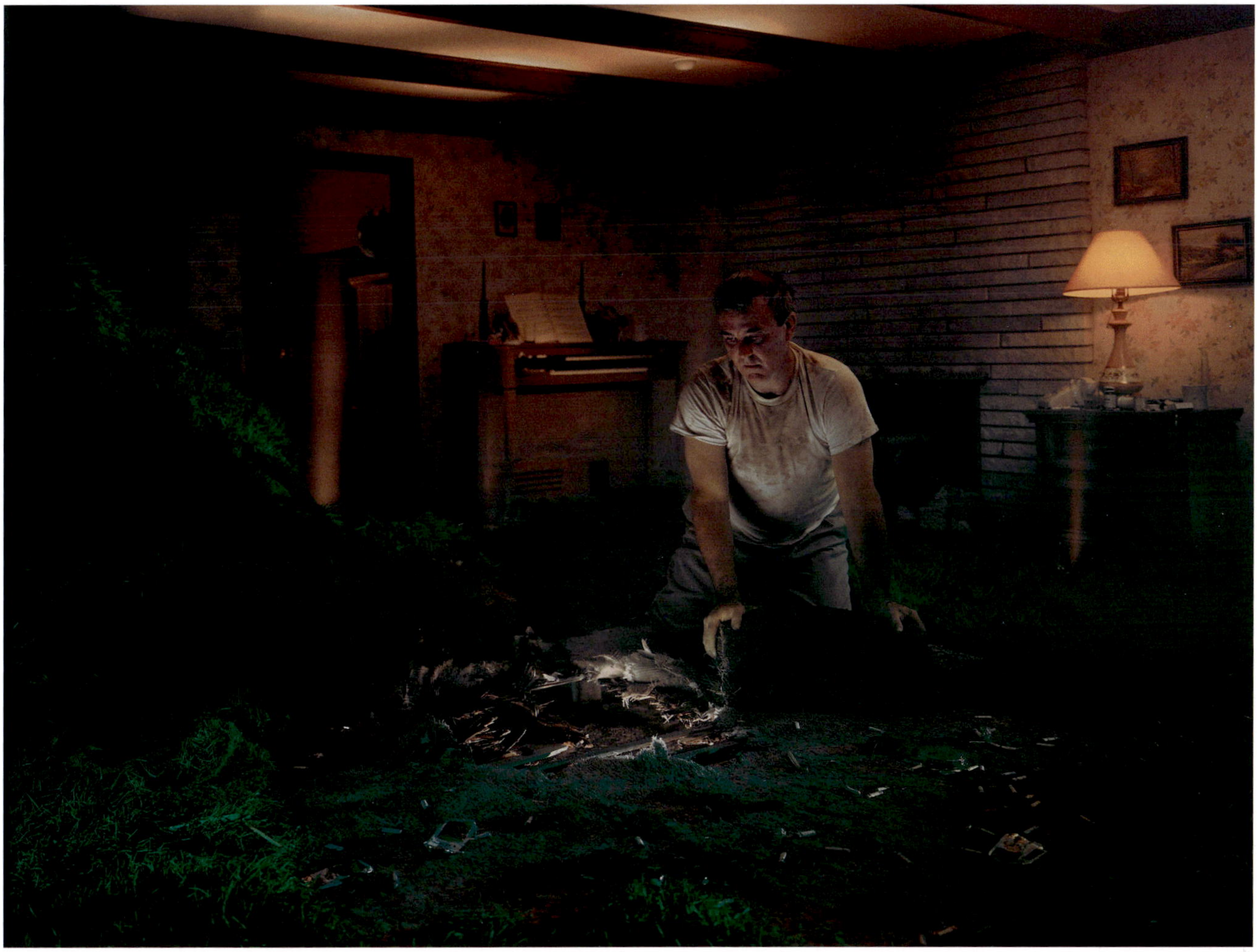

Figure 32
Gregory Credwson,
Untitled 1999
Chromogenic print,
127 × 152.4
Solomon R. Guggenheim Museum, New York

interrupt the ideology of realism. Artists like John Heartfield or Hannah Höch created photomontages that purposely dislocated these values of realism, with a considerable aesthetic and political effect. Theatricality clearly surfaced again in the 1970s, in work by artists associated with postmodernism, such as Barbara Kruger, Cindy Sherman, Richard Prince and Sherrie Levine.[28] These artists drew on a variety of media images, sometimes copying or re-presenting them unchanged, as pastiche, or others redeploying or remaking them with a critical difference, as parody. A strategy of explicit fakeness in photography tends to disrupt, ruin or even disintegrate any clear meaning. Artificiality highlights conflict inside

Figure 33 Alejandro Chaskielberg, *The Paraguayans* 2007 From the series *La Creciente* Digital c-print, 110 × 140

the picture, in its very form. Becoming allegorical, such pictures engage with the 'ruin' of photographic meaning in a way that makes the spectator ask more questions, rather than giving them answers.

In an interesting departure from the dynamics of these tactics, the Argentinian photographer Alejandro Chaskielberg uses very slow exposures on a large-format camera to dislocate the naturalism that Emerson had argued was necessary in photographs of real rural communities. Chaskielberg was formerly a director of photography for film, and he brings this sensibility to each scene, carefully lighting and sharply focussing it, balancing and blending artificial and natural light sources. The photographs are made at midnight, and the islanders pose, standing still for the long exposure. The resulting effect is a combination of focus and blur, a mix of both artificial and natural lighting, in effect reconfiguring the old pictorialist polemics between Robinson and Emerson. The series *La Creciente* (fig.33) creates a wildly visual atmosphere for these rural island communities, situated around the watery arteries of the Paraná River Delta in Argentina.[29] Chaskielberg also makes us

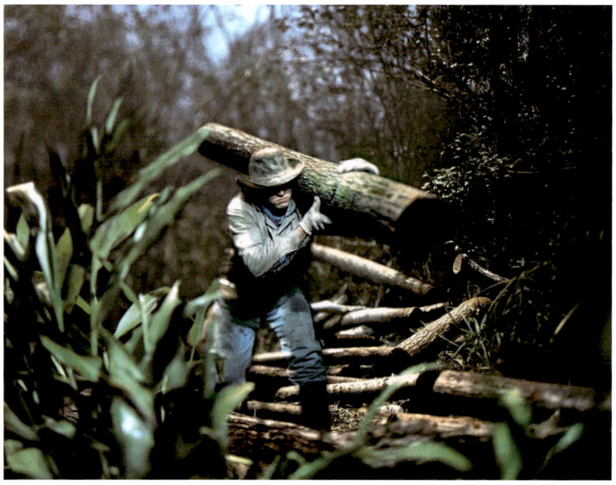

see that there is value in rethinking the techniques of photography as a means to disrupt the all-too familiar patterns of visual thinking that inhabit the wider social forms of representation. The aesthetics of Chaskielberg's images challenge the viewer's perception of a subject and its meaning, which is what tends to be forgotten as a more critical aspect of the history of pictorialism.

Historically, pictorialist photography had implicitly asked aesthetic questions about photographic meaning through use of different techniques and visual strategies. Yet, like painting, pictorialism in all its forms had not resolved these issues, but only advanced them in relation to the subject matter of particular pictures. As such, the conclusions to arguments over theatrical or naturalist tendencies are no more resolved today than the scenarios they refer to. These aesthetic debates relate to different ideas about art, and were re-articulated in the late twentieth century in a reconfigured understanding of the role of the viewer, who in one model is interrogative, actively producing meanings from an image, and in another passively consumes a preconceived message. The outcome of these strategies is crucial to contemporary art, and is perhaps nowhere

29 Chaskielberg 2011.

more acutely present than in the field of documentary photography, which increasingly turned towards art discourse. In effect, pictorialism suppressed the documentary aspect of photography, although it remained implicit to the work, and it was the aesthetics of the document that would return and come to dominate twentieth-century art photography.

Straight Images

Traditional histories of photography usually date the decline or even the end of pictorialism as 1917, when it was overshadowed by Stieglitz's New York group, who had broken from pictorialism in the final issues of *Camera Work* magazine. Yet in some ways this is something of a myth, because many photographers around the world continued to develop pictorialist ideals in their work long after Stieglitz had dumped it. In the final issue of *Camera Work*, Stieglitz promoted 'straight photography' in the work of Paul Strand, which developed from pictorialism. In the USA this straight photography was still aesthetically minded (via post-impressionism and cubism), but increasingly developed a conscious and confident view of a new modern 'photographic vision'. This vision literally saw a new role for sharp focus, depth of field and the abstraction of subject matter. Suddenly, photographic visuality was accepted on its own terms, and the painterly effect of the pictorial scene was gradually rejected for a purer 'photographic seeing'.

Today, a return to those older motifs and techniques of late nineteenth- and early twentieth-century pictorial art can be found here and there in contemporary photography. Photographers, perhaps even unaware of this older history, return implicitly to some of the aesthetic techniques and values of these earlier practices, from the *f*/64 deep-focus and sharpness of Andreas Gursky's 1990s work to the pictorialist 'fuzzography' of modern photography, like Sarah Moon's symbolist aesthetics or the middle-ground romanticism of Deborah Turbeville's pictorialism. As photography is digitised and automated, new inspiration for subject matter is found not only in photographic practices beyond art, such as fashion, photo-journalism, the internet, cinema and televisual drama, but also through a renewed interest in older historical forms of photography. Photography, once the outsider of art, has found its place at the centre. No longer a wolf in sheep's clothing, it has thrown off the coat it was given by painting and is now fully acknowledged as a default medium in contemporary art. Yet, paradoxically, photography also still dominates the non-art field of visual culture with a vast array of different uses. Art photography cannot be defined by the specificity of the medium or measured by any simple craft value, since these are all practised elsewhere in amateur and professional fields. Instead, a new art definition would evolve, picking out certain characteristics to define photography as an art of the document.

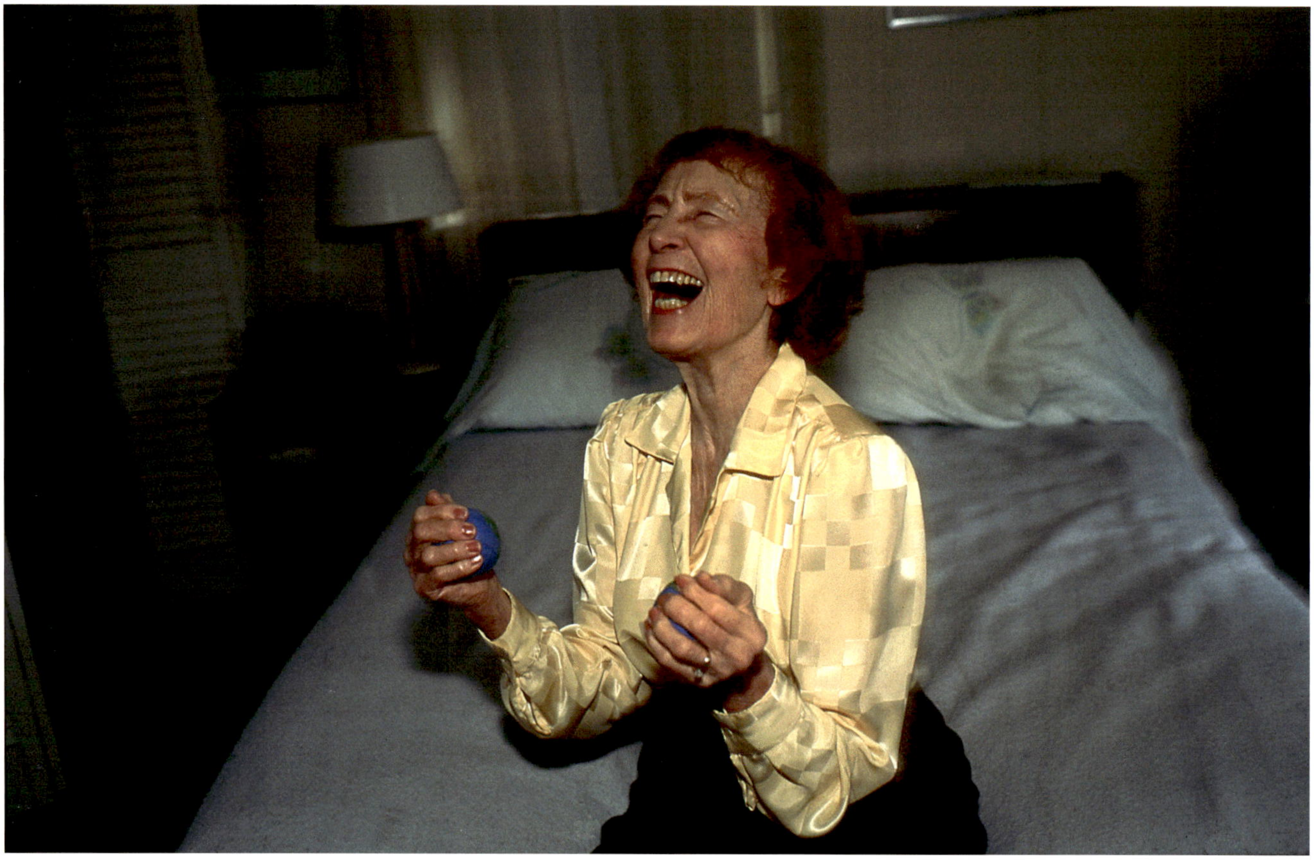

THE ART OF THE DOCUMENT

1 See Williams 1983, p.42.

2 The term 'documentation' will be discussed more fully in the next chapter.

3 Rancière 2009, pp.22–3.

4 Chéroux 2001.

5 Rancière 2009, p.23.

6 Ibid., p.27.

Figure 34
Nan Goldin, *Lil Laughing, Swampscott, Massachusetts* (also *My Mother Laughing, Swampscott, MA*) 1996
Cibachrome, 76.2 × 101.6

The photograph shows the artist's mother on the edge of a bed, gripping two 'stress balls' in her hands.

A document is usually thought of as 'artless', so that an artless photograph is one that makes itself invisible and privileges the referent of the image, the actuality that it represents. The perception of the photograph as a document flows from this notion of showing something plainly and simply, without artifice or artistic interference. Contrary to how it might sound, to be artless was once a positive attribute – even in art – implying spontaneity or a lack of guile.[1] In this sense, the snapshot, conceived as an instantaneous document, can be identified as typifying the artless artefact. To pick up a camera with the intention of showing things 'as they are' in this way can be called an impulse to document, which is the basis of documentary photography. However, the idea of the document in art introduces a number of complications, both in terminology and conception, along with the terms 'documentary' and 'documentation', which have different associations.[2] Perhaps this is why the French philosopher Jacques Rancière uses the term 'naked image' to refer to these types of photographic image.[3]

Naked Image

The example that Rancière gives of the naked image are the photographs taken at Nazi concentrations camps in 1945 by Lee Miller, Margaret Bourke-White, George Rodger and many others. These pictures represent the camps at the moment of their liberation, and all the horrors that were discovered there. Such pictures have since found their way into art exhibitions, like the 2001 exhibition *Memoirés des camps: 1933–4.*[4] Troubling as these pictures are, they convey, as Rancière puts it, 'the trace of history, of testimony to a reality that is generally accepted not to tolerate any other form of presentation.'[5] Their function is not so much to produce a dissemblance, an undoing of representation, but the resemblance of history to fact and reality. Their aim is to act as witness to a truth, and to provide a testimony to the process of human annihilation. Such pictures become a crucial trace of history, documents to prove that the bodies did exist and to reveal the extent of the atrocity. Rancière refers to a photograph by George Rodger (fig.35): 'the back of a corpse whose head we cannot see, carried by as SS prisoner whose bowed head shields his face from our eyes. This horrendous assemblage of two truncated bodies presents us with an exemplary image of the common de-humanization of victim and executioner.'[6]

While the naked image aims to show things as they are, without aesthetic pretentions, the role of the aesthetic cannot be avoided. Rancière suggests a two-staged semiotic reading of the holocaust photograph. The denoted perception is of the brute violence perpetrated on the visible human beings by absent others, with all the attendant suffering this brings. The second connoted understanding is that a process of

Figure 35
George Rodger, *Belsen: Collecting the Dead* 1945
Gelatin silver print, 20.2 × 25.4

Rodger photographed Bergen-Belsen concentration camp after its liberation in April 1945.

de-humanisation has occurred, in which the boundaries between victim and executioner, human, animal and mineral begin to dissolve. Sickening as this is, the second connotation, Rancière suggests, is the product of an aesthetic education, linked to other representations we see elsewhere.[7] For Rancière, the immediate reference is Rembrandt's painting of a skinned ox (fig.36), while for others there may be different associations with other art or media images. I am reminded, for example, of the famous photograph by Brassaï (fig.37) at a Paris meat market taken ten years before Rodger's Belsen image, the superficial resemblance offering a sort of cheerful counterpoint to the bleak nakedness of the camps.

Since a document is viewed in dialectical relations to other images, it can never be pure, or completely separated from other associations. There is a lesson here about all photographic images. Firstly, an image will always prompt associative avenues of thought in the viewer, whether consciously or not, which may divert it from its aim or obfuscate its subject

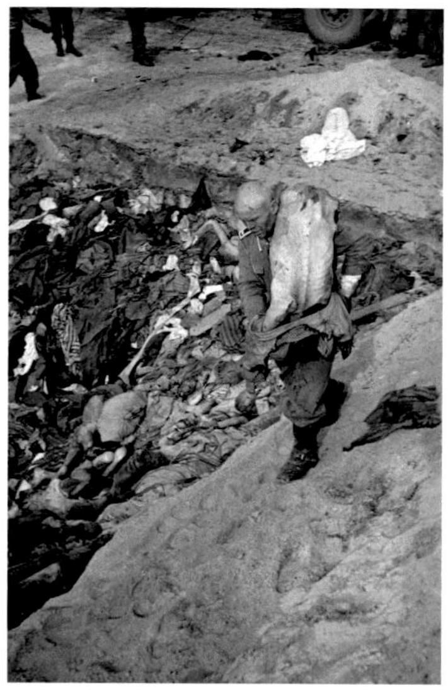

matter. Secondly, language can also lead the viewer down a very different path, just as Rancière's text leads us away from the historical Belsen moment in 1945 to Rembrandt's art. Thus the naked image poses questions about ethics and politics of images in art: how might such documents of barbarism retain their value as documents? What really is their function in this context of art? Is it to make art from the sensation or shock-effect of 'images of horror'?

In a short film about the history of art, filmmakers Jean-Luc Godard and Anne-Marie Miéville critique precisely this use of such photographic documents in an art exhibition. Photographs taken by the forensic scientist William Haglund after the war in former Yugoslavia, originally as evidence of crimes against humanity, were enlarged to show the exhumed bodies from mass graves. Godard and Miéville argue that to blow up these forensic pictures of war crimes to mural size and show them 'as if they were paintings' is to show a real misunderstanding and to transform their original function from evidence to spectacle.[8] The crucial point here is the changed situation, of documents intended for a court of law

7 Ibid., p.27.

8 Godard and Miéville 2006, p.47.

transformed and celebrated in the forum of art for aesthetic contemplation. While it might be argued that the art gallery should offer such a space for contemplation, the dangers of de-contextualisation must be clear for all to see. Such controversial examples highlight the ethical problems and social issues that are perhaps less often raised or discussed in relation to other social uses of photographs as 'documents'.

Document Image

Passport photographs, identity mug shots, police crime-scene pictures, military reconnaissance images, personal snapshots, surveillance, scientific and medical photographs, aerial shots, geographical survey and satellite images, Google Street View – all these photographic genres are intended to function as documents, but it is surprising how many have ended up in art in one form or another. This is usually precisely because of their status as documents, and they have been surprisingly more central to the formation of art photography than is often perceived.

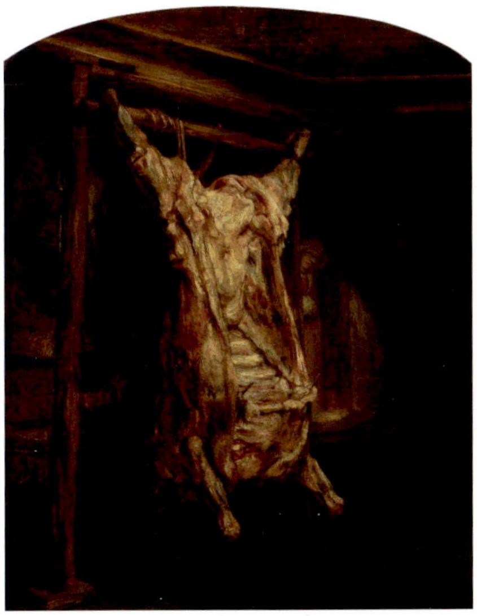

Figure 36 Rembrandt van Rijn, *The Slaughtered Ox* 1655 Oil paint on wood, 94 × 69 Musée du Louvre, Paris

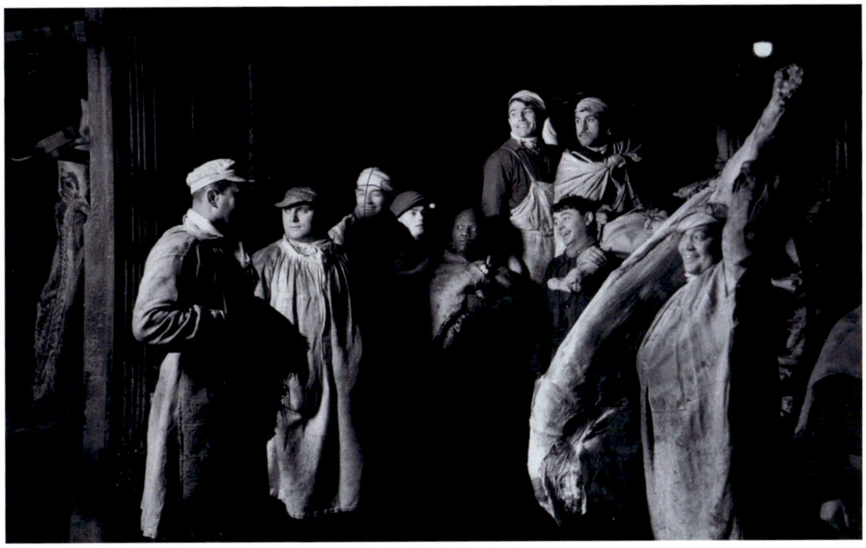

Figure 37 Brassaï, *Les fort des halles* 1935 Silver Gelatin print, 18 × 28 Musée National d'Art Moderne, Centre Georges Pompidou, Paris

Perhaps still the most obvious and significant historical instance of this is Eugène Atget's albums of photographs of Paris, which were transformed into art, despite his own claim that they were 'simply documents'.[9] Atget was an old neighbourhood photographer who earned his living by selling photographic images of shops, streets, carriages, carts, salons, staircases, bedrooms and many other spaces usually inhabited by ordinary Parisians, including Atget himself. He sold the photographs as 'studies' to customers in a variety of industries, and to magazines, museums and artists, such as Braque, Picasso and Utrillo, alongside many others.[10]

For thirty years Atget accumulated his pictures of Paris *populaire*, moving from tourist views to the outskirts of the old city, representing *Vieux Paris* and its environs (figs.38, 39). Of the thousands of photographs, most are taken frontally or with a slight oblique angle view, others at unusual angles. Overall, most of the subjects are slightly off-centre and feel as though they were not 'composed', or only unconsciously so. This variation lends the albums an air of informality and innocence. Atget

9 See Nesbit 1992, p.1. For a critique of Atget's canonisation see Solomon-Godeau 1995.

10 Nesbit 1992, p.20.

referred to his works, which are all characterised by this informal realism, as 'photographic documents'.

The Surrealists, especially Man Ray and the poet Robert Desnos, championed Atget's photographs of Paris, claiming that he was a pioneer of a new type of image-work that gave face to ordinary life. But even though the sign on Atget's door clearly read '*Documents pour artistes*' (Documents for artists), it was as though the surrealists took this to mean documents *by* an artist. In 1928, the year after Atget's death, Desnos eulogised: 'These are not the albums of an artist left to libraries, but the visions of a poet bequeathed to poets.'[11] Two years later Pierre Mac Orlan, theorist of the 'social fantastic' and of the role that photography could play in creating social mystery, described Atget as 'one of the purest poets of that anthill of small independent lives.'[12] Evidently the surrealists saw something in Atget's work that he himself had not.

11 Desnos, 'Spectacles of the Street – Eugène Atget', first published in *Le Soir*, Paris, 11 September 1928; reprinted in Phillips 1989, p.16.

12 Pierre Mac Orlan, Preface in Atget 1930; reprinted in Phillips 1989, p.48.

13 Nesbit 1992, p.26.

14 Ibid., p.27.

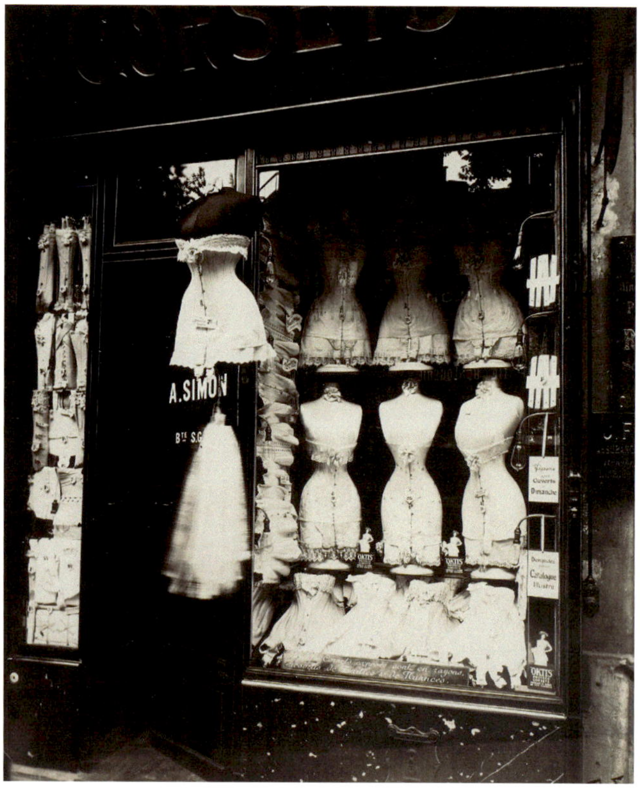

Figure 38
Eugène Atget, *Boulevard de Strasbourg (Corsets)* 1912. Gelatin silver paper print, 22.9 × 18 The Art Institute of Chicago. Julien Levy Collection

This image was featured (uncredited) in the French surrealist publication *La Révolution surréaliste*, 11, 1928. The picture accompanies a written account of a dream by Marcel Noll, as was common among the surrealists at this time. Another dream on the same page is by Andre Breton.

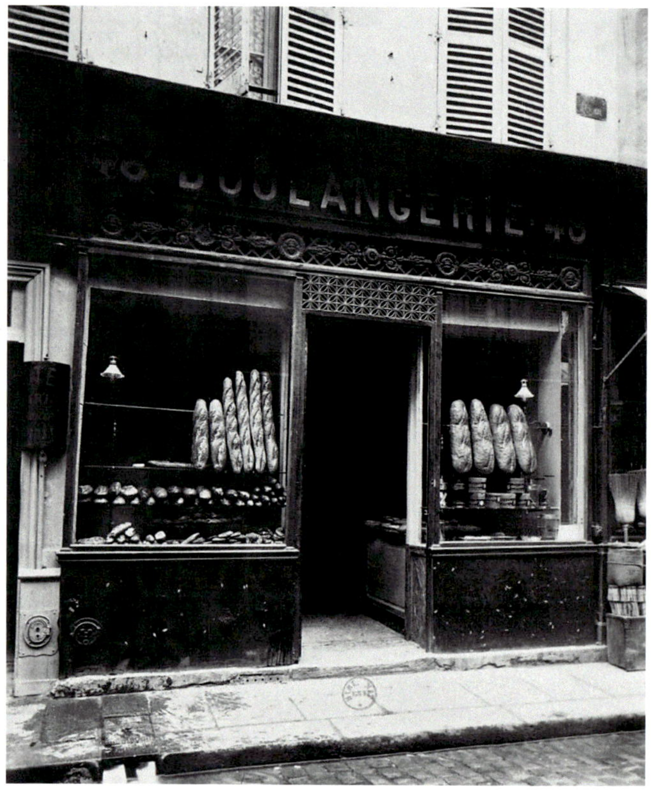

Figure 39
Eugène Atget, *Boulangerie, 48 Rue Descartes* 1910–11 Albumen print from glass negative, 21.1 × 16.5

From the album *Métiers, boutiques et ètalages de Paris* (1912)

Atget was clear that he simply earned his living selling prints of Paris in all its florid detail to any client who would buy them: artists, architects, builders, designers, interior decorators, libraries, museums, publishers, theatre set designers and more.[13] It is an extraordinary array of trades, industries and professions that he supplied with his pictures. It begins to feel as though Paris life was caught in a never-ending circle of reference, with images of the old city informing the new designs recycled via his photographs. They were the raw material from which new designs, paintings and broader aspects of Parisian visual culture were reformulated. As Molly Nesbitt notes, the photographs were 'meant to be taken up repeatedly, to have several futures, and to exist as a point of detail on the way to one of them. They were meant to be incomplete.'[14]

15 For the 'polysemic' photograph see Barthes 1991, p.28.

16 See Ian Walker, 'A Surrealist Atget', in Walker 2002.

17 See Florent Fels, 'The first Salon *Indépendant de la photographie*', 1928, reprinted in Phillips 1989, pp.23-6.

18 See '1929' in Foster et al. 2004, pp.232-7.

It is this sense of incompleteness that attracts viewers, as does Atget's intention that they be multiple in their use and plural in their meanings. As open texts - or to use a semiotic term, highly *polysemic* texts - many meanings can be attached to them, and this is certainly apparent in the diversity of Atget's clients.[15]

The story of how Atget's work entered the art museum is fascinating, not least because it gives an insight into the origins and direction of modern art photography. It was the surrealist photographer Man Ray, while living in the same street as Atget, who first obtained his pictures for publication in *La Révolution surrealiste* in 1926.[16] Berenice Abbott, the young American darkroom assistant to Man Ray, also met Atget and started buying his pictures. They became friends. Abbott was an outstanding portrait photographer in her own right and photographed Atget just before he died in August 1927.

After his death Abbott bought what remained of Atget's estate, the other half having already been sold to the Commission des monuments historiques (Historical Monuments Commission). She became a tireless promoter of Atget's cause and ensured that others would see his work too.

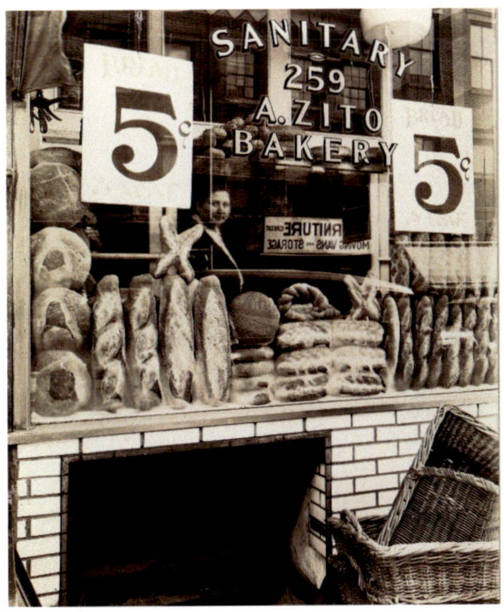

Figure 40
Berenice Abbott, *Bread Store (A. Zito Bakery), 259 Bleecker Street, New York*, 3 February 1937
From the series *Changing New York* 1935-9
Gelatin silver print, 24.8 × 19.2
The Museum of The City of New York

She submitted his work to the First Independent Salon of Photography in Paris in 1928, which was started as an alternative to the pictorialist-dominated photography salons.[17] Atget's pictures were highly popular and subsequently shown repeatedly in different exhibitions and magazines, most significantly in the hugely influential international exhibition *Film und Foto*, in Stuttgart, Germany, in 1929.[18]

Atget's photographs were suddenly connected to the new, wider international movements of modern and avant-garde photography: the New Vision of Lázló Moholy-Nagy; the New Objectivity macro photography of Albert Renger-Patzsch, Karl Blossfelt and others; the Foto-Eye of Frank Roh; and movements such as the Worker's Photography of Willi Münzenberg and the political photomontages by John Heartfield. All these innovative European movements signalled a new confidence in photography, to which an explosion of popular interest also lent its support. Just as today, with the profusion of mobile phone cameras, the visual documentation of everyday life was easily achieved by amateurs. The document photograph had come of age. Atget's 'simple documents' fed into these new ideas about the value and quality of photography, and as a precursor, also legitimated them. Thus his career as an artist was launched, involuntarily, after his death. His documents were commuted into a documentary oeuvre, an artwork, a visual atlas of Paris, which, like Aby Warburg's unfinished history project, *Mnemosyne Atlas* 1929, presented a constellation of images on the interval of life.[19] For the new avant-garde photography movements, Atget's pictures were brilliant observations of Paris. For the surrealists, Atget's pictures championed the mystery of 'everyday' life, the enigma that haunts our ordinary lives, and for them, Paris as a psychological entity. For Berenice Abbott, Atget's work provided the foundation for a new documentary practice, which she set about developing in her own photographic work in New York, after she moved back there in 1929, coincidentally just before the Stock Exchange crash. She oversaw the publication of Atget's work in *Atget: Photographe de Paris* 1930, which included ninety-six photographs, published simultaneously in three editions, in USA, France and Germany (the German one published in Leipzig was seen by Walter Benjamin).

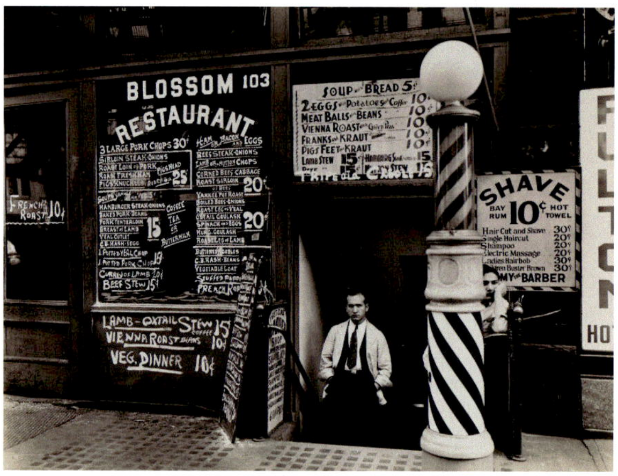

Figure 41
Berenice Abbott, *Blossom Restaurant, 103 Bowery, New York* 1935
From the series *Changing New York* 1935–9
Gelatin silver print, 19 × 24.5
The Museum of The City of New York

Back in New York, Abbott was visited by Walker Evans, whose work can be seen in a direct line from Atget and Abbott, both in the repertoire of the images and in the attitude of ways of seeing. Abbott had been a successful commercial portrait photographer, but in New York she began to borrow Atget's approach to document New York, his angles of view and subject matter, but modified for the new themes and context of the American city (figs.40, 41). She also tentatively developed a 'frontality', which subsequently became a signature trait of Evans's photography. Evans and Abbott had studios in the same street and became friends in New York. At this time Abbott was busy making prints from Atget's negatives that she had brought with her to New York for the first solo show of his photography at the Weyhe Gallery in New York in 1930, which had also sponsored the publication of her book on Atget.[20] Evans would thus have seen Atget's work first-hand in Abbott's studio. Indeed, he even reviewed the book in his essay, 'The Reappearance of Photography', published in *Hound & Horn* in 1931, although he was rather unimpressed with the quality of the reproductions.[21] He argued that Atget's pictures showed a 'lyrical understanding of the street', not simply a

19 Warnke and Brink 2000.

20 Weissman 2011, p.113.

21 Evans 1931.

'poetry of the street' or the 'poetry of Paris', but also 'the projections of Atget's person'.[22] These ideas would inform Evans's own 'documentary style', a phrase that he coined to identify his own version of photography as art. 'Documentary,' he would say, 'that's a sophisticated and misleading word. And not really clear ... The term should be documentary style ... You see, a document has use, whereas art is really useless.'[23] Evans, who had already spent time in Paris, had originally wanted to be a writer like Gustave Flaubert – the French writer famous for his unusual mode of descriptive writing – and clearly saw Atget as a kind of visual equivalent, a visual artist who could 'write' the real world in poetic 'photo documents'.[24]

Abbott, on the other hand, despite having met many avant-garde artists, writers and critics in Paris, and in New York before that, maintained that documentary was more important as the mode and means of recording life.[25] She did not move towards surrealism or Duchamp's brand of conceptualism, but stayed with the project of documentary photography, inspired by Atget's photographic work as being 'simply documents'.

22 Walker Evans, 'The Reappearance of Photography', in Trachtenberg 1980, pp.18-6.

23 Evans 1971; see Naomi Rosenblum, p.340.

24 Evans 1980, p.188. For Gustave Flaubert and description, see Barthes 1986.

25 Weissman 2011, p.43.

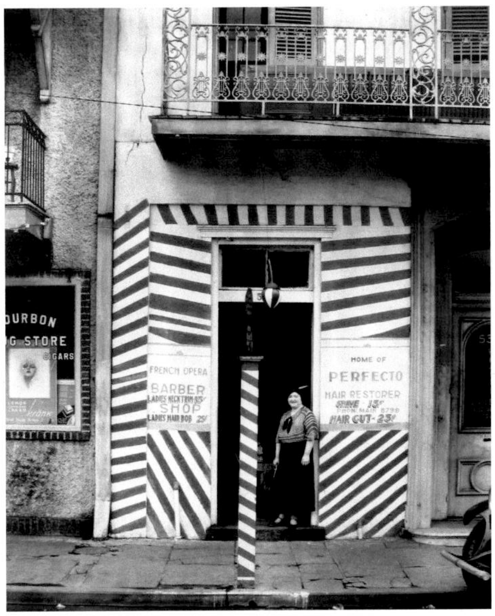

Figure 42
Walker Evans, *Painted Doorway of 'French Opera' Barber Shop on Bourbon Street, New Orleans, Louisiana February-March 1935* 1935

Writing much later in 1951, she was still opposed to the aestheticism of photography, of pictorialism and picturesque equivalents, and does not even mention the avant-garde surrealism of Man Ray and his friends, which she had seen at first-hand in Paris, nor indeed any other new tendency. Proudly American, she argued that photography should be thoroughly 'documentary': 'To chart a course, one must have a direction. In reality, the eye is no better than the philosophy behind it. The photographer creates, evolves a better, more selective, more acute seeing eye by looking ever more sharply at what is going on in the world. Like every other means of expression, photography, if it is to be utterly honest and direct, should be related to the life of the times – the pulse of today. The photograph may be presented as finely and artistically as you will; but to merit serious consideration, must be directly connected with the world we live in. 'What we need is a return, on a mounting spiral of historic understanding, to the great tradition of realism. Since ultimately the photograph is a statement, a document of the *now*, a great responsibility is put on us.

Today, we are confronted with reality on the vastest scale mankind has known. Some people are still unaware that reality contains unparalleled beauties. The fantastic and unexpected, the ever-changing and renewing is nowhere so exemplified as in real life itself. Once we understand this, it exercises a dynamic compulsion on us, and a photo-document is born.'[26]

Even though Abbot rejected surrealism, its influence is apparent in her reference to the 'fantastic and unexpected', and the issue of aesthetics also inevitably returns too, since her formulation of realism and reality include the term 'beauty'. Perhaps there is a distant echo here of surrealist aesthetics, of their formulation of the convulsive beauty in everyday life. The surrealists could certainly see this in Atget's documents: the marvellous in the everyday and dream-like enigma of human experience.[27] The surrealists chose photographs from Atget's albums to suit their project, as did his other clients – a surrealist interest that the brilliant German critic Walter Benjamin would name as an experience of the 'outmoded'.[28]

Affective Documents

Atget's photographs remind the viewer of the fashionless and *passé*, of timeworn buildings, the old products in shops and the residues of life that are made redundant by industrial progress. Such images warp the sense of modern time and space, turning the idea of progress back on itself, into an uncanny return of the past. Benjamin noted, 'almost all these pictures are empty ... They are not lonely, merely without mood; the city in these pictures looks cleared out, like a lodging that has not yet found a new tenant.'[29] The pictures are absent of any action, yet full of description, wherein Benjamin saw their revolutionary experience. He says in 1931: 'Not for nothing were pictures of Atget compared with those of the scene of a crime.'[30] Writing two years before Benjamin, the Belgian surrealist Albert Valentin had already remarked on the location of Atget's pictures: 'those dead-end streets in the outlying neighbourhoods, those peripheral districts that his lens recorded, constituted the natural theatre for violent death, for melodrama...'.[31]

In fact, the streets in Atget's images already had moving stories attached to them through popular cinema, because, as Valentin noted, these outer Parisian locations 'were so inseparable from such matters that French filmmakers, Louis Feuillade and his disciples – at a time when studio expenses were what was skimped on – employed them as settings for their serials'.[32] Feuillade was the director of *Fantômas*, a popular series of mystery films based on the pulp novels by Pierre Souvestre and Marcel Allain and loved by the surrealists. Feuillade set his movie scenes in the very same peripheral districts of Paris that Atget photographed in *Vieux Paris*. So while it is not surprising that the surrealists experienced déjà vu when watching these scenes, such filmic sources do not account for the subsequent continued fascination with Atget's photographs. Nevertheless, in this way it was the surrealists who were the first to aestheticise the non-aesthetic 'document' photograph. (The French writer Gustave Flaubert, so admired by Evans, can be said to have done the same thing for description in literature.)[33] Even today, these inert documents of empty spaces can still become dream-spaces, images formed in imaginary action with protagonists activated in events invented by the spectator.

26 Berenice Abbott, 'Photography at the Crossroads', 1951, in Trachtenberg 1980, pp.183–4.

27 David Bate, 'What is a Surrealist Photograph?', in Bate 2004.

28 Walter Benjamin, 'Surrealism: The Last Snapshot of the European Intelligentsia', in Benjamin 1985, p.229.

29 'A Short History of Photography' in Trachtenberg 1980, p.251.

30 Ibid., p.256. See also Ian Walker's discussion of this comment in Walker 2002, pp.100–1.

31 Albert Valentin, 'Eugène Atget', first published in *Variétés*, Brussels Dec 1929; reprinted in Phillips 1989, p.20.

32 Ibid., p 20.

33 See Barthes 1986.

34 'A Short History of Photography' in Benjamin 1985, p.251.

35 Ibid., p.256.

36 Ibid., p.252.

Benjamin's readings of Atget's photographs differed from the surrealists', though. He saw their potential for 'giving free play to the politically educated eye, under whose gaze all intimacies are sacrificed to the illumination of detail.'[34] For Benjamin, the devil is in the detail, and the art of the document revels in it for sure. Benjamin goes on to suggest that in this 'new way of seeing' it is the anonymous aspect of the photographs that is illuminating. 'Is it not the task of the photographer', he asks rhetorically, 'to reveal guilt and to point out the guilty in his pictures?'[35] Atget's pictures, he seems to say, solicit in the spectator the curiosity of a detective. Of course, the images may not literally depict crime scenes, but the viewer construes meaning from them as such, scrutinising them as signs, to ask 'what is happening here?' But how do spectators interact with document photographs to produce a meaning? The mystery and adventure that Mac Orlan and the surrealists saw in Atget's work, the 'decidedly strange places where there appeared to be nothing of the slightest interest', as described by Valentin, is what creates a 'certain malaise' in the viewer. This malaise arises from how spectators find themselves split between being both the accused and the accuser. The common sense of guilt felt by every voyeur interacts with the curiosity of the detective, who aims to gain knowledge from seeing. This is the interplay of emotions to which many documentary photographs lend substance: a set of conflicting feelings, which pervade the effect experienced by the spectator when looking at the subject matter. 'Should I be looking at this?' 'What does this picture mean?' Sometimes the viewer's sense of guilt can be displaced or passed on to the photographer, or even on to the subject of the picture, who may be blamed for being depicted, and more easily so if they have elected to display themselves. These dynamics of identification are volatile and mutable, often aired with all the force of any intersubjective human relationship.

Benjamin considered the potential of Atget's work to elicit such conflict to be radical, and extended this to other documentary-orientated photography too. In August Sander's extensive series of German social portraits, *People of the 20th Century* (fig.43), Benjamin also recognised their value as 'comparative photography', as a veritable 'atlas of physiognomy'. Their level of detail in documenting otherwise anonymous persons of different social strata, professions and classes had its use: as 'a training manual', as exercises in how to see others.[36] From Sander's pictures one could learn about the people who make up society, and about their differences. This was the value of the art of the photographic document: the legibility of the world to its viewer.

In contrast to these two distinct modes of photography – Atget's documents of human spaces and Sander's comparative human portraits – a third form emerged: the action document or 'snapshot'. As cameras had become simpler to operate, the dynamic snapshot came to rival these older forms of document, and outstripped them, aided by automation of the camera and imaging technologies, with the digital form being most dominant today.

Writing in the early 1930s, when photography was industrialised, Benjamin was keenly aware of photography changing the definition of art and was eager to shift the argument away from the old debates. The old question of whether photography was art was exhausted, he argued, the new question was about *how* art was now photography. Benjamin

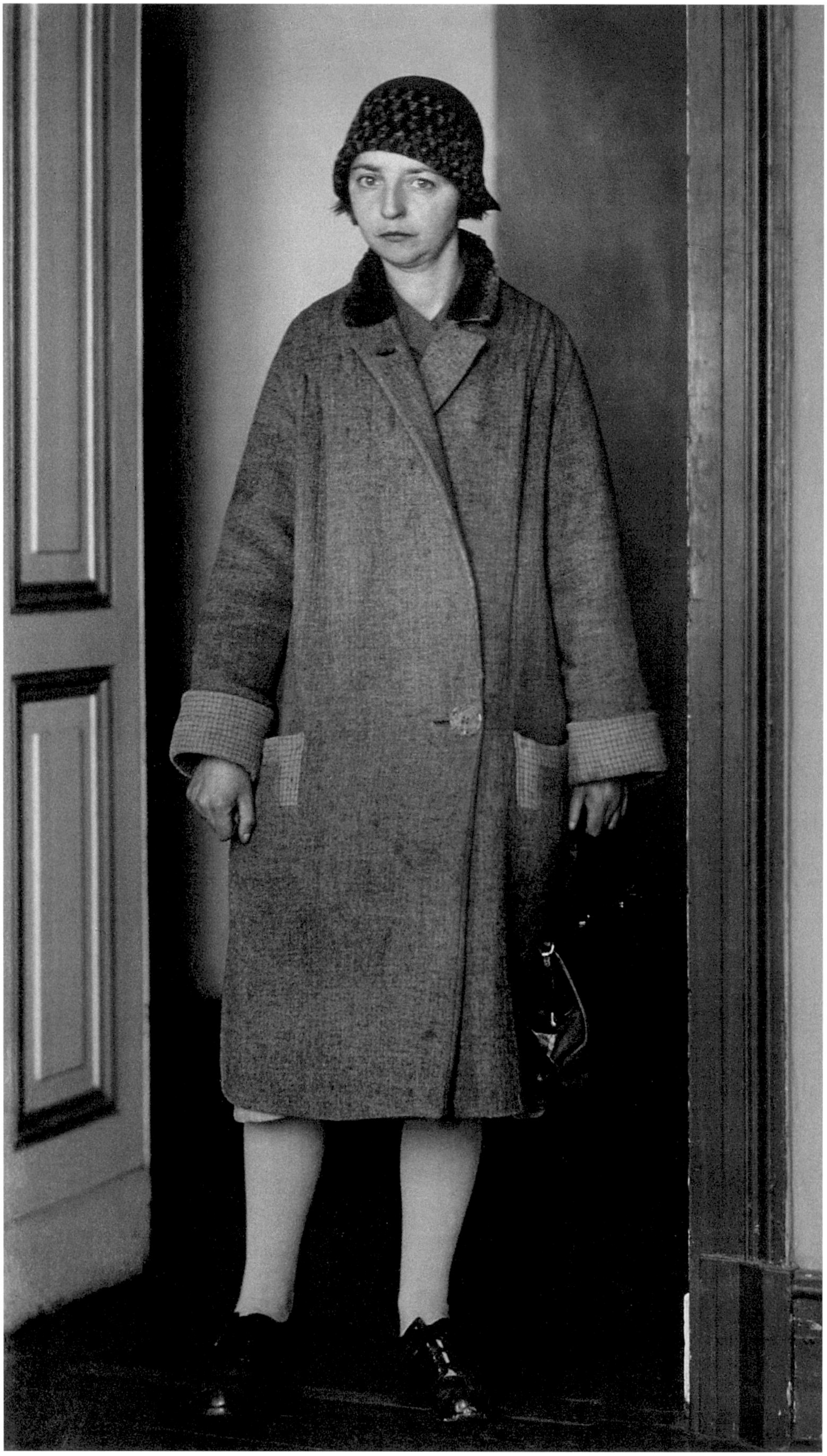

37 Ibid., p.253.

38 Alexander Rodchenko, 'Against the Synthetic Snapshot, For the Snapshot', 1928; reprinted in Phillips 1989, p.239.

39 Stalinism, however, would turn this realism into idealism, and the document into an advertisement for the right Soviet life.

40 Baudelaire 1965, p.162.

developed his own thesis regarding art where, he argued, photographic documentation was changing the viewing conditions, context and availability of art, and therefore the very meanings of paintings and sculptures. He wryly remarked: 'Everyone will have noticed how much easier it is to get hold of a picture, more particularly a piece of sculpture, not to mention architecture, in a photograph than in reality.'[37] Photographic pictures were becoming the primary means of encountering objects and places, and the actual experience of them was now secondary. In this sense, it was believed that photography could replace the experience of the original artwork and we would begin to live in a world of reproductions and re-presentations. Photography heralded a new era, in which to be photographed meant everything.

Indeed, in the new revolutionary Soviet Union, photographers like Alexander Rodchenko had hailed the end of art altogether, declaring snapshot photograph to be 'factography': 'Art has no place in modern life', he argued. 'It will continue to exist as long as there is a mania for the romantic and as long as there are people who love beautiful lies and deception ... Photograph and be photographed!'[38] Rodchenko championed the snapshot as a democratic form of image over the values of art. Factography was more concerned with an urgent sense of the present, not posterity, with the multiplicity of images more than any singularity, and with reality over any romantic vision. To make a photo document was indeed to be realistic, but in a modern and socially relevant sense.[39]

Figures 43
August Sander,
Beggar 1930
From the project *People of the 20th Century*
Gelatin print, 27 × 16.4
Die Photographische Sammlung/SK Stiftung Kultur, Cologne

Imagination and Realism

The magnitude of the shift in attitude towards photographic realism becomes clearer if we look briefly back to the nineteenth century and the assertions that a document was not – and could not be – art. Documents were seen as related to the accumulation of 'facts', and cameras, as copying machines, were predisposed to gather them in depictions of mundane reality, rather than to appeal to the human imagination. This idea about photographic realism, however, was not peculiar to debates on photography, since it also applied to painting, literature and all the other arts too. Charles Baudelaire characterised the issue well, when reflecting on the work of painters in the Paris art salon of 1859. Having already complained of painters making their pictures too photographic in their taste for the 'True', he praised those who seek the beautiful, and subsequently divided artists into two camps: realists and 'imaginatives': 'There are those who call themselves "realists" – a word with a double meaning, whose sense has not been properly defined, and so, in order the better to characterize their error, I propose to call them "positivists", and *they* say, "I want to represent things as they are, or rather as they would be, supposing that I did not exist." In other words, the universe without man. The others however – the "imaginatives" – say, "I want to illuminate things with my mind, and to project their reflection upon other minds".'[40]

In the early 1930s Benjamin reconfigured this distinction between positivist realism and human imagination, turning it upside down. The 'positivist' realism of the photograph could do far more for the social imagination of humans than Baudelaire had ever conceived. For Benjamin, it was the document that could be at the service of the spectator's imagination. Gone was Baudelaire's view of realism as static, absolute and

Figure 44 Carl Mydans, *Mountaineers 'spelling' themselves in front of store, Pikeville, Tennessee March (for the Farm Security Administration)* 1936 Gelatin silver print, 22 × 16

mere external fact; for Benjamin, the document embodied an art of the modern age: a democratic visual knowledge and the visual imagination as a wonder of modern twentieth-century culture itself. Just as the surrealists argued that Atget's documents created a radical dream world with images from ordinary city life, so Benjamin saw the radical potential of the photographic document to inspire a 'profane illumination'. What Benjamin saw in these images was something that he claimed would charge the human experience of them with 'bodily innervations of the collective'.[41] Perhaps he was over-optimistic about the emancipatory capacity of photographic images. His essay on the irreverent imagination of the surrealists was published just as the effects of the economic crash of 1929 were

41 'Surrealism' in Benjamin 1985, p.239; Badger and Parr 2004, pp.114–15; Burgin 1986.

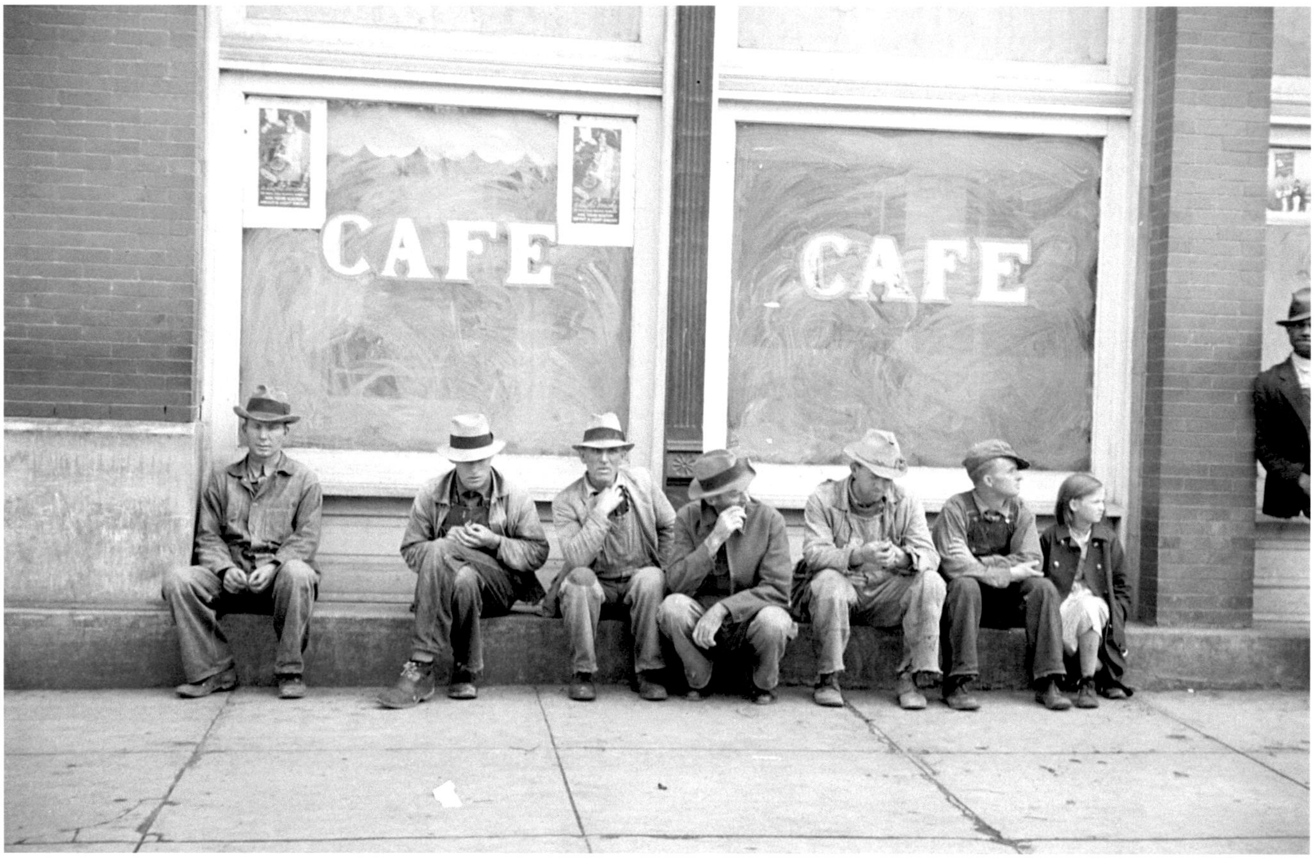

really beginning to hit home. Tragically, his own life ended a few years later, as he fled from the Nazis. But he was right about the importance of the photographic document: the 1930s became the age of documentary, an era when photography and film became the new arts. The birth of the photo-document also gave rise to the modern photography book in an explosion of new and different profane illuminations.

Social Documents

The Great Depression of the 1930s made many pictorialists and artists rethink what to photograph. Under the United States' New Deal programme, the Resettlement Agency was set up in 1935 to help unemployed and displaced farm labourers by providing loans, jobs and land for the migrant Americans. Setting up an 'Information Division' to publicise the

42 Hurley 1972.

43 Roy Stryker took up employment with Standard Oil to set up and run the photography project to 'document' its work.

agency's work, Roy Stryker, an economics tutor at Columbia University, who had already worked with the social reform photographer Lewis Hine on the book *American Economic Life*, was employed to gather visual evidence to record and publicise the activities of the Resettlement Agency (later renamed the Farm Security Administration, or FSA). Stryker, as chief editor, employed photographers to collect the visual data: first Arthur Rothstein, who like Stryker had worked at Columbia University, then Carl Mydans (fig.44), an experienced Wall Street photographer reporter, and Walker Evans, quickly followed by the appointment of painter and graphic artist Ben Shahn and photographer Dorothea Lange (fig.45). This core group accrued an astonishing record of rural life during the Depression years.[42] Many other photographers came and went after 1937 too, and the project continued until it was hit by the impact of the Second World War, when the FSA was transferred to the Office of War Information, and finally closed with Stryker's resignation in late 1943.[43]

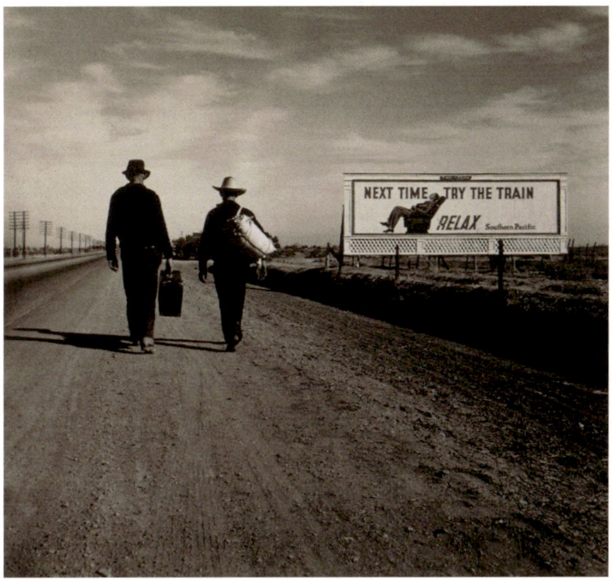

Figure 45
Dorothea Lange, *Heading towards Los Angeles, California* 1937
Gelatin silver print, 22.6 × 23.4

Through the FSA, the idea of a social documentary project became honed, organised and institutionalised. Shooting scripts and questions were designed to lead photographers towards specific themes and arguments. The photographers were asked to fulfil assignments, to record particular events and activities and to keep written records of them too. Inevitable conflicts erupted over what, how and why to record particular social events and processes rather than others. Such disputes aside, the resulting archive of photographs and related material is immense, and a variety of meanings can be elicited from this vast photographic archive. These meanings and the stories derived from them are as diverse and multiple as the term 'propaganda' (a term often levelled at this project because it was state funded) is supposed to be certain and fixed. While the initial aim had been to highlight and publicise the problems with which the Resettlement Agency were dealing – desperate rural poverty, eviction, unemployment and hunger – what remains is a massive repertoire of photographs, the collective meaning of which exceeds any single function or purpose. No doubt the general aim of the photographic work was to

Figure 46
Raghubir Singh, *Employees, Morvi Palace, Gujarat, India* 1982

Raghubir Singh was strongly influenced by Cartier-Bresson's photography, using his mode of 'the fleeting moment' to create a social view of India.

show how and what the Agency was doing to help, but they also displayed the dignity and deprivation of those suffering to those who were not. Creating wider public awareness of the existence of these issues was intended to breed compassion and care among viewers, but no matter how much bitter reality it made visible, the unjustness of the social situation remained. Although different participants had varying views on the role, effects and use of all this visual material, nevertheless the FSA is one of the key founding projects in which social documentary photography was used as a sociological method. It is from such projects that documentary photography quickly gained much of its reputation and currency in social studies and photography, and in art.

Document Art

In 1938 Roy Stryker was invited to submit a selection of FSA photographs to the International Photographic Exhibition in New York, held at the Grand Central Palace and sponsored by the USA Leica representative, Willard Morgan. The FSA photography section of the show was so immensely popular that the Museum of Modern Art (MoMA) in New York offered to tour the work throughout the USA, and so social documentary photography came into wider circulation via the art museum.

The same year MoMA also held the first solo exhibition of a photographer's work. *American Photographs* showed work by Walker Evans, including some of his FSA photographs.[44] As what Evans called his 'photo documents' were installed in the modern museum of art, it also installed the prototype for art photography. Single prints in frames on the wall functioned as individual art objects, but also belonged together in a sequence. Under the guise of an exhibition catalogue, the layout of photographs in the book also became a permanent photowork in its own right. Like the book of Atget's photography, edited by Abbott and published eight years before, Evans's book followed the same clean and simple layout, and established the photobook as an artwork in its own right. The reproducible status of photography meant that viewing pictures in the book and visiting the exhibition could be seen in parallel, as equivalent, if different, experiences. The viewer of the exhibition and the reader of the book could move back and forth from one picture to the next, or browse across them in any order or direction, although sitting in a chair with a book is a more intimate experience than strolling around a public exhibition. The double-page spread of the book was designed to privilege the single picture on a plain white background, just as on the white-cube gallery wall. There were no captions or text on the image plate page, only page numbers, with contextual information appearing as endmatter and an introductory essay at the front. This would become the prototype for art photography books, conceived not only as a reproduction of photographs as prints, but as a type of popular art object or artwork in itself.[45] Benjamin had been right: photographs could supplant the visit to an exhibition. Art had become photography.

The accompanying essay in *American Photographs* by Lincoln Kirstein described the pictures as 'intensely dramatic'. This seems wrong, however. Like Atget (or August Sander for that matter), Evans had not been interested in drama, but in description. The frontal characteristic attributed to his photographs serves to emphasise this descriptive purpose, and when

44 Badger and Parr 2004, pp.114–15.

45 See the critique of this ideal by Victor Burgin, 'Seeing Sense', Burgin 1986.

carried across from one photograph to another creates a visually descriptive journey across America.

Evans was notorious for rejecting his FSA assignment briefs, often disappearing for weeks at a time to produce his own poetic commentaries on situations, environments, circumstances and events. Here was the idea of a personal mode of expression with documentary effect. Evans demonstrated how a photographer could pursue in depth and at length a body of work made up of a series of images that worked individually, but also together, like a visual novel. The photographer thereby becomes an author, a conveyor of 'facts' strung into a visual narrative, which Evans himself would later name 'lyrical photography'. If this art photography is

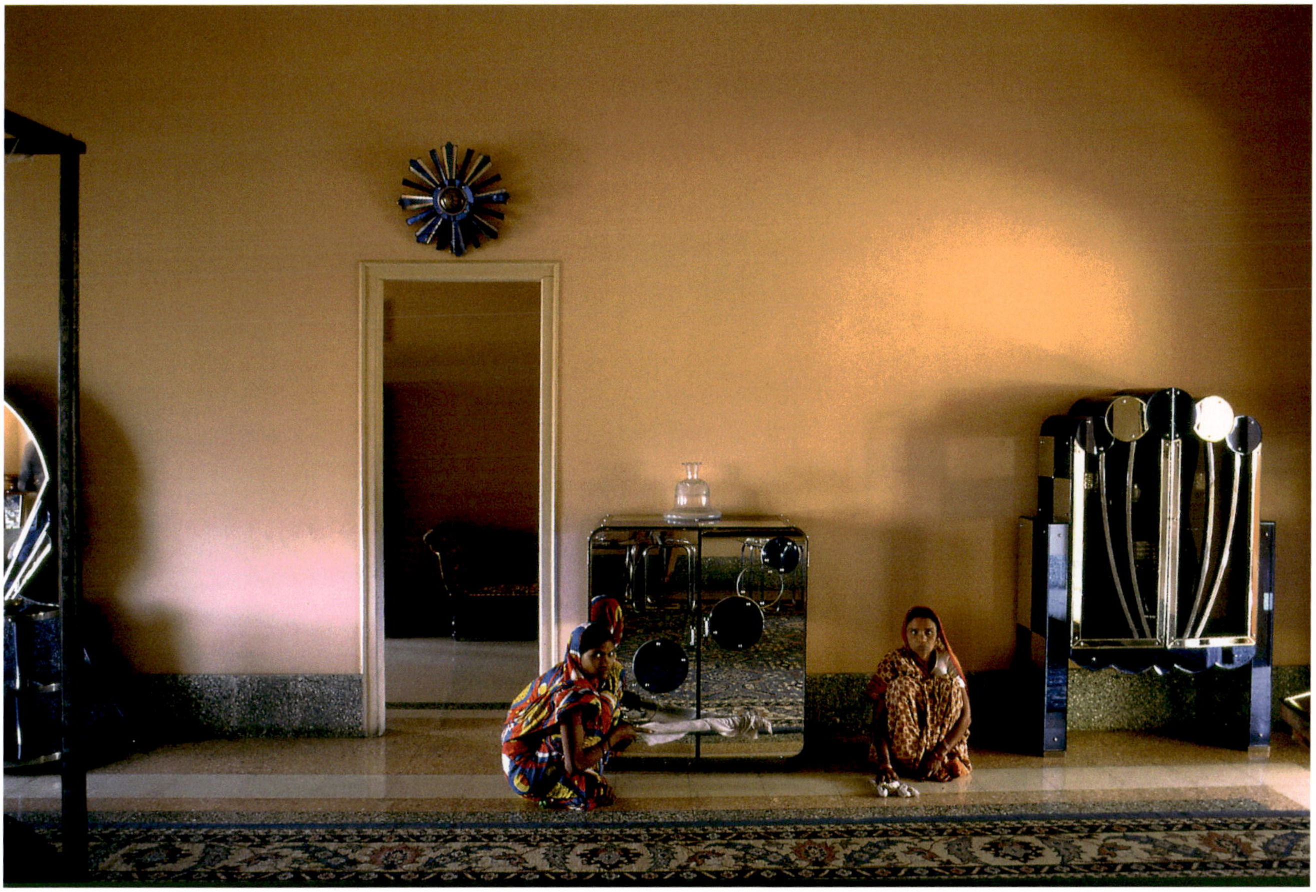

like poetry, why not make a poem about poverty? Should any life experience be excluded as a theme for art? In a way, the idea of photography as a poetic realism enabled the photographic artist to blur the distinction between a personal view and a social view, rendering the imagination of the artist and the depiction of facts as a common goal, although this distinction haunted modern art photography for many years to come.

Forty years later, *Mirrors and Windows*, the 1978 MoMA exhibition curated by John Szarkowski, addressed these competing tensions inherent in this approach to documentary art photography with two contrasting clichés: art as a 'mirror of the artist's soul' or as a 'window on the world'. The exhibition in effect fused these attributes together, with the resultant 'expressive realism', a composite idea implicit still in much art

Figure 47
Doug Rickard,
#41.214669, Chicago, IL 2007
From the series *A New American Picture* 2010
Archival pigment print,
52.7 × 84.5

photography today. The most exemplary popular and globally significant photographer of expressive realism in twentieth-century photography was Henri Cartier-Bresson. His form of poetic documentary photography, organised to narrate social events, has been developed by many others ever since (see, for example, fig.46).

However, this poetic image lyricism was not at the forefront of the ambition of the FSA social documentary project. Dorothea Lange's FSA photography book *American Exodus*, for example, published in 1939, a year after Evans's *American Photographs*, was quite different in emphasis. Lange's book included captions and quotes from those who featured in her pictures, giving them a voice. (Her most famous photograph, *Migrant Mother*, was not included in this book.) The accompanying essay by sociologist Paul S. Taylor emphasises the plight of farmers forced to migrate in the search for work. Evans's book, on the other hand, emphasises his own voice as an artist, although it included some of his FSA pictures. The people are all unnamed, remaining as enigmatic as the eponymous sitter in the world-famous *Mona Lisa* painting. The differences between the modes of presentation in Evans's book and Lange's documentary make clear the distinctions between the 'documentary style' of Evans's poetic document work and the FSA social documentary purpose in Dorothea Lange's photography – even if their image styles of description can be seen to overlap in some ways.

We can point here to a very long list of well-established practitioners who continued the poetic documentary tradition. Robert Frank's *The Americans* 1956, for instance, had a profound international influence. Frank, a Swiss émigré to the USA, made a book that was critical and poetic, but which also used the snapshot in a new way. The pictures were dark and moody, ephemeral, yet razor sharp in their social observation and critique. William Klein's photographic series *New York* 1957 comprised a less polemical but even grittier visual style, almost graphic in appearance, which had a special impact on the look and style of the photography of Daido Moriyama and other Japanese photographers, as can be noted in Japanese photography books from the late 1950s onwards.[46] The 1967 New York exhibition *New Documents*, curated by John Szarkowski at MoMA, featured the work of three younger American photographers – Diane Arbus, Gary Winogrand and Lee Friedlander – and was followed a decade later by an exhibition of new colour photography by William Eggleston, which included his desolate yet beautiful scenes from the Southern States in the 1970s. The social document of the 1930s had evolved into the art of street photography, with the photographer as a *flâneur* of modern life (or less frequently the female equivalent, *flâneuse*), as the one who 'botanises on the asphalt' as an 'unwilling detective'.[47]

Perhaps one technological terminus of this type of street observation practice can be glimpsed in Doug Rickard's *A New American Picture* 2012 (fig.47). Rickard's work reproduces images grabbed from Google Street View. To construct its 'world' archive, Google uses vehicles and people mounted with multiple cameras to map terrains – in those parts of the world where this is politically and practically viable – and then transposes them into a fully virtual, photographic version of space, which can be navigated by anyone with a computer connected to the internet. But Rickard turns this into a new type of digital street photography, as a form

46 See Kaneko and Vartanian 2009.

47 Benjamin 1989, p.40. For a founding critique of the male *flâneur* see Janet Wolf 1990.

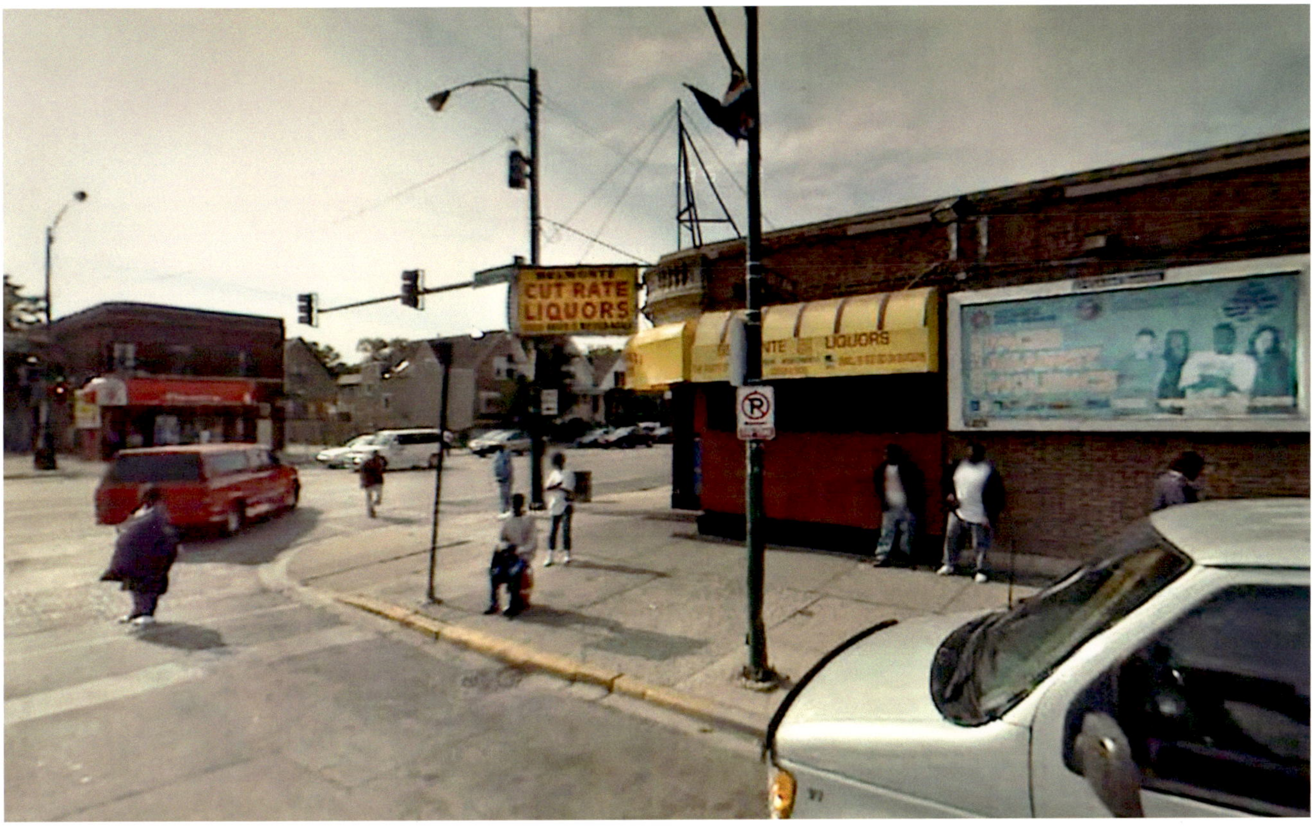
CUT RATE
LIQUORS
LIQUORS

of documentary. Indeed, the book's title discreetly suggests an update of Walker Evans's *American Pictures*, since the scenes he chooses also focus on dispossessed and marginal figures. The automated cameras of Google have accidentally caught the American 'homeless' and transient life. In some pictures pedestrians gape at the passing camera. These exchanges of looks between people and cameras in ghettos and run-down streets points to a general sense of social neglect, and to the irony that a highly sophisticated device designed to map streets has also recorded the activities and poverty of neighbourhood life. Although these scenes were automatically captured and digitally stitched together using computers, Rickard's pictures are nevertheless chosen and composed. To navigate Street View the user/viewer has to click their way down the street and select a point of view, a camera angle from which to record the scene of choice. The click of the shutter has been replaced by the click of the mouse. What is curious is how even an automated process can produce pictures that look as though they might have been sought out by a human, and this ambiguity of intent has a curious effect on the viewer. The pictures have a renewed sense of the authentic, as a new aesthetic actuality, driven by the computer taking a picture as a document. Yet while this long tradition of street photography continues, it has also mutated, drawing on the snapshot aesthetics of is origin to return towards that other domain, the opposite of the public sphere – private life.

48 Barthes 1984, p.98.

Private Lives

In the 1980s Nan Goldin's intimate and brutal *The Ballard of Sexual Dependency* and Larry Clark's monochrome series *Tulsa* sparked an international explosion of projects investigating the privates lives of photographers or those around them. In the 1990s, highly intimate themes, often sexually explicit, were explored through a focus on difficult situations or dramatic personal events in life.

With the increasing accessibility of fast, automated film cameras during the 1990s, many practitioners from a wide range of social backgrounds began to address personal experience as a social issue. The automated camera was less visible, the taking of a photograph a less intrusive event. Some might see this tendency to make work about our intimate lives as a general sign of social change, hailing the destruction of privacy through the public exposure of personal dirty linen – quite literally in some cases – and heralding a new transparency or an openness to showing private lives in public. This was compounded by the rise of paparazzi photography and their intrusion into the lives of celebrities, suggesting that private life was no longer 'private'. Roland Barthes already hinted at this demise of privacy in *Camera Lucida* in 1980, when he wrote, 'publicity of the private: the private is consumed as such publically'.[48] On the other hand, such intimate work can be seen as a sign of social enlightenment, which is perhaps how Benjamin might have understood it to be, as a demythologising of the realm of private and personal life. The dynamics of sexual relationships, private habits and dramas are, it could be argued, regarded as less shameful precisely because their photographic visibility has normalised them. The neorealist exposure of the details of intimate lives, whether autobiographical or biographical, has certainly been prevalent internationally in art photography since the

49 The critique of such forms of practice is well known; see for example Martha Rosler, 'Post-Documentary, Post-Photography?', in Rosler 2004.

late twentieth century. The sexually explicit scenes in Araki's photographs of women, Boris Mikhailov's radically 'anti-aesthetic' snapshots of homeless people, in a documentary of what he calls 'Russian capitalism' (fig.48), or the abject depictions of Richard Billingham's family in *Ray's a Laugh* are all different, but recognisably related by their depiction of intimate lives, as an art of the private document.[49]

Figure 48
Boris Mikhailov, untitled photographs from the series *Case History* 1997–8
Chromogenic colour print, dimensions variable

Public and Private

It is interesting that the distinction between private and public space did not really preoccupy the early pioneers of the photographic document, such as Atget, Sander or even Evans, who photographed across different spaces as if they were one continuous place. It is only in later documentary photography that these distinctions appeared, reformulating the relations between them. In Mikhlailov's work, for instance, the idea that social and private spaces are distinct and opposed is abolished and deconstructed, so that personal tragedy is recognised also as a social tragedy.

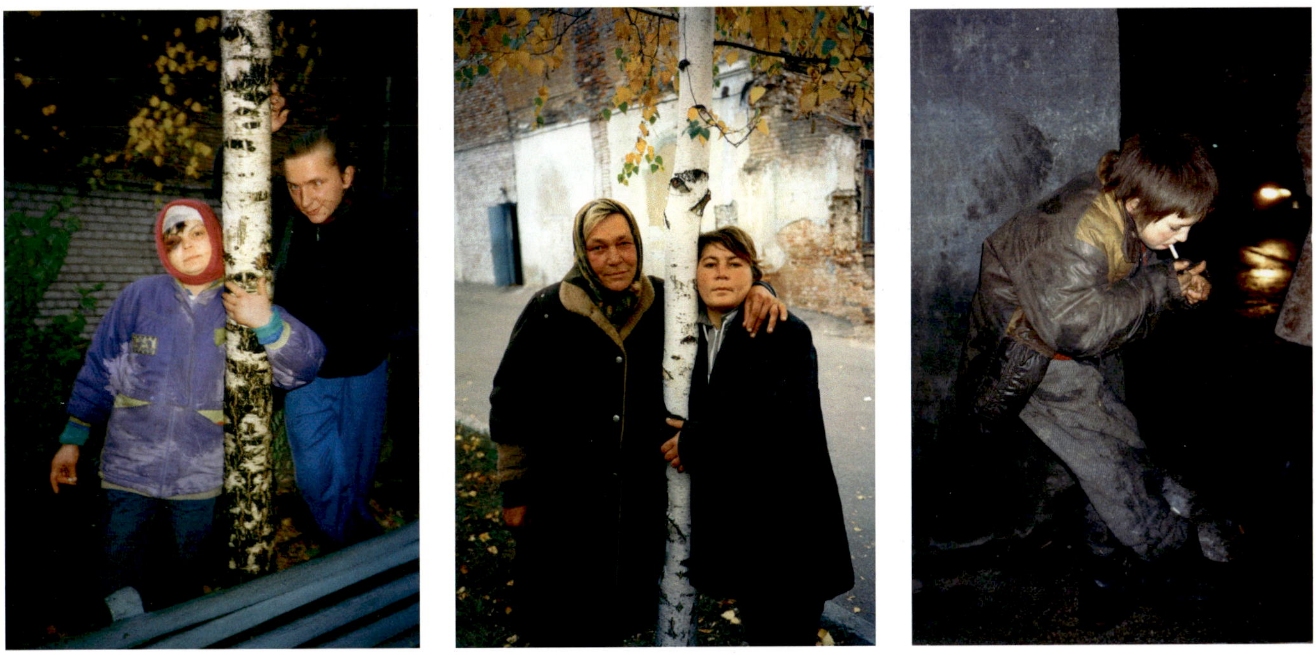

Perhaps this deconstruction of public and private was already implicit in street photography, which usually shows individuals in an intimate moment within the given social space. David Goldblatt's photographs taken in apartheid South Africa (fig.49) hint at hidden feelings in the face of racial segregation at a public event, showing the complex dynamics at work in the regime's social relations.

It would be possible to write a number of different historical narratives of the use of photography as document, using other selections of art photographers, whose emphasis on social conflict and private personal relations vary according to the specific aims of the work: Bruce Davidson, Stephen Shore, Joel Meyerowitz and Alec Soth in the USA; Mohamed Bourouissa's photographs of ethnic culture in Paris's suburbs; Yto Barrada in the Tangier straits; Allan Sekula's photographs of globalisation protests; and Bruno Serralongue's refugee camps in northern

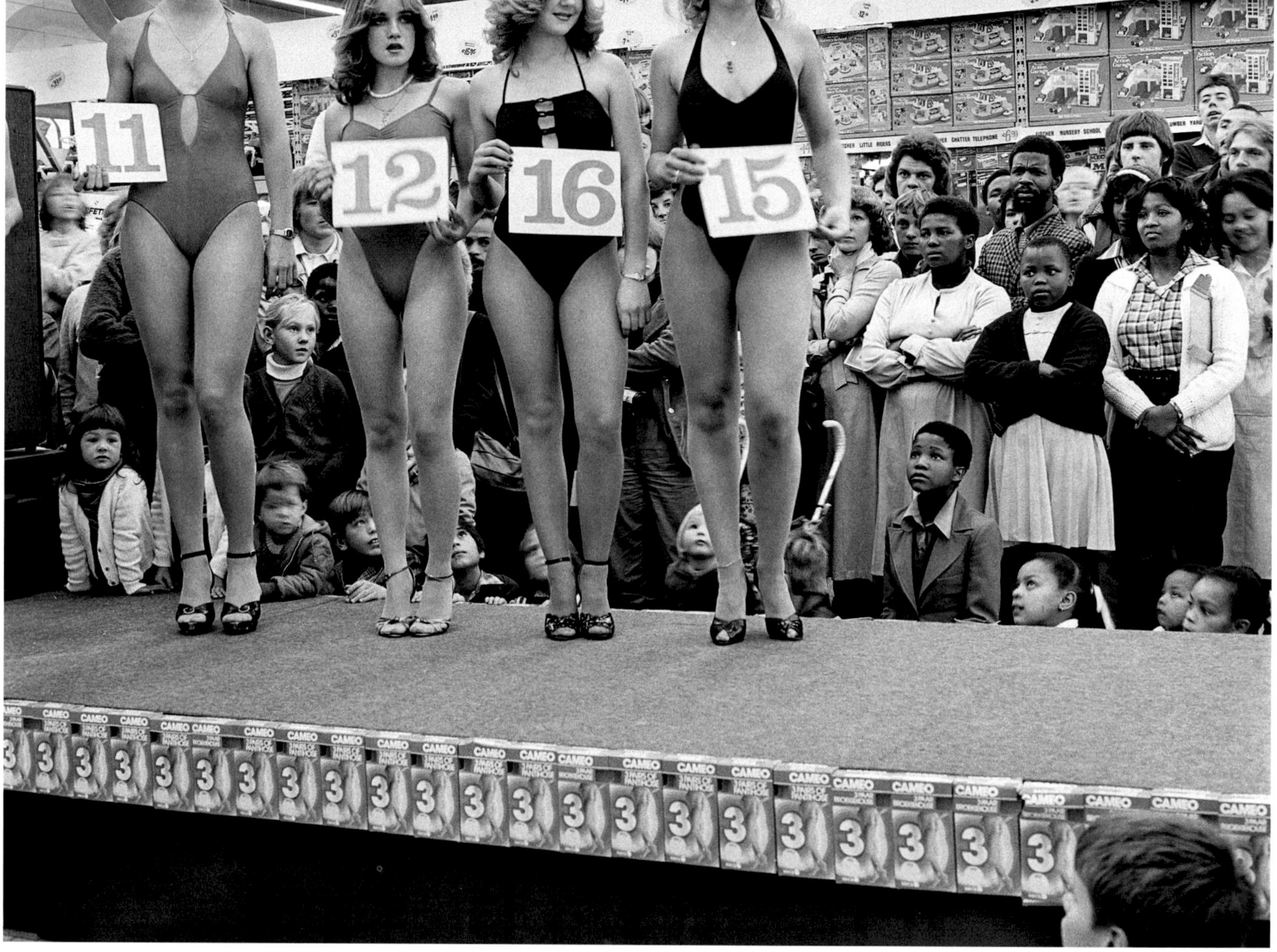
MEO
11
12
16
15
CAMEO
3

France. All these photographers take social issues as the explicit basis of their work and emphasise its documentary function, yet navigate and manage the nuances of social and political problems and tensions within a variety of visual forms. Contemporary photographers are often all too aware of the limitations of specific visual strategies and the problems they pose. On the one hand there is the risk of imposing old forms on new problems, the same world-weary repetition of conventions and tropes applied to different situations and events. On the other, a sense of unfamiliarity through radical compositions may also alienate the viewer from the photographic document altogether, making them too uncomfortable or precipitating a loss of interest in the theme or issue. Some try to question these conventions directly and develop new strategies and tactics to avoid them, to reconstruct the idea of what a document is. We might include here Jeff Wall's pictorial tableau photographs too, since he describes them as 'near documentary', bringing a sense of social conflict to the realm of staged 'fictional' photography. Wall frequently bases his staged scenes on actual events that he has seen, and restages them, as it were, with ideal photographic models (see pp.42–3).

Figure 49
David Goldblatt,
Saturday morning at the Hypermarket: Semi-final of the Miss Lovely Legs Competition
28 June 1980
Gelatin silver print,
60 × 60

What all these practices have in common is a sense of advancing the idea of the document in different ways, away from an entirely sociological ccount of reality and from the bureaucratic accountancy of facts, towards a more psychological effect, aiming to trigger a set of thoughts in the imagination of the viewer. Artists and photographers have thus found other ways to dissociate the photograph from simplistic ideas of evidence or truth. Mike Mandel and Larry Sultan's book *Evidence* (1977/2003), of anonymous photographs from the photographic archives of corporations, implicitly addresses the question of how far any photograph is a document at all; and Sophie Calle's quasi-realistic stories test the viewer's limits of credibility (see p.117). In some instances these strategies involve language; in others it is photography itself that is handled differently. The examples that follow are but a selection to highlight the ways in which the logic of the photograph as document has developed. The first tactic is the 'hyper-document', through which a viewer is saturated with an excess of visual information; the second uses collage and seriality or narrative to emphasise critical questions about the definitions of reality, and the third uses language, where a text lays photographs open to the interrogation of meaning.

Hyper-Document

A clear example of the 'hyper-document' is Thomas Ruff's series of huge facial portraits (fig.50). These large photographs of anonymous Germans (we are given their first names as subtitles but nothing more) comprise high-definition images of the subject's head and shoulders, their face mostly filling the frame. We can scrutinise the details, the very pores, hair, skin and flesh of their faces. But while we are offered everything to see, we realise how little we actually know about these people. The document displays its own limits through our surveillance of it. The format, if not the scale, is that of a passport photo; it prompts associations of nationhood and identity, as well as state surveillance and the control of free passage. While Ruff's sitters are given a choice of background colour, he asks them to look expressionless, as a passport photo requires.

Figure 50
Thomas Ruff,
Portrait 1986 (Stoya) 1986
From Portraits
C-print, 160 × 120
Tate. Purchased 1998

The viewer is then placed in the position of a passport control officer, asking: who is this, what are they like as a person, why are they here? Are they nice, honest or whatever else might be in the mind of the spectator? Inevitably, the viewer finds some sort of expression, reading friendliness, coldness, warmth or malevolence in their features. We become aware of our own complicity in constructing the meanings of the so-called documents.

The document seems blank, inert and denotative, despite the information it clearly contains. But it refuses to give up any meaning, unless we invest it with one ourselves. Mostly, spectators cannot resist and inevitably betray their thoughts and feelings as the interpretation of what they see. While they are apparently given the possibility of visually controlling the image through looking, the hyper-document reveals the ambiguity in the source of this process of making meaning. The huge scale of the pictures on the gallery wall converts these would-be victims of our scrutiny and surveillance into towering, dominating presences. There is no one-to-one relation here: our heads are tiny in comparison, and they look out from their pictures - and through us - with an imperious gaze. The whole value and meaning of the portrait becomes tenuous and uncertain, yet the lure of the document brings us back to the facticity of what we see.

In another series, Ruff enlarges pornographic and newspaper images, but with the opposite effect. The blurred or pixelated scenes are disguised, frustrating all attempts to see the details or to identify and deduce any significant meaning. These works draw on an art/non-art relation of what Rancière calls the 'metamorphic image', where media images are quoted or reworked in order to question their original function. The danger of these strategies for Rancière is that the aesthetics of such work may be recuperated by the very systems of meaning they set out to contest.[50] Perhaps this was not the positive social future of the document that Walter Benjamin imagined, but we shall never know. It is certainly hard to see Ruff's cool descriptive portrait series in any kind of continuity with, say, Diane Arbus's warm, expressive portraits of people, where faces and gestures are central to the meaning of the work, even if they are about pain. Nor are Ruff's pictures like the much earlier social typology portraits of August Sander, for whom the link between the appearance of his subjects and their profession or trade was a matter of certainty. In this sense, Ruff's work is postmodern, sceptical of the certainty of meaning. It throws the idea of the document into question precisely through its excess of visual information claiming to be a document of something.

50 Rancière 2009, p.27.

Collage and Seriality

The Atlas Group, an imaginary collective founded by Walid Raad, set out to document, study and question the contemporary history of Lebanon. The artworks often use found photographs alongside other documents, treated as one family of artefact amongst others. *My Neck is Thinner than a Hair: Engines* 2000–3 presents, in a grid in the gallery, one hundred framed inkjet prints of the remains of car bombs detonated in Lebanon between 1975 and 1991, each accompanied by a documentary-like caption, with details of the explosion, the photographer if known and notes transcribed from the back of the picture.

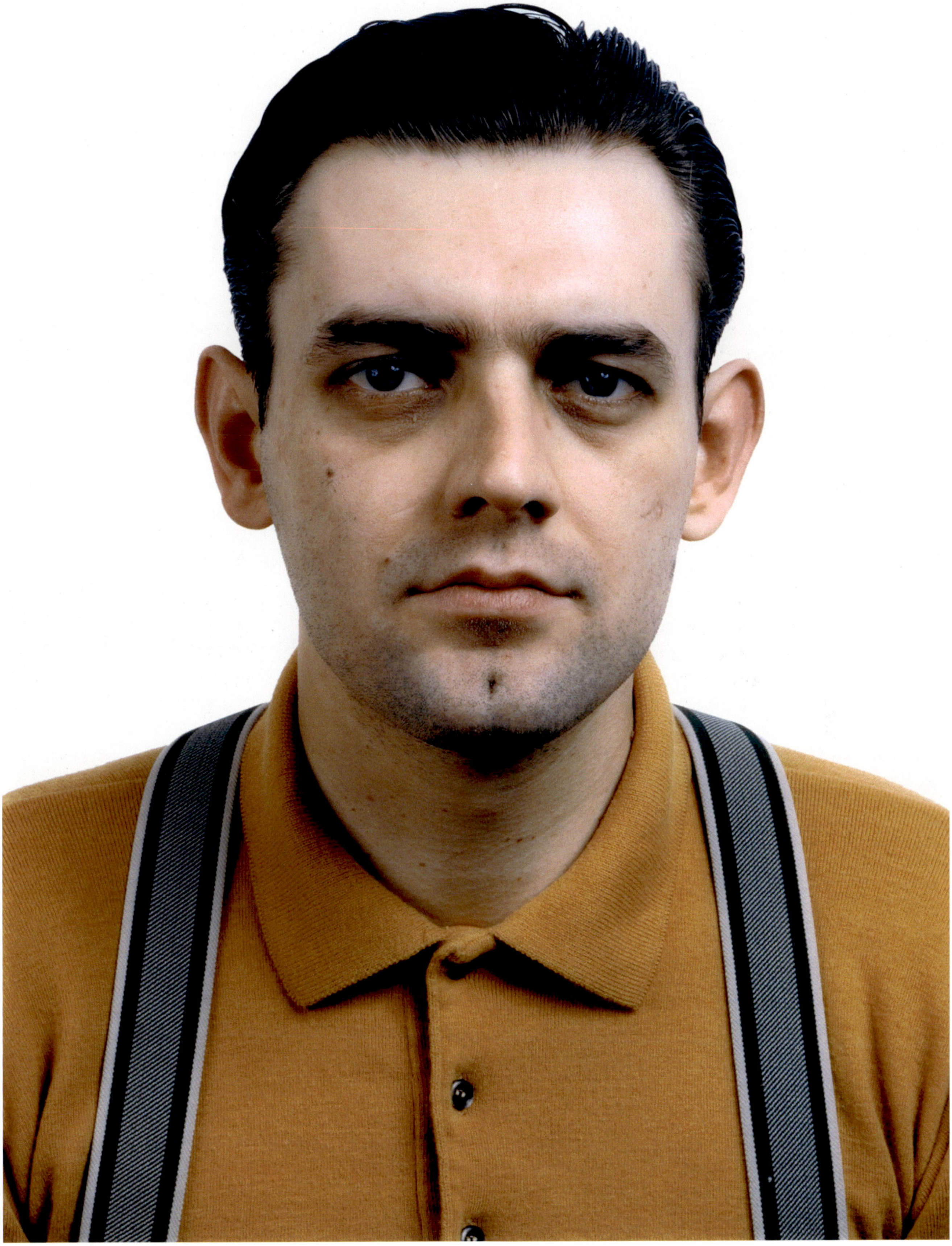

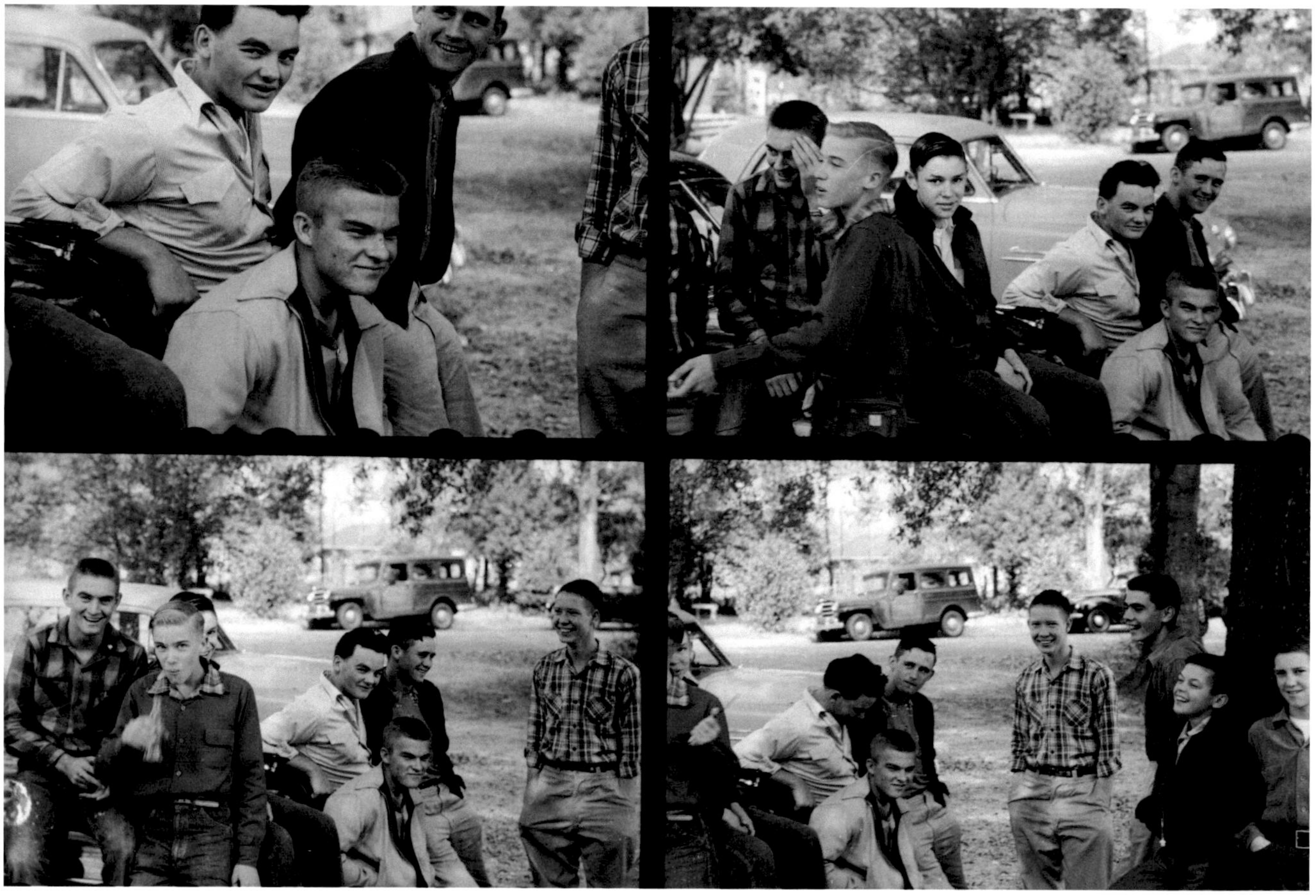

Commonly featured in newspaper reports, the original naked photographs are thus recuperated for scrutiny in the art gallery. This process introduces into art a new iconography of modern conflict – the car bomb – and refutes the media's narrative of them as singular events. The seriality of the work creates a 'comparative photography', to use Benjamin's phrase, much as Sander's portraits did, constituting something that is more than the sum of its parts, like bricks in a wall. What may have seemed like separate events, random acts of violence become a unified, potentially knowable whole. The spectator is challenged to find consistencies and therefore answers, just like detectives in crime movies who pin up pictures of suspects to look for patterns in their behaviour. Indeed, the collective's name echoes Raad's ambition to collect and group together these photographs into an atlas of auto engines, which in turn documents violence. But then the fictional status of the group's authorship also serves to cast doubt on the authenticity of the documents themselves, which plays against the photographs' apparent journalistic artlessness. The factual claims for the work strongly echo earlier conventions in conceptual art. Indeed, the work is very knowing of art-historical references to conceptual art (Walid Raad teaches art in the USA), yet the work also pushes against them, bringing something new into the field of art through the use of documents.

Figure 51
Robert Frank, *Port Gibson, Mississippi in front of the High School, September 1955* 1955

Written and Visible

For the work of language and image, consider Robert Frank's *Port Gibson, Mississippi in front of the High School, September 1955* 1955 (fig.51). The four pictures of young men, with their friendly humour, are clearly interacting with the photographer. These scenes take on a different meaning after we read Frank's text: 'He must be a communist. He looks like one'. The brief exchange between photographer and subjects betrays the apparent innocence of these youths, and lays bare a slightly more hostile set of values within their group. The reading of the words changes what we think about what we see. The naked image is contaminated by language, creating a dissensus. Frank counters the friendly visual scenes with a different sense, which undoes assumptions about the picture's subjects, and giving a different meaning to it as a document. The use of language can derail the anticipated reading of any picture, taking the reader/viewer by surprise.

And so we find ourselves back at the issue with which this chapter began: the question of the role of the 'artless' in art and how it brings something new to art. The artless document brings a kind of virtue or purity back into a practice, reaching or striving towards a new actuality. The fact that this is a kind of work that still exists, which today finds it hard to escape the world as already represented and totally photographed, means that art is far from exhausted when it looks outside itself. This idea of the document as a type of modern art also comes into view from another direction – the history of conceptualist art.

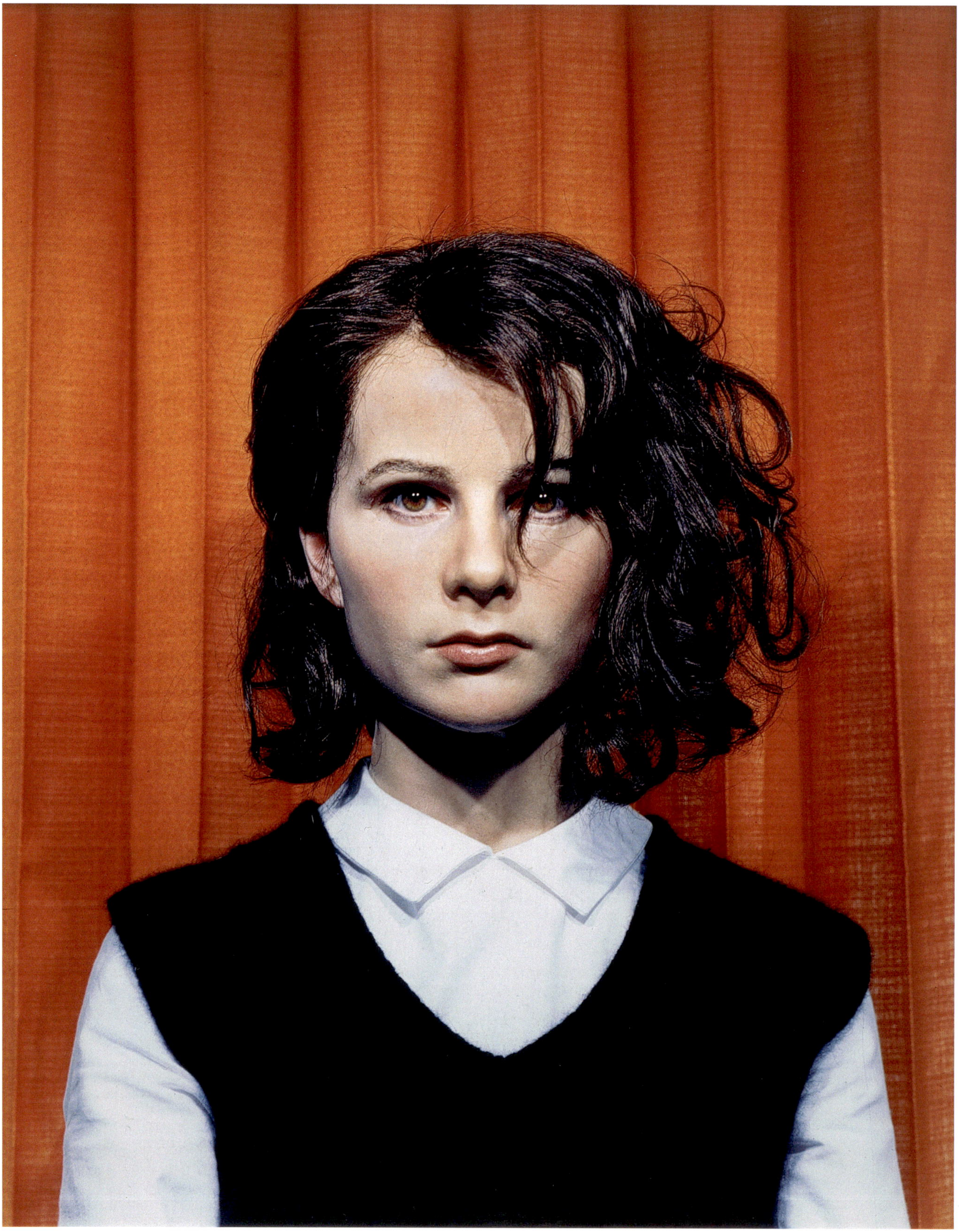

CONCEPTUALISM AND ART PHOTOGRAPHY

1 See Camnitzer, Farver, and Weiss 1999.

Figure 52
Gillian Wearing, *Self Portrait at 17 Years Old* 2003
Framed c-print, 115.5 × 92

Is all art photography today post-conceptual? If so, what does that mean? Conceptual art has become a category so general and is applied to such a broad range of works and ideas that these terms may appear to be meaningless. The history of conceptual art, however, tells a different story, of a series of significant changes to the historical forms and functions of art which, importantly, appeared with photographic images, ostensively of conceptual rather than perceptual ideas.

A preliminary historical distinction will be useful here, between the term conceptualism and conceptual art. 'Conceptualism' is now usually associated with the general post-Second World War avant-garde art, whereas 'conceptual art' designates the specific new attitudes in art that emerged in the period after 1968. The dramatic student protests and political radicalism of 1968 – riots in Paris and events in Chicago, London, Mexico City, New York, Prague, Tokyo and Warsaw to name but a few – are regarded as marking these two post-war periods apart. As traditional social authority was discredited or questioned by waves of feminism, civil rights and political discontent, these critical attitudes also appeared in art. The dates are not exactly the same everywhere, but the specific term 'conceptual art' began to appear in different places at about the same time, with the 1970s considered its apogee.[1] Conceptual art is widely considered to be the last avant-garde. Unlike the pre-war avant-gardes, like constructivism and pre-Stalin Soviet art, dada and surrealism, which all had a centre and spread outwards, conceptual art was multi-polar and of global origins, emerging more or less simultaneously across North and South America, Europe, New Zealand, Australia, Korea and Japan. It is important to stress, however, that these were different versions of conceptual art, multiple and diverse, not unified. Conceptual art was as decentred as its geography, and emerged long before many art institutions came to recognise it as existing at all. Looking back at these practices today it is clearer how central photography was to them in complex and different ways, as will be seen in what follows.

Conceptualism

The pre-1968 conceptualisms are many and include artists and collective tendencies such as Andy Warhol and pop art, Yves Klein and the French nouveaux réalisme, the international group Fluxus, Viennese actionism, minimalism, eccentric abstraction and arte povera. Minimalism in particular is usually recognised as key to conceptual art, but the work of the other earlier avant-gardes is often neglected. Photography was involved in some of these early conceptualisms, as source material, for example, in Andy Warhol's pop art, but also as a new medium to convey the concept of the work in its own right.

Figure 53
Yves Klein, *Leap into the Void* 1960
Photographed by Harry Shunk
Gelatin silver print, 25.9 × 20
The Metropolitan Museum of Art, New York

Within the nouveaux réalisme movement, the famous image by Yves Klein, *Leap into the Void* 1960 (fig.53), was published in the mock newspaper *Dimanche* (a parody of the *Journal du Dimanche*), which the artist printed himself and distributed during the second Festival of Avant-Garde Art in Paris in 1960. Klein's photo-text work calls into question the believability of the photograph and, by association, the truth of newspaper reporting too. The picture also proposes the artist's body as a gesture, like a paintbrush in space.

All these movements and moments fed, overlapped and mutated into aspects of conceptual art, which was, as a result, far from being a unified, localised project. Despite New York's position at the centre of art discourse in the 1960s, divergent practices elsewhere must also be acknowledged as crucial in Europe, South America and Asia. As a rather chaotic and un-unified category, the term 'conceptual art' strains to contain its different contents, practices and tendencies, which varied between geographic

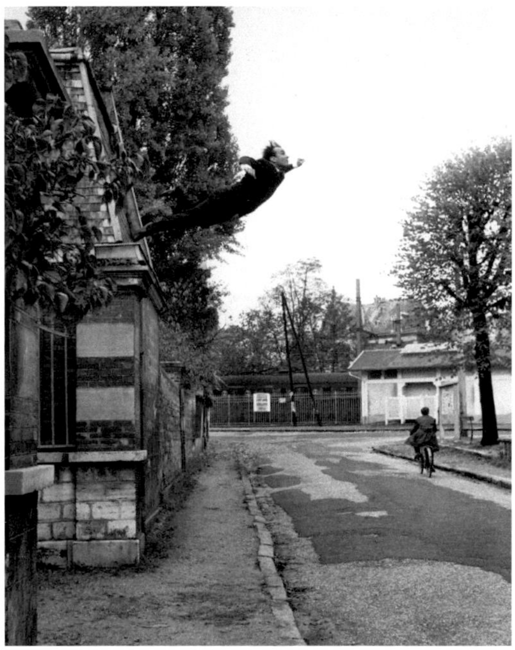

contexts that were often oblivious of one another. So while the key features of conceptual art are usually cited as the dominance of philosophy, text and performance and the absence of objects, these are by no means exclusive or globally applicable. Even so, photography could be used to signify the absence of objects, through their sole presence in a photograph. Yet similarly, photography in conceptual art has no universal, singular function or aim either, although it was commonly used to document performances and events, with these types of historiographic images becoming a particularly widespread component of this often ephemeral sector of art production.

Conceptual Art

Terms like 'concept' or 'ideas art' can be found much earlier than 1968 but, as Lucy Lippard, one of the key critics and curators involved in conceptual art argued, 'around 1960 Henry Flynt coined the term "concept art", but it was a different kind of "concept" – less formal, less rooted in

2 For a succinct view of the emergence of 'conceptual art' from an insider, see Lippard 1997, p.ix.

3 Lucy R. Lippard, 'Preface: Six Years ... Forty Years Later', in Morris and Bonin 2012, p.xi.

4 Crow 1996.

5 Lippard and Chandler 2000, p.46.

6 Lippard and Chandler 2000, p.47.

7 Ibid., p.48.

8 See Kotz 2007.

the subversion of art-world assumptions and art-as-community'.[2] Writing much later, Lippard reflected: 'Anti-establishment fervour in the late 1960s focused in the art world on demythologizing and decommodifying art, on the need to be independent of the greedy sector that owned everything and was promoting the war in Vietnam.'[3] If social unrest characterises this period – with its civil rights movements, the Vietnam war, the rise of feminism and the Women's Liberation movement, ecology, anti-colonial, decolonising and postcolonial issues – then conceptual art was its corollary in the art world. 1968 was also the year that rocked the USA, when Robert Kennedy and Martin Luther King were assassinated. Although art of this time did not necessarily take politics as its direct subject matter (in North America and Europe at least), its implicit dissatisfaction with the elite art market and established modernist values was echoed among the angry young men and women across cinema, literature, architecture, theatre and popular music.[4] Independence was in the air and the arts were embroiled in a social and cultural revolution. As indicated by Lippard, artists also embraced the anti-establishment attitude of this period, affected by the same desire for social liberation.

The phrase 'de-materialization of the object' as used by Lippard and John Chandler in 1967 described what they saw as the response of an 'ultra-conceptual art' that wished to 'emphasize the thinking process almost exclusively'.[5] The focus of artists was shifting away from making objects, they were 'losing interest in the physical evolution of the work', so that the object might even become 'wholly obsolete'. Less detail in the work, they argued, gave the spectator 'more participation': 'the time spent looking at an "empty" work, or one with a minimum of action, seems infinitely longer than action-and-detail-filled time.'[6]

Photography, text and performance played important roles in this process of disrupting the traditional conventions of painting and sculpture, if not displacing them entirely. Time and space devoid of objects could encourage the thoughts, experience and thus the participation of the viewer. This was not anti-aesthetic, as is often claimed, but post-aesthetic: 'Dematerialized art is post-aesthetic only in its increasingly non-visual emphasis.'[7] What this meant was that rather than the perceptual absorption and retinal pleasure of modernist artworks, art was turned into a realm for thinking. Making objects was no longer the primary aim of art, rather it was the idea and the experience enabled by it that formed the focus of work. During John Cage's performance of *4'33"* in 1952, for instance, in which the musicians sat silently, playing an almost blank score, the sounds of the room, the audience breathing, shuffling noises and intrusions from the world beyond the venue became the content of the piece.[8] As long as it was not traditional painting or sculpture, the artwork that stimulated thought and experience could take many forms: writing, actions, events, photography, texts and performances. Many of these time-based events and actions were completely unrecorded and persist only as written memoirs or descriptive texts, but others were documented with photographs or recorded on video and film. Some works were later remade precisely because of this situation.

Whereas minimalism drew on the iconography and materials of modern industry, like aluminium, bricks, glass, fluorescent lights, iron and steel, conceptual art preferred the office and study. The studio was

Figure 54
Vito Acconci, *FOLLOWING PIECE 'Street Works IV' Architectural League of New York; Activity, New York City; Oct 3–25 1969* 1969
All photos by Betty Jackson

'Each day I pick out, at random, a person walking in the street. I follow a different person every day; I keep following until that person enters a private place (home, office, etc.) where I can't get in.'

'again becoming a study', Lippard argued.[9] Works often purloined and repurposed office or academic paraphernalia: think of Robert Morris's index cards and files; Art & Language's filing cabinets; Hans Haacke's reports and financial records; Victor Burgin's typewriters, desks and lamps; Adrian Piper's speeches and lectures; and all the myriad clocks, lists, diaries, meeting notes, letters, noticeboards and diagrams on graph paper that appeared elsewhere across conceptual art. Artists would also operate as if they were office managers, writing scripts and instructions for others to follow; Iain and Ingrid Baxter in Canada even defined themselves as a corporation, as N.E. Thing Co.

In another type of iconography, conceptual artists would frequent the streets, using photography to document the everyday life events, actions or performances they witnessed there, although some of these actions and events were based on written instructions created by the artists. Vito Acconci, for example, in *Following Piece* 1969 (fig.54) established the rule that he would randomly choose people to follow on the street until they went into a private space. The people being followed, although a point of focus, remain anonymous in the black-and-white documentation photographs, while the pictures' conceptual framework is elucidated by the accompanying text. With the actual event lost to history, its documentation *becomes* the work, and photography is more aligned with information and immediate description, rather than painting or the aesthetic interpretation of an event.

Without the conventional object-based practice of modernism, where artists dedicated themselves to a specific medium, conceptual artists let new ideas emerge, no longer maintaining formalist innovation or art for art's sake as the main aim of art. The value of art as a dimension of culture was freshly interrogated, with language itself seen as a material form, probed via philosophy and semiotics, not only to question in theory what art is, but to open up new terrains of art as cultural practice.

The Performative Photograph

The analytical philosophy of the linguist J.L. Austin, as outlined in his 1962 book *How to Do Things with Words*, identified a particular class of performative language. This was a 'speech act', an utterance where the spoken word does not describe something already existing, but performs an act by saying something that employs very specific terms. In other words, language 'is, or is a part of, the doing of an action'.[10] Austin gives the examples of saying 'I do' in a marriage ceremony or 'I name this ship Queen Elizabeth' when smashing the bottle against the ship at its launch. The utterance of the words themselves is the action that signifies the event. It was possible to translate this theory into non-linguistic actions, like a photograph or a performance. Indeed, it might be argued that wedding photographs have already become a required performative element of the event of marriage, the photographic act an essential means of signifying its completion. In this spirit, photography could be thought of as a performative act that makes statements and generates events that produce evidence of their own actions too. While this idea of the performative photograph could clearly be related to documentation, whose purpose is usually seen as secondary, now the very act of photography became a primary form, constituting an event or performative act in

9 Lippard and Chandler 2000, p.46.

10 Austin 1975, p.5.

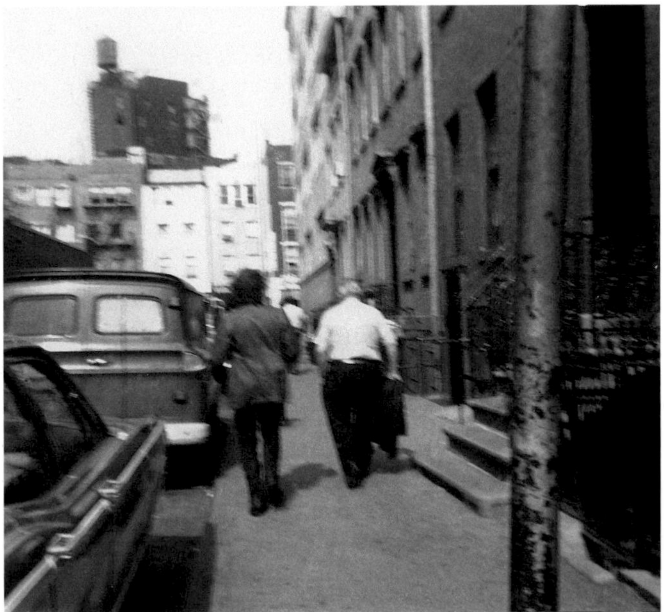

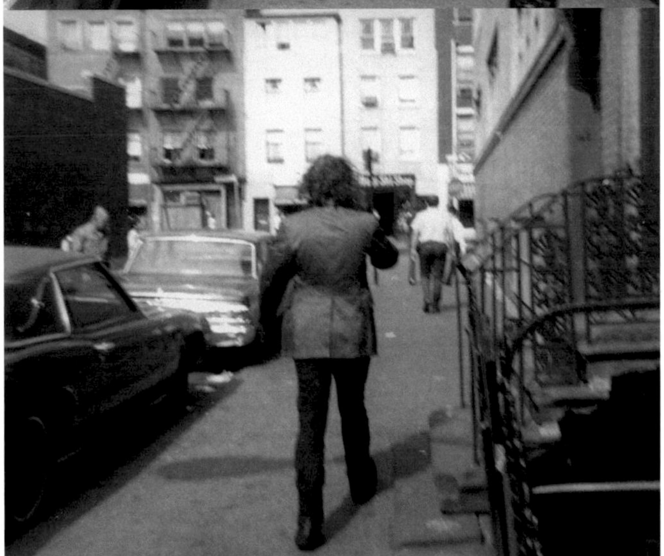

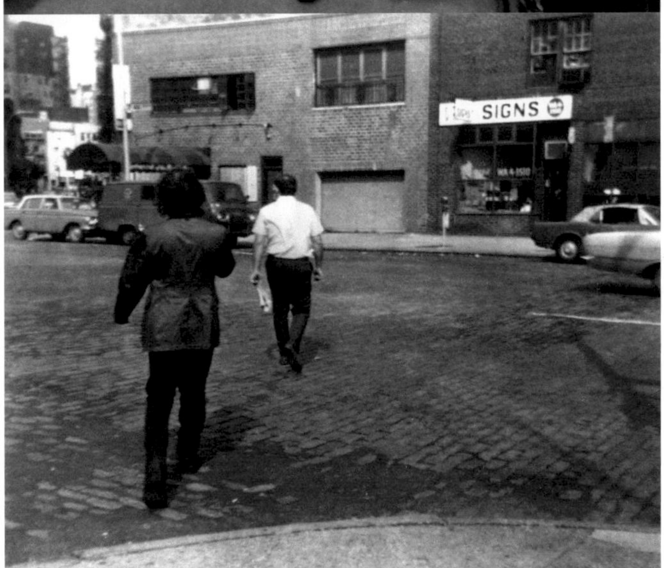
SIGNS

Figure 55
Joseph Kosuth, *One and Three Saws* 1965
Two black and white photographs and saw mounted on board, 51 × 96

its own right. As such, photography was implicitly a key component in the construction of the very concept of art. In 1960s New York, Joseph Kosuth brought all these various components together – that is, language, objects and photographs – to create a new kind of philosophical avant-garde: conceptual art.

Each iteration of Joseph Kosuth's gallery piece *One and Three* series (later renamed *Proto-Investigations*) included three components: a real object, a printed dictionary definition of that object and a photograph of it as it appeared in the gallery (fig.55). Juxtaposed together, these three parts define the artwork, which is nothing other than a definition of a thing as its representation.

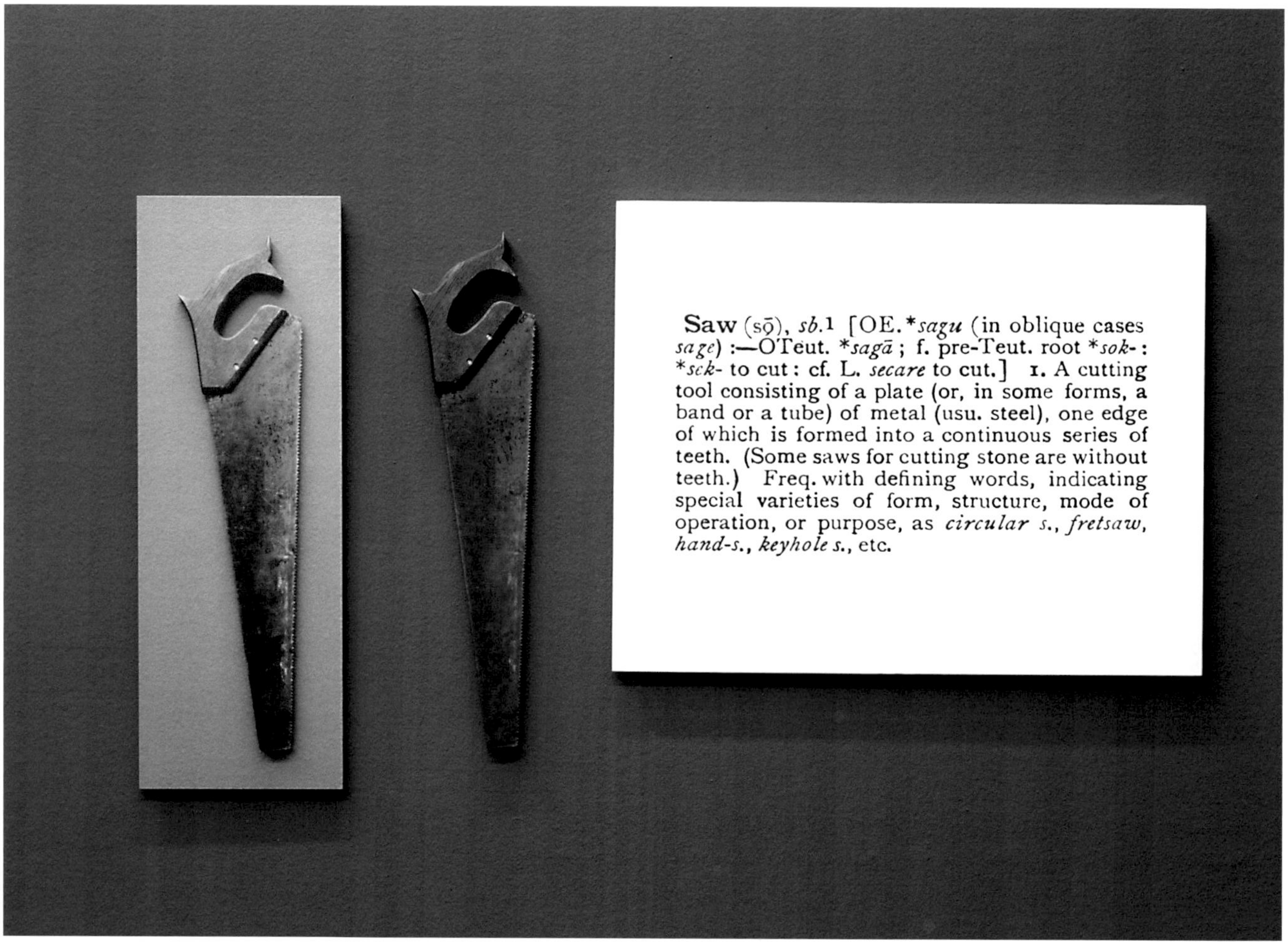

Kosuth had read the linguistic theory of the analytical philosopher A.J. Ayer and adopted his term 'propositions' as a way to interrogate the artworks' validity.[11] Statements about art, he realised, could be made as a proposition to question its legitimacy as a conceptual idea and as a way to establish its new identity. If *One and Three* described or proposed a chair or saw, what else was there to be said about it? To ask if it was a good or bad artwork, beautiful or interesting, no longer seemed relevant. For Kosuth, *One and Three* were like meta-linguistic propositions, which in their brute factualness resisted statements against them. The relationship between a dictionary definition, the presented object and a

11 Kosuth 1991.

photograph of it appears obvious, since the three representations all refer to and denote the same concept-object, whether a chair, broom, saw, etc. Here was an artwork intended to be purified of aesthetic judgement and which anticipated art criticism by rendering it null and void with the sheer propositional status of the work. The work creates a kind of tautology, each component confirming the existence of the other. In semiotic terms, the same concept, 'saw', is represented and reiterated within three different signifying systems, with each element of the work a different type of sign: words as symbols, the object as indexical and the photograph as iconic. Together, the *One and Three* works make a series of statements, which, like the performative linguistic act, asks: is this art? And this is the question that the work opens up as a space for the spectator to consider.

Kosuth's work also inadvertently demonstrates how art is a discourse combining objects, language and photographs, set in the institutional context of the art gallery or museum. Together they constitute art, and Kosuth's propositional artworks then take up the question that Marcel Duchamp's much earlier readymade had posed: what can be art? The answer: what the artist nominates as art. The art 'proposition' becomes art. *One and Three* was the product of the artist's intention to say what art is. Art was no longer about appearance and beauty, but the *conception* of what art is. In effect, this became a new version of modernism's art for art's sake, and while it introduced a new emphasis on text and image and very different everyday objects as 'readymade' art, it fell short of radically breaking the boundaries of art values, which others were seeking to do at this time. Other artists would eventually break through this tautology by placing their work within the wider social and semiotic environment of culture, as will be seen later, and photography was central to these processes.

With its capacity to register information and record what was in front of the lens, photography and its moving equivalents, film and video, brought the social and referential dimensions of art to the fore. In hindsight, the implicit move towards issues of social representation that the use of photography brought about may seem to have been inevitable, hastened by the fact that the social and cultural realms were faced more and more with mass-produced photographic images throughout public and private life. Culture's saturation with advertising, fashion, news and wider media images brought photography firmly into the centre of a new media sphere, as something to be addressed. Conceptual art rejected the values of these media industries and practices, but found itself using photography as a component of its armoury and as a means to recognise the existence of its activities and manifestations. Yet none of this seemed by any means inevitable at the time. It is important also to acknowledge that the cultural critique developed beyond the philosophical interrogations of conceptual art. Furthermore, conceptual artists came to photography via different routes, interests and directions.

The Absence of Presence

Let's consider works by artists who were in the ground-breaking exhibition *When Attitudes Become Form* 1969 at the Institute of Contemporary Arts in London.

Figure 56
Richard Long,
A Line Made by Walking 1967
Photograph and graphite on board, 37.5 × 32.4
Tate

Richard Long's image-text piece *A Line Made by Walking, England* 1967 (fig.56) was completed while he was still an art student in London. It involved his going to the countryside and walking up and down on a patch of land until a path appeared. Given that the performance was conducted outside the gallery, the photograph and its caption, as documentation of the performance, became the constituent artwork. The act of walking itself remains invisible to the spectator of the photograph, until they read the title, at which point the action that animated the photographic scene can be reanimated in their imagination. Since the line in the landscape, which was directly caused by the artist's action, is long gone, the photograph is all that remains of the work, apart from its other, secondary representations in interviews, reviews, etc. Long's photo-text documentation has become a familiar format in conceptual art, with the presence of a photographic image paradoxically signifying the absence of the actual event.

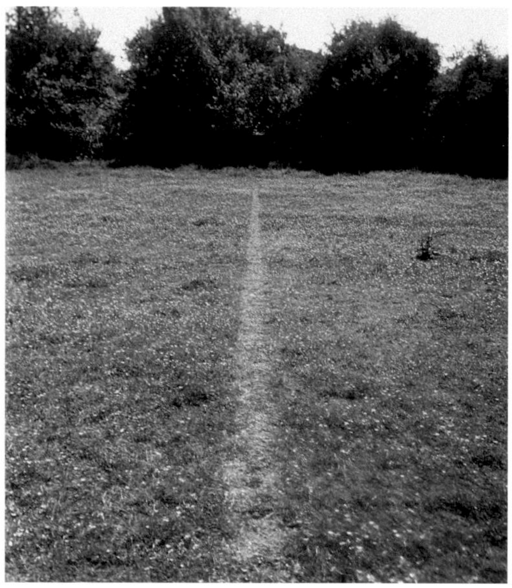

Contrast this with Victor Burgin's minimalist *Photopath* 1967/9 (fig.57), where photographs of the floorboards of the gallery have been placed over the precise area they represent. Reproduced at a scale of 1:1, photograph and floor correspond faithfully, making the work site-specific, functioning only when installed in a particular gallery floor. This abolishes the art object as commodity, because to buy *Photopath*, you would also have to buy the gallery floor. Of course it may have been possible to commission the artist to make another work like it, as a site-specific installation elsewhere, but then this would be another work.

Photopath hides the real floor beneath its photographic representation and, besides the use of the camera, there is no implicated physical presence of the artist. Long's photograph of the path, on the other hand, includes a more traditional trace of the artist – his footsteps in the grass are analogous to the artist's signature, an indexical trace in the path image. Arguably, Long's 'intervention' on the land is also making a point about human interference in the ecosystem, as much land art often does. Burgin's *Photopath* was written as instructions on an index card in 1967, and enacted with photographs in 1969 for *When Attitudes Become Form*, where it invoked a presence of absence in the gallery.

So, on the one hand, both artists have abolished the traditional art object as sculpture, replacing it with photographic images of something that is 'not there'. On the other hand, Long's work retains the artist's presence, since his walking created the path that is photographed, whereas Burgin's work abolishes any reference to the artist's presence in the photograph, resisting processes of commodification.

Keith Arnatt's *Self Burial* 1969 (fig.58), also in *When Attitudes Become Form*, makes the conceptual disappearance of the artist a direct act; literally burying himself becomes the work. The sequence of photographs was shown one image per night on German television, reporting the disappearance of the artist. The attitude of Arnatt's conceptual piece was concurrent with arguments in critical theory, exemplified most clearly by Roland Barthes's 'Death of the Author'. This controversial essay, which

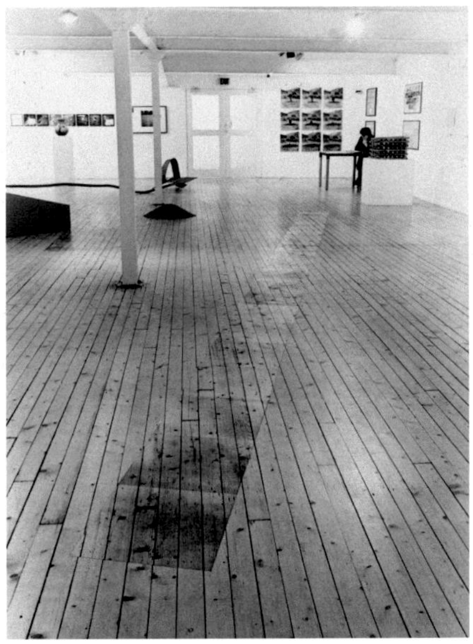

Figure 57
Victor Burgin, *Photopath* 1967
Shown as installed in the exhibition *When Attitudes Become Form* at the Institute of Contemporary Arts, London, 1969

was translated into English for the New York magazine *Aspen* in 1967, argued for the liberation of the reader from the tyranny of the author's intentions in the work.[12] This new liberty of the reader or spectator to do what they think with an artwork not only recognised the potential plurality of meanings of artworks, literature and cinema, but also chimed with the arguments of conceptualist art, which stated that the structures of the artwork should be open too.

However, eradicating objects and artists from the artwork was not an end in itself. As Burgin later argued, conceptualism was an attack on what he called the 'primacy of *presence*'.[13] In his essay 'The Absence of Presence: Conceptualism and Post-modernisms' 1984, he stated that conceptualism allowed a glimpse 'of the absence of "presence", and thus the possibility of *change*'.[14] The fetishism of the modernist art object – which in the pictorialist and fine-art modernist photography traditions belonged to the visual high-craft value of the print – was rejected by conceptualism in favour of the question of representation itself. Since the absence of presence was ultimately an issue of representation and

12 See Barthes 1981 and Lippard 2012, p.43.

13 The essay was republished in Burgin 1986, p.47.

14 Ibid., p.48.

Figure 58
Keith Arnatt,
Self Burial (Television Interference Project) 1969
9 gelatin silver prints on board, 46.7 × 46.7. Tate

This sequence of photographs was broadcast on German television in October 1969. One photo was shown each day, for about two seconds, sometimes interrupting whatever programme was being shown at peak viewing time. They were neither announced nor explained, so viewers had to make what sense of them they could.

signification, photography was bound to be prevalent in its exploration, given its pervasive social use. Burgin's argument resonates with what Jacques Rancière recently called an 'ostensive image' in contemporary art. The ostensive image is one that provides a meaning through the absence of something, presented as an obtuse presence, something that photography is particularly good at doing.[15] The example that Rancière gives is a photograph of Marcel Duchamp's readymade *Fountain* 1917 (fig.59) – the proto-conceptual artwork – taken by Alfred Stieglitz, the New York-based pictorialist photographer and champion of early modern art.[16] We can in fact date the relevance of photography in conceptual art back to this much earlier time, and to the founding work of Duchamp. With his theory of the readymade at the beginning of the twentieth century, Duchamp is the figure to whom many conceptualists, like Kosuth, referred to as a source for inspiration. Indeed, the centrality of Duchamp's work in art history today is indebted to the conceptualists' revival of his ideas, around the time that Duchamp died, in October 1968. The story of the urinal is a crucial anecdote in the history of avant-garde art.

15 Rancière 2007, p.23.

16 Hoffman 2004.

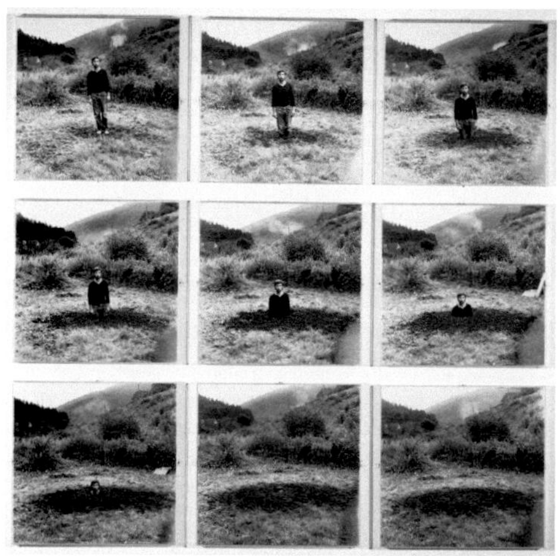

Duchamp's designation of industrial objects as art created havoc, when in 1917 he submitted *Fountain* to the first exhibition of the Society of Independent Artists in New York. The exhibition was supposed to be open to any work submitted by any artist, without censorship, but the organisers, who were mostly artists, refused its entry. Surely this mass-produced urinal with the pseudonym 'R. Mutt' scrawled on it was not art? The lack of evident craft made it contentious, and even more so because it was a toilet, which was felt to be an insult, deemed vulgar and immoral. What sense of beauty or craft-value did this so-called ugly object produce? Surely none? What is more, this was plagiarism – or theft – of someone else's work, of the people who had made it. A further irony was that Duchamp had a hand in formulating the very rules that his submission had set out to test, hence the use of a pseudonym. Duchamp's game, or stunt as some might see it, begged a question: what was art in this new century and modern era?

Fountain is often seen as an early art world prank, a dadaist provocation or conceptual prototype, but Wanda Corn argues that Duchamp was teaching his fellow American artists a lesson: 'Duchamp in 1917

17 Corn 1999, p.46.

18 *The Blind Man*, no.2 May 1917.

19 The US had just joined the First World War, so *The Two Warriors* title of the painting could be viewed as being linked to that context too.

was as interested as Stieglitz in the possibility of a newly independent, non-Europeanized, American art. *Fountain* was a Duchampian lesson to the American art world in what such an art might look like. The means Duchamp used differed from those of Stieglitz – Duchamp was a non-national provocateur, Stieglitz a native-born evangelist – but his ends were similar.'[17]

In response to the rejection, Duchamp brought the urinal to Alfred Stieglitz's studio to be photographed. The subsequent photograph was then published in the 1917 dada journal *The Blind Man* and captioned as 'The Exhibit Refused by the Independents'.[18] It was accompanied by a text written by Duchamp and artist Beatrice Wood, which responded to the 'Richard Mutt Case'. Reasoning against the rejection, they argued that the accusation that it was just some plumbing 'is absurd. The only works of art America has given are her plumbing and her bridges.' Also, it did not matter that Duchamp had not made the urinal, after all he was the one who had *chosen* it, making it useless as a functional object and giving it a 'new thought'. This argument was echoed in the way Stieglitz

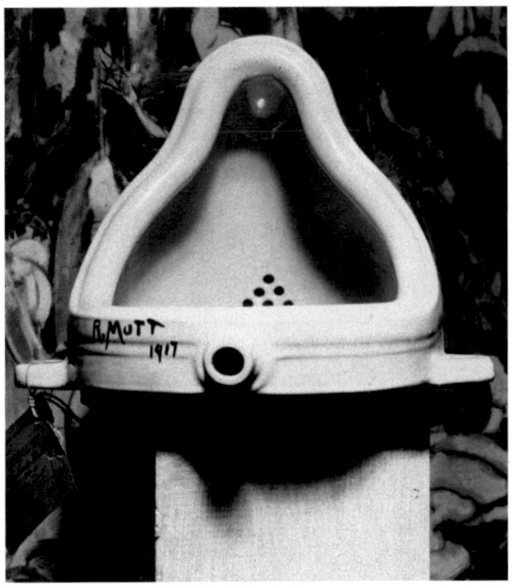

Figure 59
Alfred Stieglitz, *The Fountain by R. Mutt* 1917
Gelatin silver print, 11 × 17.9

photographed the object, positioning the urinal so that it looked unfamiliar, its usual function obscured. The shadow repeated an outline shape of the object and the drain holes within it. A second essay, by Louise Norton, argued how beautiful the object was. The ensuing debate over its interpretations seemed, in the end, more important than the artwork itself. Many artists have learned strategies of publicity and attention from this episode, about how setting a 'language game' discourse around an artwork helps to form its meaning and clarify the intention of the artist. Some conceptual artists, like Kosuth, were later to distance themselves from this type of 'scandal' conceptual art in preference for a more reflective form of cultural critique.

However, it was through Stieglitz's photograph that Duchamp's object was mostly seen: the photographic presentation of an image instead of the absent object. The photograph has its own effect on the object. Stieglitz photographed the urinal in front of a painting – *The Two Warriors* 1913 by Marsden Hartley – thus already making a sort of rhetorical point about art: that painting is literally put in the background, upstaged by the readymade object.[19] This chimes with Burgin's argument about the absence of

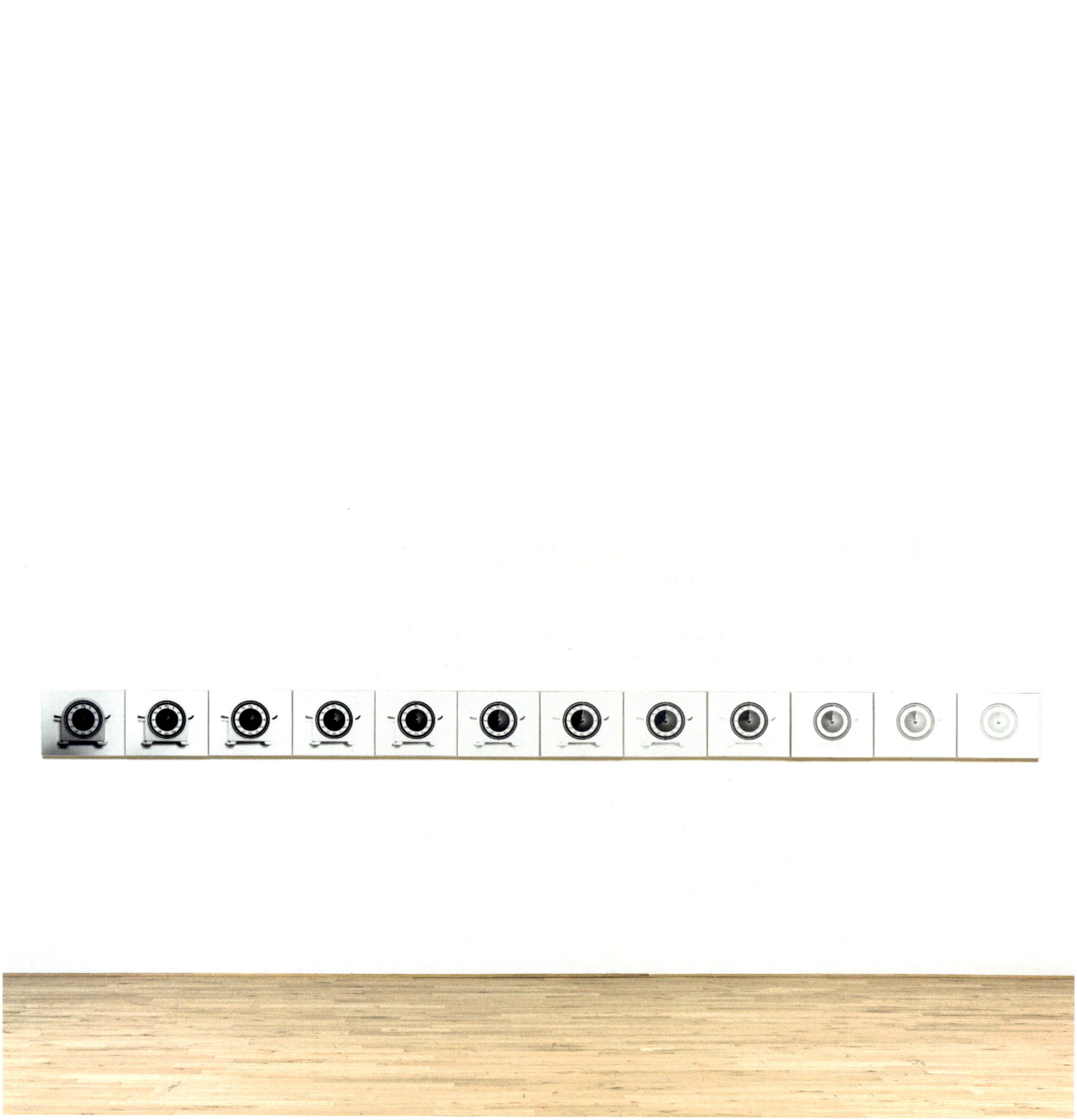

20 Roland Barthes introduced the idea of an 'obtuse' meaning in photographic images, which was discussed in relation to film stills in his essay 'The Third Meaning'. See Barthes 1981.

21 Rancière 2007, p.24.

presence in conceptual art, and with Rancière's ostensive art image, an image of 'sheer presence'. Stieglitz's photograph faces up to the media circulation of images, but also drags the discourses of art into it too. This is how the ostensive image functions: circulating the presence of that which is 'obtuse', not obvious, and difficult to name exactly.[20] In later conceptualisms we can see a similar process or chain of events. First there is the idea, followed by the event of the work and the photograph of it. Stieglitz's photograph, Rancière argues, 'becomes a display of a presence', which 'makes it possible to identify the dissemblances of art with the interactions of hyper-resemblance.'[21] On the one hand, the photograph of the urinal is an obvious representation of Duchamp's artwork, creating its presence; on the other it forces a distance from the thing itself. The photograph maintains a nervous dialectic between the object's self-identity and obtuse difference to itself. Photography, thus linked to dominant forms of media and visual representation in society, begins to undermine the resemblance of the world through the dissemblance of reality involved in conceptual art's use of photography.

The role and look of photography in conceptual art has varied enormously, depending on the skill, inclinations, interests and values of the artists involved. For some, photography was simply a handy tool, for others it became a question of examining what it was, allegorically, in itself.

John Hilliard's photographic works, for example, initially explored how photography works, how it constitutes its images, technically and formally, but turns towards investigating its social meanings too. *Sixty Seconds of Light* 1970 (fig.60) comprises twelve horizontally arranged photographs of a darkroom clock taken using exposures increased incrementally by five seconds. Although perhaps seen superficially as a formal experiment, with the extent of the blurring of the clock hands indicating the length of exposure time for each image, the series demonstrates how the way we see something is determined by the photographic process. The work points to the growing interest in and recognition of the role of photography in this period in critically organising how we *see* reality, especially through mass-media depictions. Reality is refracted via representation, mediation is not only what we see, but also how we see it.

John Hilliard's later work *Plundered/Dug/Prepared/Dry* 1975 directs this investigation of photographs towards the social meaning of pictures via their context. Here the same photographic image is cropped in four different ways to reveal how the same basic picture elements can be used to construct various meanings. The captions of each image, repeated in the title of the whole piece, anchor the scenes to types of action. The artwork becomes more directly about the performance of meaning and interpretation, not necessarily just in art, but in the wider social and semiotic world.

Victor Burgin developed this direction in a more explicit fashion, integrating the use of photography with cultural criticism. Art was not merely to be a tautological questioning or proposition about what art is, but could make links to other fields, such as advertising, literature and cinema. Art could be mobilised to dissemble the assumed meanings of advertising, fashion or other mass media imagery.

In his series *UK76* Burgin took documentary style formalist photographs and added text borrowed from advertising copy, in what he called

Figure 60
John Hilliard, *Sixty Seconds of Light* 1970
Twelve black and white photographs taken using 120 film, each 39.2 × 49.2
Tate

The photographic darkroom clock was photographed twelve times, each exposure five seconds longer than the previous one, ranging from five to sixty seconds. This resulted in under and over exposure of the clock compared to a so-called normal or correct exposure. The work thus highlights the way the reality presented in the image is a product of different aspects of photographic mediation – in this case light exposure.

Figure 61
Victor Burgin, *Today is the Tomorrow You Were Promised Yesterday* 1976
From the image-text (or *scripto-visual*) series *UK76*
Gelatin silver print, 101 × 152.4

a 'scripto-visual' practice. The picture *Today is the Tomorrow You Were Promised Yesterday* (fig.61) depicts a slightly desolate contemporary suburb, but overlaid with an optimistic text: 'The early-morning mist dissolves. And the sun shines on the Pacific...'. The piece demonstrates a gap between the conflicting values of idealised fashion copy text and the reality of everyday life, as seen in the photograph. Here, the question is no longer concerned with 'what is art?' but is replaced with a broader critique of culture through the very image systems and language that media ideologies use to sustain it.

We can make a link here back to the earlier avant-gardes, particularly the early radical Russian photography of the 1920s and 1930s – Alexander Rodchenko's 'factography' and the ideas of 'Art into life!' – where photography

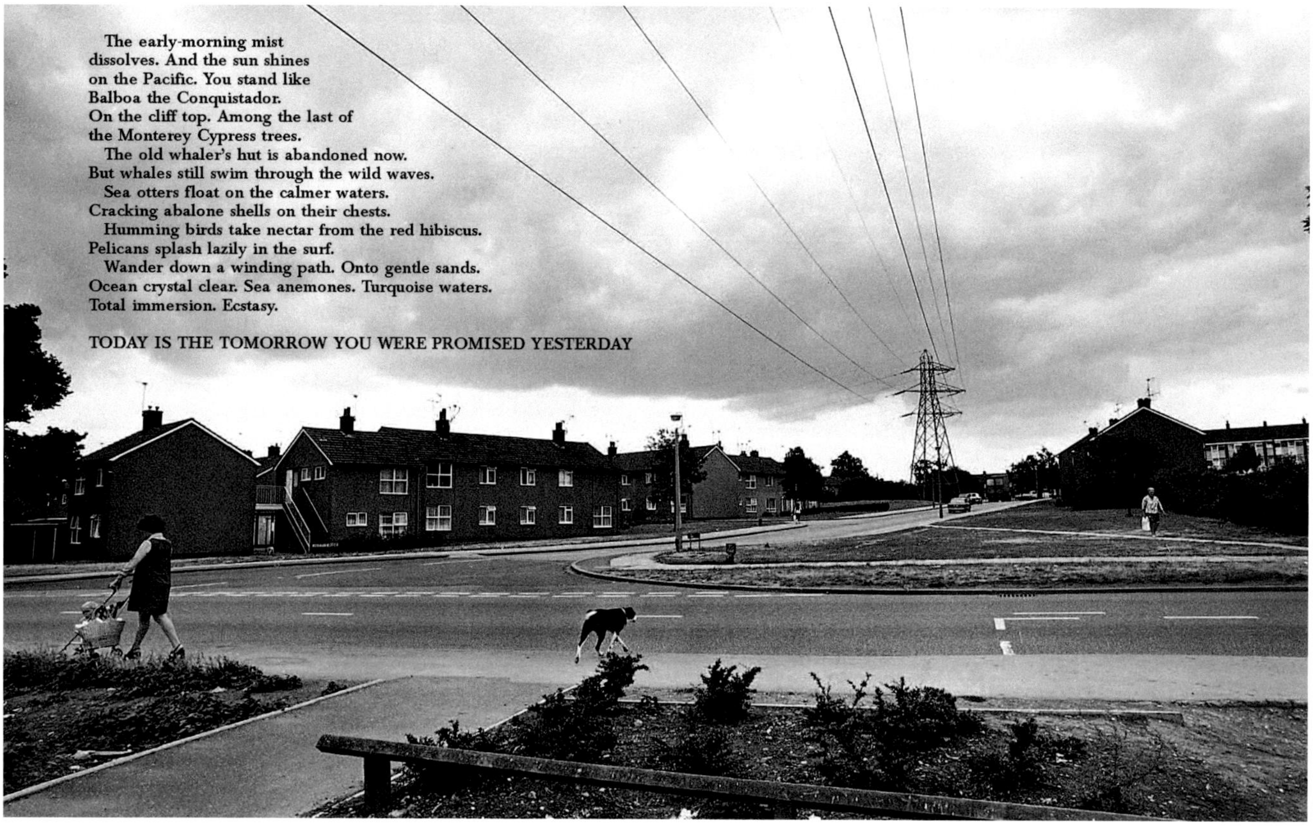

was merged into a new post-art critical practice of analytical-documentary. Indeed, Burgin later wrote about such practices in his essays.[22] Drawing on the essay of the Russian art theorist Victor Shklovsky, 'Art as Technique', and more recent film theory, Burgin developed a sophisticated theory which argued that any critical practice had to take account of not only the mechanisms of visual desire in the viewer, but also the art institution and its formation of discourse around the work. Radical forms or contents, Burgin concluded, were not in themselves 'progressive' unless the artist recognised the way an institution confers power and meanings onto them, especially if such work aimed to be critically effective.[23]

Of course, not all artists travelled the route towards an expanded field of art practice, recognising the importance of wider media images and systems of cultural meaning in the new modern world. But we can link such

22 See Burgin 1982, and Burgin 2009.

23 Burgin 2009, p.144.

24 Mulvey 1984.

interests forward, to more recent generations of artists, many of whom, significantly, are women. While many male conceptual artists employed the language and apparatus of the office and study, women artists also often used the home as material for their work. Martha Rosler's 1975 video 'Semiotics of the Kitchen' tackled the domestic kitchen directly. In a direct address to camera, Rosler shows the viewer a range of kitchen tools, each one announced verbally with its name. Spoken with implicit malice, her performance highlights the potential violence that ordinary instruments like 'knife' can imply. Mocking both the television cookery programme and the instruction manual style of advertising for kitchen appliances aimed at women, Rosler ironises the woman-in-the-kitchen televisual genre, emptying it of its traditional values. Laura Mulvey's essay 'Visual Pleasure and Narrative Cinema' 1975 heralded a new theoretical base for the 'destruction of pleasure' – already evident in the so-called anti- or post-aesthetics of conceptual art – with the rejection of traditional pictorial values of beauty as a feminist strategy too.[24] Conceptual art was put to work to question the representations of women and their relation to social identity, whether through celebration or critique, liberation or analysis. A 1970 performance by multi-ethnic, African-American

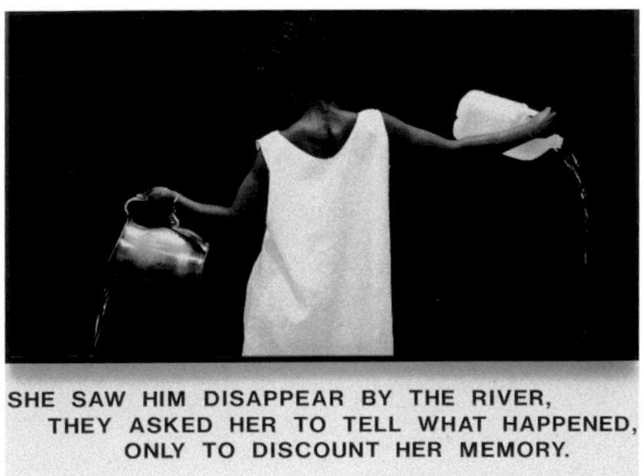

Figure 62
Lorna Simpson, *Waterbearer* 1986
Gelatin silver print and vinyl lettering, 114 × 196

conceptual artist Adrian Piper, for example, involved walking the streets of New York bearing the sign 'wet paint', alluding to the idea of surface appearances and ethnic identity. The work of Lorna Simpson, a younger generation conceptual artist, relates the issue of feminine identity to African-American history. *Waterbearer* 1986 (fig.62) alludes, as a metonymical fragment, to a story that might be imagined from the history of slavery. Tantalising in its obtuse presence and invocation of the woman as someone who is not listened to, the work again draws together image and language into a scripto-visual practice. Already, from these few examples, it can be seen that the social experience of artists in these works has become relevant, but in plural ways that highlight social and cultural differences. It would be hard to describe any of these works as 'political' in any direct sense of the term, but it is clear that they address and involve wider social and cultural values.

All of these techniques were, in some sense, opposed to modernism, as defined by the dominant ideas of the US critic Clement Greenberg, whose main thesis was to separate painting, sculpture and, by extension, photography, into their own medium specificities. Conceptual art mixed up these media with other genres and categories of practice, such as performance, absent objects, photography, documentation, video, use of the body, expressive gestures, signification of mass media forms and even the very medium used by critics – writing.

In the later generations of so-called 'postmodern' artists during the 1980s, these hybrid forms of art diversified even further. Photography remained central, just as it was in culture and the mass media, but it seemed that artists had taken on board the tactics of the media with which they were so saturated and adapted them for their own purposes. After the monochromatic tendencies of conceptual art, colour and visual pleasure returned, no longer the demonic other, as the mark of mass media, which high culture had previously excluded and despised. Like pop art, these new practices seemed to be ambivalent about mass-cultural sources. It was not quite clear if they were being celebrated, enjoyed as part of the culture, or whether this ambivalence was part of the aim of the work (as it had been in some pop art), asking the spectator again to think for themselves about these things, as a form of cultural critique.

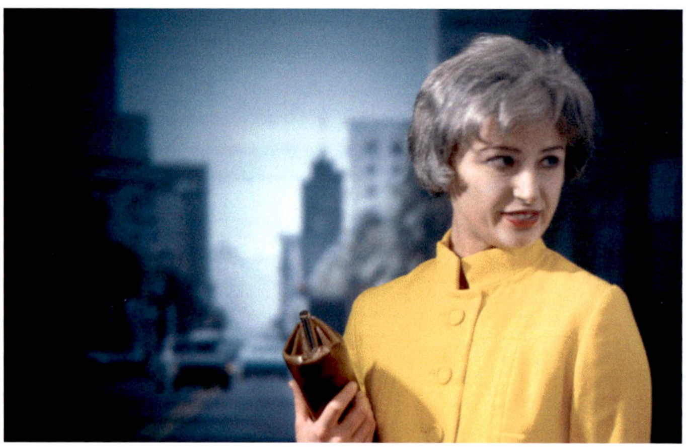

Figure 63
Cindy Sherman, *Untitled* 1980
Chromogenic colour print, 40.6 × 61

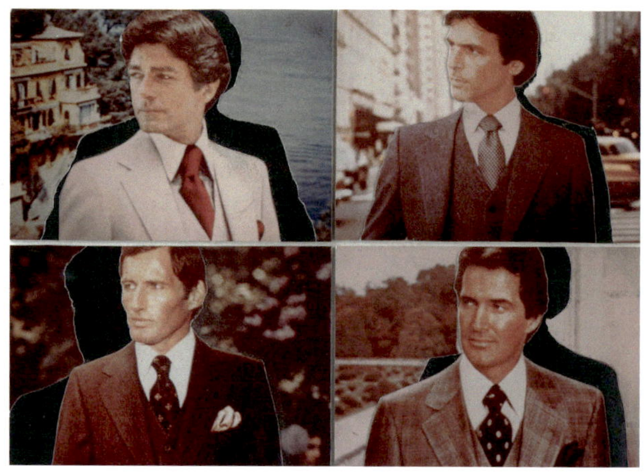

Figure 64
Richard Prince
Untitled (four single men with interchangeable backgrounds looking to the right) 1977
Mixed media on paper, 58.4 × 48.3
The Metropolitan Museum of Art, New York

We might ask here whether this was a fusion of conceptualism and modernism, or the absorption of conceptualism by modernism. This art-historical narrative has yet to be fully written. Did the marginal become the centre and in the mainstream? One way to consider this issue would be to look at the recent return to popularity of Ed Ruscha's photographic work, as indicative of a historical shift. Ruscha's early 1960s conceptualist photographic books were a precursor to the conceptual art of 1968, but today they seem to have taken a more central place in that history. Perhaps this is because something in Ruscha's work and its form of conceptualism speaks to what has been happening in recent contemporary art photography, and the notion of a post-conceptual photography.

Conceptualism can be seen as a response to the failure of 'modern' art, including fine-art photography, to engage significantly with or address any of our wider social experiences. Modernism, it might be argued, became a reclusive practice, separating itself from other social spheres of modern existence. The tension of this separation between art and popular culture was nowhere more fraught than in photography. While art photography had begun to draw documentary into it, this has been seen, in terms of the artist's aesthetic vision produced, as a 'signature style'. On the other hand, the so-called crude amateurism of photography in conceptual art rejected these obvious notions of artistic visual creativity and expression. Photographs were usually lacking in conventional aesthetic ideas of beauty, such that they attracted accusations of being anti-aesthetic or banal.

25 See Sylvia Wolf, *Ed Ruscha and Photography*, New York 2004.

26 Ibid., p.69.

27 Ibid., p.115.

28 Ibid., p.112.

Ed Ruscha and Post-conceptual Photography

As is well known, Ruscha's method was first to give the book a form, as a design, then a theme, and then to take photographs to fill them. So the subject matter of the pictures was determined by the concept/title of the book.[25] His first and best-known book, *Twentysix Gasoline Stations* 1963 (figs.65, 66), had forty-eight pages with twenty-six monochrome photographs positioned on the right-hand page. Ruscha acknowledged that his simple and small (approximately 12.7 × 17.8 cm) publications were influenced by the clean typography and uniform format of European books he had seen on earlier trips.[26] Ruscha photographed the many gasoline stations on Route 66, between Los Angeles and Oklahoma City (Ruscha's home town and city of choice), to find the right twenty-six for the book.[27] The pictures were not in any geographical order, but chosen, cropped and placed in sequence according to the feel and design of the book, rendering a sense of visual progression. While any book implies a narrative or chronological progression because of its form, as a sequence of pages, Ruscha's book exploits this too, even if not intentionally.

Ruscha applied this game of conceptual form over the content of his other books – *Some Los Angeles Apartments* 1965, *Every Building on the Sunset Strip* 1966, *Thirtyfour Parking Lots* 1967, *Nine Swimming Pools and a Broken Glass* 1968, *Stains* 1969, *Real Estate Opportunities* 1970 and others – which all rely on photographs to enunciate their themes. While each book elaborates a set of photographs on a theme, so every book adds to a larger collection of motifs and themes, accrued across the whole series.

Early reviewers regarded Ruscha's book as a dadaist joke, while some reviews were unable to see anything other than the pointless banality of showing ordinary gasoline stations (in a time when they were plentiful), others were unable to see any point in the work at all. Today, critics read the work in other ways. In *Twentysix Gas Stations*, Sylvia Wolf has argued, each of the photographs depicts a particular manifestation of vernacular American industrial architecture and their different ideals.[28] For example, the slanting roof in 'Phillips 66', Wolf notes, signifies the dynamic architectural 'spirit of hope, mobility and speed' of America, whereas the flat utilitarian shape of 'Texaco, Verga' or the minimal 'Hudson, Amarillo, Texas' resemble the architecture of a border town, as in Orson Wells' classic 1958 film noir movie *A Touch of Evil*. Or we might even add Alfred Hitchcock's popular 1960 thriller *Psycho*. The general idea of a gasoline station is particularised by each of the photographs, whose specific descriptive differences are fed back into the title of the book. There is a clear sense of continuity in Ruscha's approach to these themes. Each picture is a variation on the theme, making it clear that he is far from a naïve or 'anti-photography' artist simply preoccupied with vernacular subject matter. We know this much from his biography.

In 1956 Ruscha had begun studying at Chouinard Art Institute (now CalArts) in California, where, as well as the new conceptualist art of the

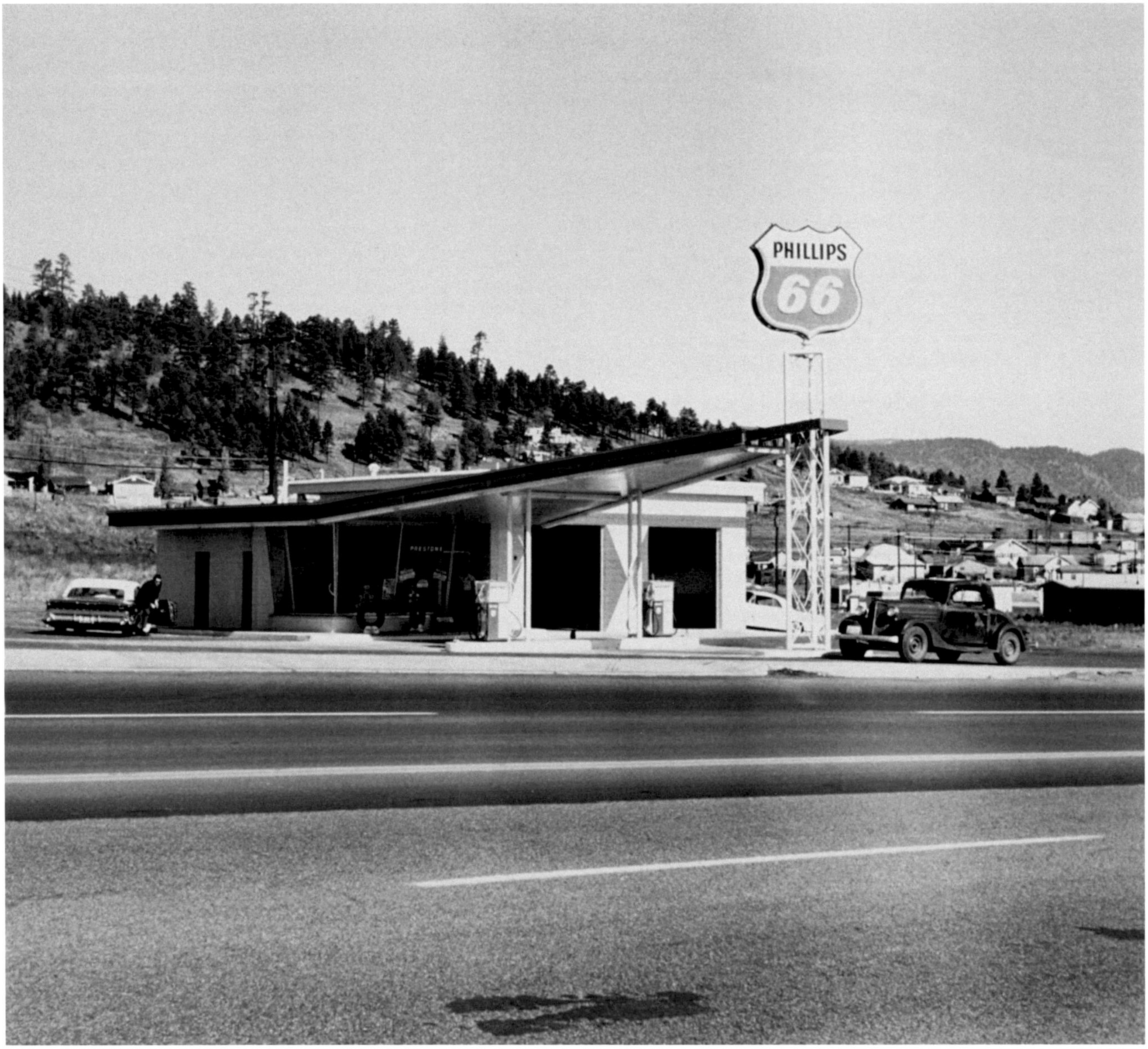
PHILLIPS
66

29 Ibid., p.37.

30 'This devotion to a deadpan, anonymous, amateurish approach to photographic form corresponds exactly to Ruscha's iconographic choice of the architectural banal', Buchloch 1997, p.134.

31 Wolf 2004, p.111.

32 Ibid., p.127.

day, through the likes of Jasper Johns and Robert Rauschenberg, he was also introduced to art photography and its history. Amidst the different bodies of work that he encountered at this time were seminal American photography books: *American Pictures* by Walker Evans, *The Americans* by Robert Frank, and the epic international exhibition *Family of Man*, which he saw in Los Angeles in 1957. Organised by Edward Steichen, it comprised 503 photographs by 273 photographers (over half of whom were American) from 68 countries. On graduation Ruscha briefly worked in a Los Angeles advertising agency on graphic design and layout. Within a year he left for New York, where he later laid out pages for *Artforum* magazine. It is interesting to see how these different experiences converge in Ruscha's later work, the clear articulation of his interest in language, the use of graphics and lettering, a wry humour and taste for offbeat subject matter, cultivated into a dry and neutral style of photography. These all provided the foundations for a text and image practice, a scripto-visual conceptual art that included photography.

Five years later, in April 1961, aged 24, Ruscha sailed with his family to Europe for a family holiday and personal road trip.[29] Taking in seventeen countries in seven months, Ruscha photographed throughout the journey, getting the films developed along the way. Clearly inspired by Eugène Atget, Walker Evans and Robert Frank, Ruscha was far from being an 'amateur', as his use of a 6x6cm-square, medium-format Yashica camera at that time, and the pictures he took with it, indicates. Given this training and background experience in photography before he started the book series, he was well qualified to take his own pictures for them - although in one exception, *Thirtyfour Parking Lots in Los Angeles* 1967, he did hire a commercial photographer, Art Alenis, for an aerial view shot. Ruscha is unusual among conceptualist artists in having this specific training in art photography and, more importantly, a familiarity with its history. Many of the other conceptual artists only became familiar with the history of photography much later.

While Ruscha's books have their own charms, and the art critic Benjamin Buchloch once described his photographs as 'amateurish',[30] they are certainly not easy to place. The photographs are not quite deadpan, nor do they follow the rigid taxonomic formal rules of Bernd & Hiller Becher's pictures of European industrial architecture. Ruscha's books do not narrate or describe any real journey, as in Frank's *The Americans*. Ruscha describes his own books as collections of facts and, borrowing Duchamp's term, identifies the gasoline stations as 'readymades'. Indeed, Ruscha was greatly influenced by Duchamp's work first-hand, having seen a major retrospective of his work at the Pasadena Art Museum in 1963.[31] In Ruscha's own account, he explains how his books represent something that is absent, but made present: 'Instead of going out and calling a gas station "art", I'm calling its photograph art ... But the photograph isn't the art. The photograph by itself doesn't mean anything to me; it's the gas station that's the important thing.'[32]

Yet there is something disingenuous about this argument. How can the photograph be art, and then not art too? Is the photograph only secondary to the absent subject matter, when it is the photograph that brings it? Where is the art? How can the gas station be art without the photograph enunciating it in Ruscha's book? In Ruscha's dry, paradoxical claim, the

Figure 65
Ed Ruscha, *Phillips 66, Flagstaff, Arizona* 1962
From the series *Twentysix Gasoline Stations, 1963*
Gelatin silver print

ostensive image emerges: the image of a gasoline station is fused within the codes of the photograph, yet imagined and produced as separate from it too. Ruscha's argument plays on the fundamental paradox of photographic images as a 'message without a code'.[33] The photograph disappears when you think about the referent of the picture, but this subject matter, which is elsewhere, is only enunciated in Ruscha's books through the photograph. Like many paradoxes, this one cannot be resolved, the image and referent are bound together, one determines the other, and this is in fact the very condition of meaning of all photographic images. What is shown as present is also absent. In this sense, the work of Ruscha also shows something of the passions of collecting, in that the language-image activity of the photobook exceeds the utilitarian function of the objects concerned. Photography enabled him to collect things that are otherwise difficult to collect: gasoline stations, swimming pools and so on. So while the various series seem at first glance random and quirky, they do relate to specific aspects of social life and carry connections that are not so random: gasoline stations and swimming pools, for instance, both revolve around fluids, albeit very different ones, and both are places where casual encounters can occur.

33 For the 'message without a code', see Barthes 1991, p.5.

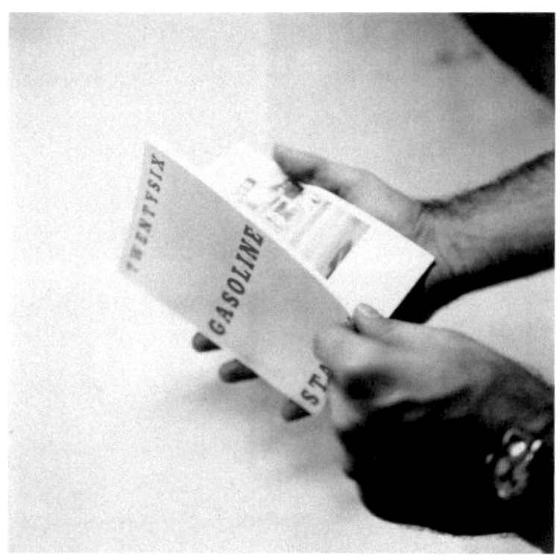

Figure 66
Ed Ruscha, *Hands Flipping Pages* 1963

Stains 1969 continued this liquid preoccupation, but is further linked to *Thirtyfour Parking Lots*, of which Ruscha says it was the oil stains left by the automobiles that interested him most, as indicators of the best parking spaces. Although not aiming to be anthropological, Ruscha's books draw obtuse links between the apparently disparate social spaces represented across his books. Perhaps through these little books the satisfaction of the collector is transmitted to the curious viewer, who can feel some kind of enigmatic kinship with their themes and motifs. A collection, like an archive, is a way of photographically organising the world, while identifying it as art, and photography is also a way to visualise the collection. Ruscha's books give a kind of aesthetic dignity to the things they depict, which of course elevates these usually neglected everyday spaces and places above their utilitarian function. So ignored in ordinary life, the themes he chooses are not glamorised through his photography, nor are they criticised; but, like Duchamp's urinal, therein lies the old twentieth-century question: what is art?

Ruscha is unusual as a conceptual artist in the early 1960s for his consciousness of photographic tradition *and* interest in formal design. It makes him an ideal prototype for the combination of photographic modernism and conceptualism, despite those who say his work is simply 'amateur'. Contemporary photographers are now far more conscious of these histories of art and conceptual uses of photography. So it might be possible to argue that the once separate fields of conceptual art, modernism and documentary are now, in effect, more or less combined in what might be called post-conceptual art photography.

Post-conceptual Photography?

Certainly, today the new centrality of photography in art has seen a revived interest in the older conceptualist works as discussed above. It is easy to see many of their features returning, and often within modern still and moving photographic images. The new works revise older arguments about the role of 1960s conceptual art, since what were once innovatory methods and ideals about anti- or post-aesthetic conceptual art are now established museum concepts in contemporary art. On the one hand, this means that art is more open to the wider semiotic and media environment of the social world; on the other, it means the critical status and function of conceptual art is no longer necessarily the same. A discussion of two photographic works can help elaborate this issue: one a conceptualist piece by John Baldessari in 1963, and the other a documentary work by the photographer Chris de Bode in 2011.

John Baldessari's *The Backs Of All The Trucks Passed While Driving From Los Angeles to Santa Barbara, California. Sunday 20 January 63* 1963 (fig.67) uses a grid of snapshot photographs to visualise the action of passing trucks. Like Ruscha's book, Baldessari's exhibition artwork is language-image based too: the title defines the concept that is elaborated upon and made visual by the photographs. The ordinary event of an automobile passing other vehicles, specifically trucks, is elevated to signify something important – at least important enough to be represented. We might consider the pictures to be pointing to something that we cannot see, something beyond the obvious event. Repetition of doing something again and again leads to boredom. On the other hand, in some cases it can lead to satisfaction (no matter how temporary), as with eating from hunger. Passing trucks might involve satisfaction and its opposite, the pain of boredom, the monotony of a car journey, punctuated by only an occasional overtake.

Chris de Bode's *Exodus from Libya* 2011 (fig.68) depicts the exodus of migrant workers (mostly Bangladeshi) from Libya during the 2011 uprising, as they leave for Tunisia and beyond. De Bode's documentary work for the Refugee Commission, an NGO, initially appeared in newspapers. Like Baldessari's, de Bode's piece also uses repetition to show streams of people, all headed in the same direction across each photograph. Visually this accumulation makes the point that the exodus was massive. One might argue that both works have a documentary aspect, using photography to make new visual arguments. Baldessari's uneven sequencing of the photographs and rough cuts between frames create a disjunctive temporality, which is also found in de Bode's work. This strategy of repeating a theme with disjunctive relations relates a passing of time and space that is fractured. In both works, a moment of everyday life has become an event to be photographed. Their common strategy is 'conceptual', but with different ends. The migrant exodus is the more urgent political issue, and it

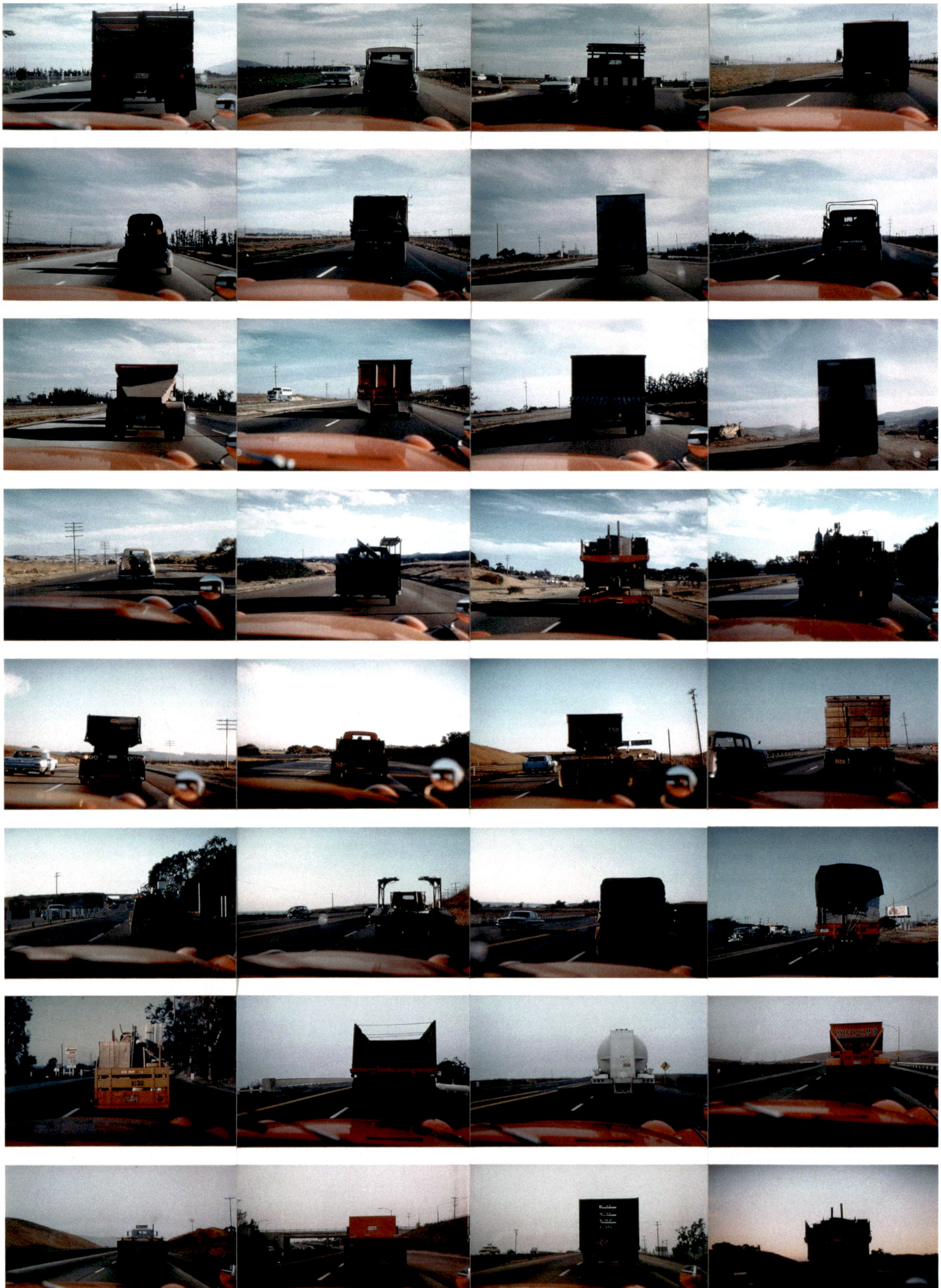

would seem wrong to reduce this to being merely an exercise in conceptualism. Baldessari's work, on the other hand, has a sense of humour and an ambivalence. And so it becomes clear that any given visual strategy or technique, when handled differently in dissimilar times and places, cannot be identified with a singular critical purpose. Like those in de Bode's photographs who flee for their lives, each has a story that, while it may be possible to universalise, is nevertheless singular and particular. We might say the same of contemporary art, so that the mobilisation of categories such as conceptual, modernist, pictorial and documentary all become problematic, fused together in many ways in particular instances by different artists and photographers. Post-conceptualism in photography, then, if such a term is to have any meaning at all, must, like all the

Figure 67
John Baldessari, *The Backs Of All The Trucks Passed While Driving From Los Angeles to Santa Barbara, California. Sunday 20 January 63* 1963
32 colour photographs from 35mm slides, 152.4 × 108

Figure 68
Chris de Bode, *Exodus from Libya* 2011

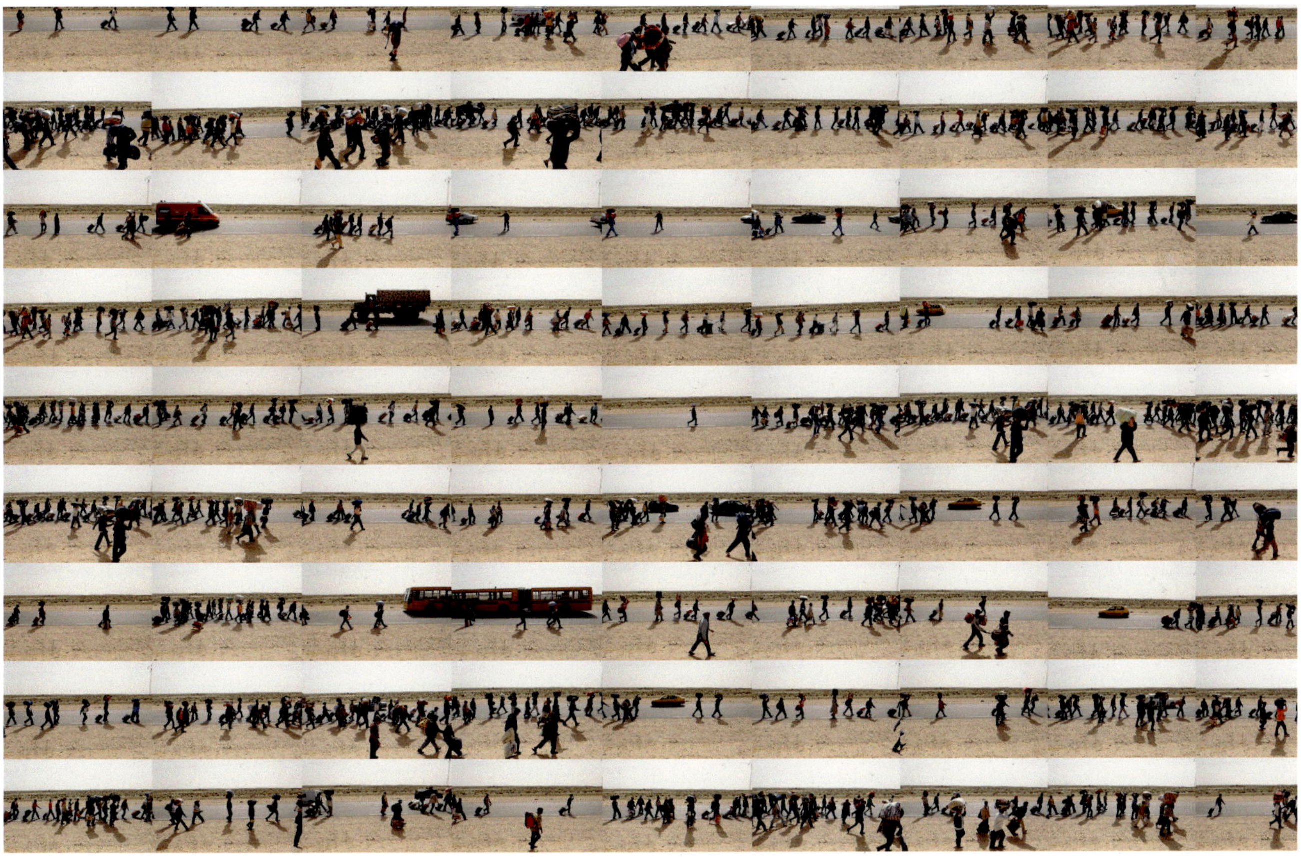

previous -isms, be taken to task by its specificity. Art absorbs the -isms of the past, so that post-conceptualist art is nothing but the absorption of conceptualism into the pluralist tactics of contemporary art.

We may note here that now probably everyone has a greater consciousness of the role of visual images, especially photographic ones, in the making of all or any event in the world. Contemporary art photography is a space that can operate to dissemble or reassemble non-art photographic values, to struggle against them in their mass-media forms, interrogating them afresh and, like earlier conceptual art, finding new ways to describe the different critical events that matter in the time and spaces of life.

The photographs show the mass departure of Bangladeshi migrant workers from Libya across the border to Tunisia. Taking more than 500 photos in a single day, de Bode's strategy was to utilise the repetition to show the intensity of the exodus.

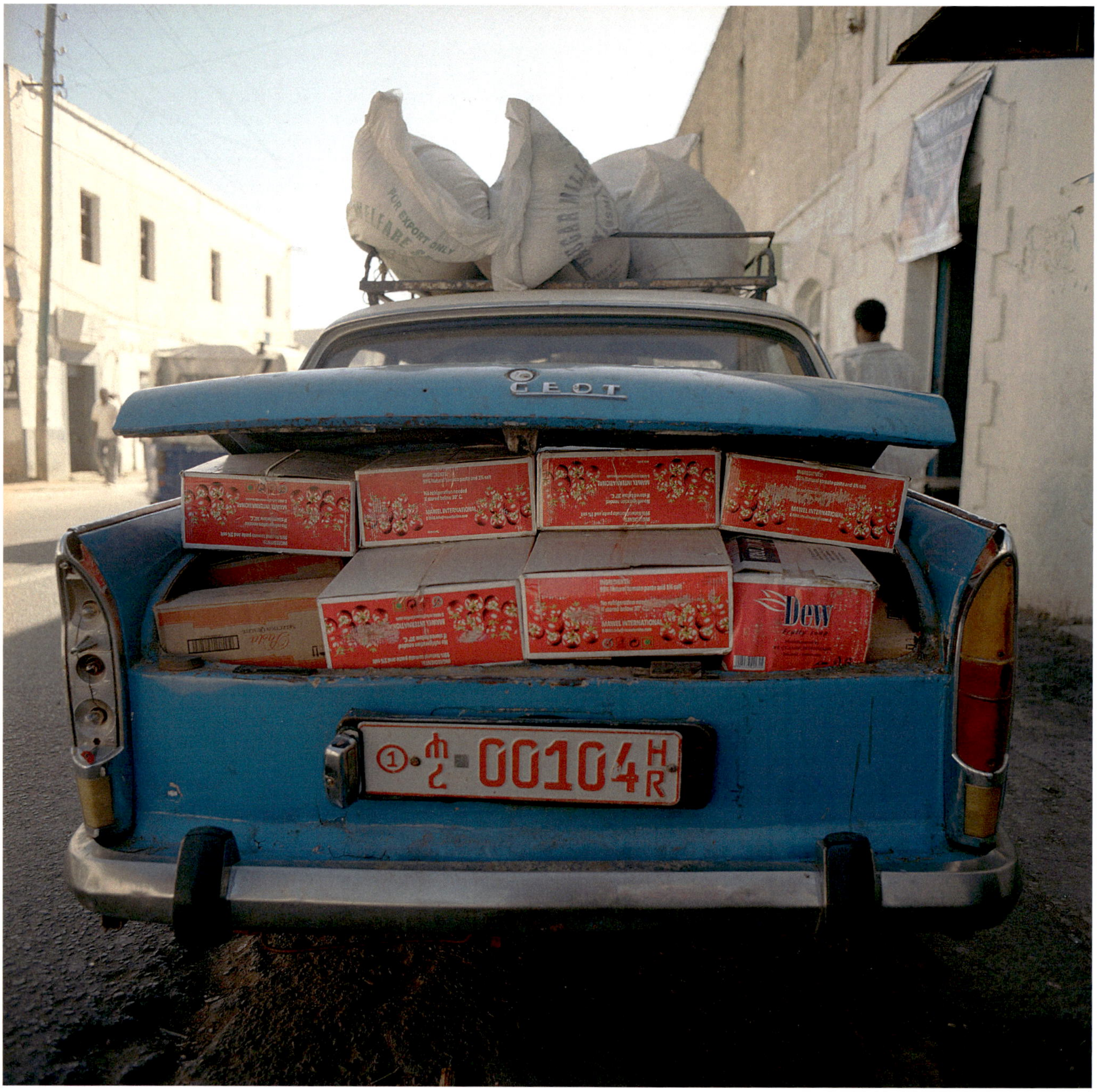
FOR EXPORT ONLY
Dew
00104

ARCHIVES, NETWORKS AND NARRATIVES

Figure 69
Raymond Depardon,
Harar Ethiopia
2013

Awareness of the historical accumulation of photographic archives has expanded exponentially since the invention of the internet. Whether private or public, anonymous or authored, photographic images now form a massive new presence as a type of archive material. It is not only that the internet has given greater access to existing archives, but that it has also begun to radically change what we think an archive is. No longer are photographic archives merely filled with dusty piles of boxes, although these certainly still exist, but the digitisation of photographic images online has also generated new networks related to each other through software systems. These systems are beginning to change the way we experience the relations between images in a number of different ways: the changing values of public and private, image and text, past and present, and the links between one image and another in narrative formations. The internet itself functions as a new type of meta-archive, linking vast quantities of individual archives. However, we might start with the institution that houses the dusty boxes, and which relates most obviously to art archives: the art museum.

Museum Archive

Museums and art museums are far from universal and are a relatively recent invention. Yet every museum has a history. The Louvre in Paris is one of the oldest art museums and remains a classic example of a European history: at first it was a private collection of art in a royal palace, then, following the 1789 French Revolution, a national public museum. Under Napoleon it also briefly became a repository for artefacts from imperial conquests, at once creating an image of self and others, including those conquered. The Hermitage in St Petersburg has a similar history, first as a private royal palace, before its conversion into a public museum. In England, the royal family still has its own private art collection, but the National Gallery in London, established by the state in 1824, is based on a separate collection of private paintings. Since 1838 it has been housed in Trafalgar Square, so named after the 1805 sea battle with Napoleon's fleet, placing national identity and a cultural museum in direct proximity.

Collections of artefacts for private or public display are thus never a neutral activity. Museums aim to serve particular interests, whether personal, cultural, regional, national, international or global. Museums act as repositories of cultural memories of the past, the present or implied futures, and organise historical narratives of culture. While the function of museums is to organise and display artefacts and materials, they also inevitably create inventories and interpretations of them along the way. The items selected and arranged - both within the architecture of the museum and its online platforms - are often chosen from a vast repository, aiming to construct a particular story or a pattern of engagement with

Figure 70
Roger Fenton,
The Third Graeco-Roman Saloon on Artists' Day in the British Museum 1857
stereoscopic photograph,
7.1 × 7.6 (each image)

objects, images and texts for the strolling or scrolling spectator. This basic scenario of complex factors can be taken as the typical situation for all kinds of museums and archives.

Photography performs a peculiar double role within these institutions. Photographs can function as both a collected artefact that might be put on display and as a way to collect the museum and its artefacts, since the photograph is a form of archive in its own right. A number of museum artefacts can be collected in a single photograph.

Consider the first photographs taken in the British Museum in London. The museum was established as a state collection in 1753, when Sir John Sloane bequeathed it to the nation. The museum's first official photographer, Roger Fenton, was employed in 1854 to document its artefacts.[1] Fenton had attended Gustave Le Gray's photography studio

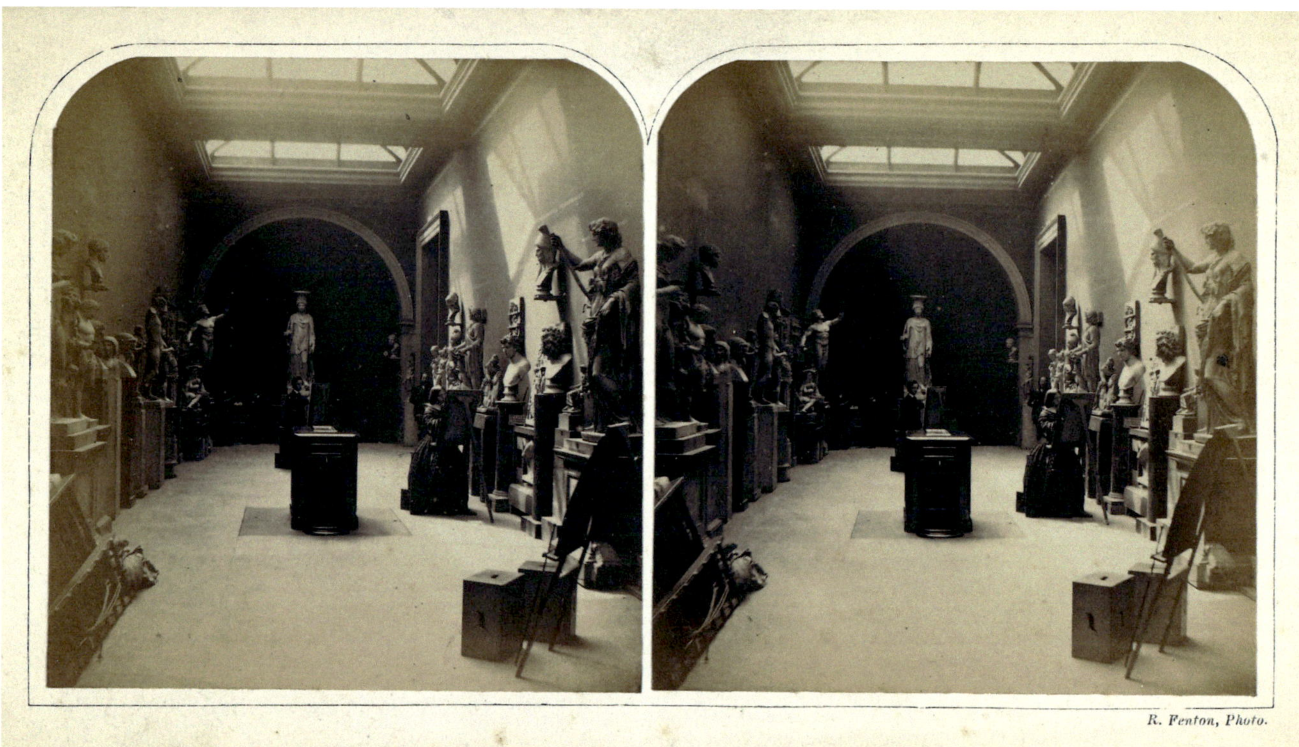

school in Paris in 1851 and, like Le Gray, had also studied as a painter with Paul Delaroche in Paris almost a decade earlier, albeit briefly. Again like Le Gray, Fenton tried to sustain himself as a professional photographer in these early years of the medium. In addition to his infamous Crimean war pictures, his photographs of the royal family at leisure won him the commission to set up a new photography studio in the British Museum. Fenton considered this commission of museum photography to be a most 'useful an application of the photographic art'.[2] To photograph the artefacts of the museum, he noted, would benefit everyone, and demonstrate how 'photography could help the museum catalogue, classify, and disseminate information about its burgeoning collection and prove photography's usefulness to the other arts'.[3]

Fenton photographed the moveable objects in a rooftop studio for maximum light, but for other, larger objects he had to settle for

1 Baldwin et al. 2004, p.16.

2 Roger Fenton quoted in Baldwin et al. 2004, p.16.

3 Ibid., p.16.

4 On the general history of photography in MoMA, see also Phillips 1996.

5 See, for example, Louise Lawler and Helen Molesworth (eds.), *Twice Untitled and Other Pictures (looking back)*, London 2006.

photographing them in the museum's interior. His photographs create an impression of how it was to see these objects in the Victorian era. The photographs evoke a 'pastness', which shows the effect a photograph itself can have on how we see the things in it. The pictures themselves create an atmospheric space, with a kind of silence around the artefacts, a stillness of the historical museum. This is what Walter Benjamin called the 'aura' of an object, created by the historical distance that is experienced in relation to it. With historical time, Fenton's photographs have become famous and feature in museum shows and exhibitions as artefacts in their own right. The effect of such photographs is not necessarily nostalgic, provoking a desire in the viewer to return to some imagined past invoked by the image; rather, the meaning of the image is also intertwined with the present. Archive photographs not only record objects and events, they also produce a meta-archive, with meanings that can be mobilised in other times and new contexts.

Public museums, increasingly conscious of different audience demographics, link the display of archives to various categories of cultural memory, but also to types of forgetting. In this sense, museums make implicit and explicit choices about how to arrange artefacts and what to say about and through them. Archives, reconfigured into museum displays, construct narratives of what can be held to be art or culture (or whatever the rubric of the collection is), as we have already seen on pp.59–60, where Berenice Abbott's collection of Eugène Atget photographs came to provide a foundation for the values of modern art photography in the Museum of Modern Art in New York.[4]

Cultural Memory

Museums accumulate archives and mobilise them to meet cultural-institutional goals. In recent years, artists have become more conscious of these institutional roles, sometimes taking them as the focus of their work. Louise Lawler's photographs feature artworks in private homes, public museums or auction houses and other key institutions that organise taste and evaluate art aesthetically, critically and economically. Her pictures show how art is contextualised or de-contextualised by these environments, and contrasts them in relation to one another.[5] Her photographs of exhibition installations of art highlight the institutional production of value through a sort of museology of art as art photography. Lawler's pictures cast a keen anthropological eye, with a visual framing that is attentive to the institutional aspect of display, from behind the scenes of a museum or auction house presentation, to domestic settings. They offer mostly fragmentary glimpses of artworks in these spaces and make a gently critical judgment. Quietly pensive, the photographs draw the spectator into a mesh of questions about spatial relations, taste and value of these objects. Lawler's photographic work does not so much judge the museums or galleries as ask questions about the relations between artefacts and the underlying logic that drives the degree to which a work belongs to its setting. In observing this, her works begin to highlight the subtle ways that cultural values such as gender, ethnicity, social currency, political affiliation and sexuality are brought out in or projected onto a work. Look at Lawler's photograph taken in the Metropolitan Museum of Art, New York, in 1983.

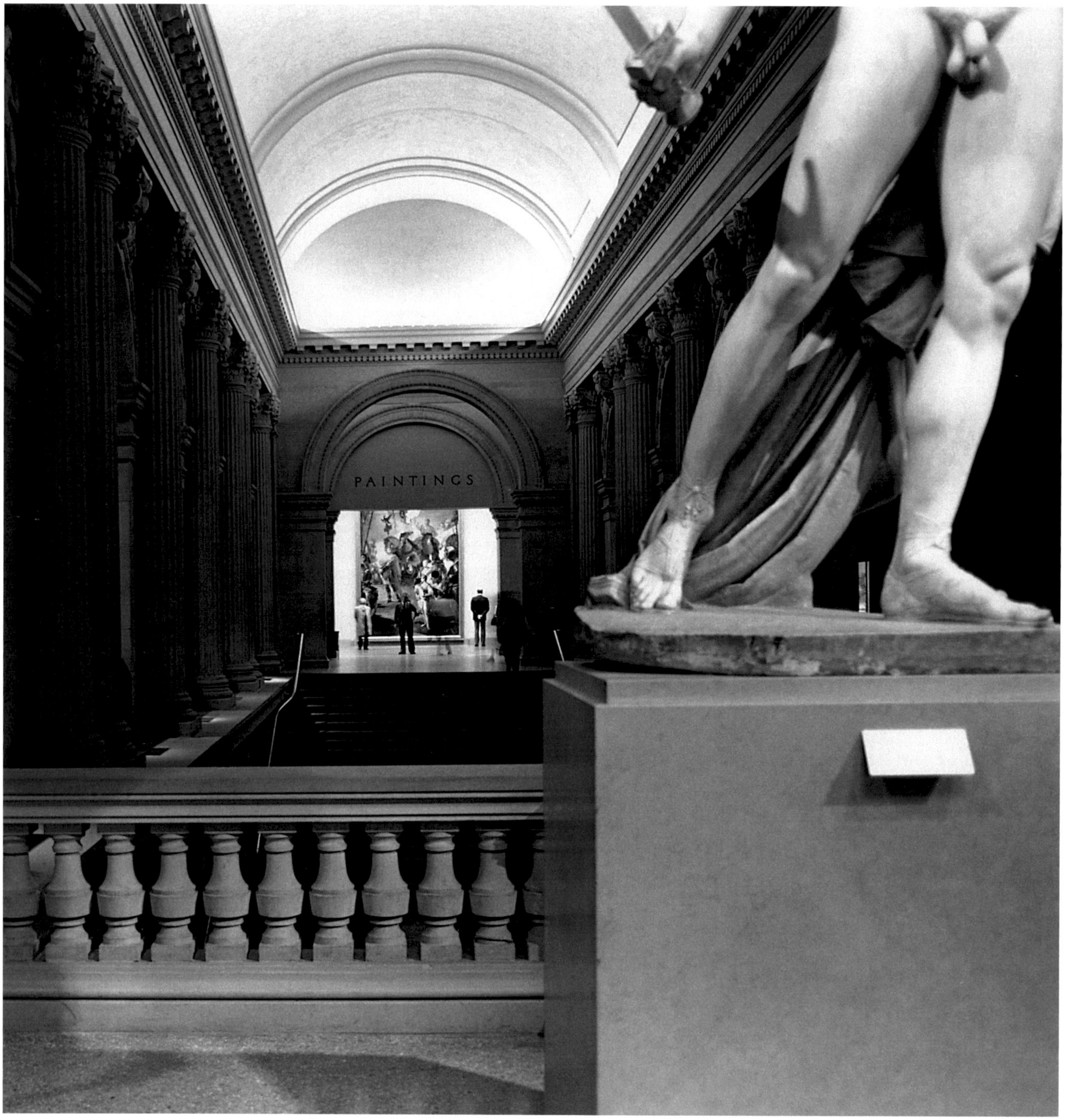
PAINTINGS

6 The specificity of the audience addressed in historical paintings is beautifully outlined in Michel Foucault's essay on Velázquez's *Las Meninas* 1656 in Foucault 1980.

The foreground space of *Statue before Painting* 1982 (fig.71) is dominated by the legs and genitals of Canova's Mycenaean warrior *Perseus* 1804–6 and its plinth, which Lawler has cropped to echo a rectangular lit space in the background, through which Giovanni Battista Tiepolo's painting *The Triumph of Marius* 1729 can be seen. Between Perseus's genitals and his hand – which holds the sword with which he severed the head of Medusa, held in his other, out-of-frame hand – the museum's architrave leads the eye straight to Tiepolo's depiction of the Roman general's victory over the African king Jugurtha. Among this neo-classical symphony of violence and victory, tiny figures – museum visitors – stand before the vast painting. We can see how the sightlines within the museum architecture frame the spectator, while Lawler's own framing and cropping strategically emphasise the archival potential of photography, as the sculpture and painting recede from the surface of the photograph itself. The photograph, alongside others, makes an 'imaginary museum', a montage of objects collected in one space, as once posited by André Malraux. A 'museum without walls' has come to fruition, materialised in photographs, websites, art books and photobooks (as they have become known).

Figure 71
Louise Lawler,
Statue Before Painting, Perseus with the Head of Medusa, Canova 1983
17.1 × 16.5

Thomas Struth's museum-based photographs turn this idea of the photograph as a museum into a question about the art museum itself (fig.72). Lawler's work looks at the organisation of artworks in relation to each other in the museum space. Struth's photographs, on the other hand, look at the social interactions between a modern audience and historical artworks in different world-famous museums. His pictures examine these patterns of viewing art in museums, and show a clear interest in the sociological dimension of the audiences of art. Mixed groups and individuals crowd together in front of and around paintings to form tableaux-like arrangements. Some photographs hint at a curious disjuncture between the time of the historical paintings and their modern mass audiences. Struth seems to see that his own photographs are creating pictures of these museums, with the audience integrated as part of their image. While tourists and school groups do not quite seem to belong to the same time as these historical pictures, this also reminds us that the paintings' original, intended audiences are long gone.[6] The life-size scale of the paintings and the restless flow of passing visitors exacerbate the contrast between the culture of the past and the modern museum visitor. The visitors seem, and indeed are, transient compared to their static, painted counterparts, which are powerfully fixed in their pose and instance of light forever. However, no museum is timeless. In fact, it is precisely the encounter with these historical artefacts that gives the experience of, and generates thought about, time and temporality.

We may contrast these works, which are so explicitly concerned with the politics and aesthetics of the cultural art museum, with work by artists and photographers who address the museum by contributing in other ways to its archive. These are, for instance, made by creating different image taxonomies, using existing archives or constructing new ones from a variety of other cultural artefacts not usually considered of museological value, giving them new value and cultural significance by bringing them within the museum as an artwork.

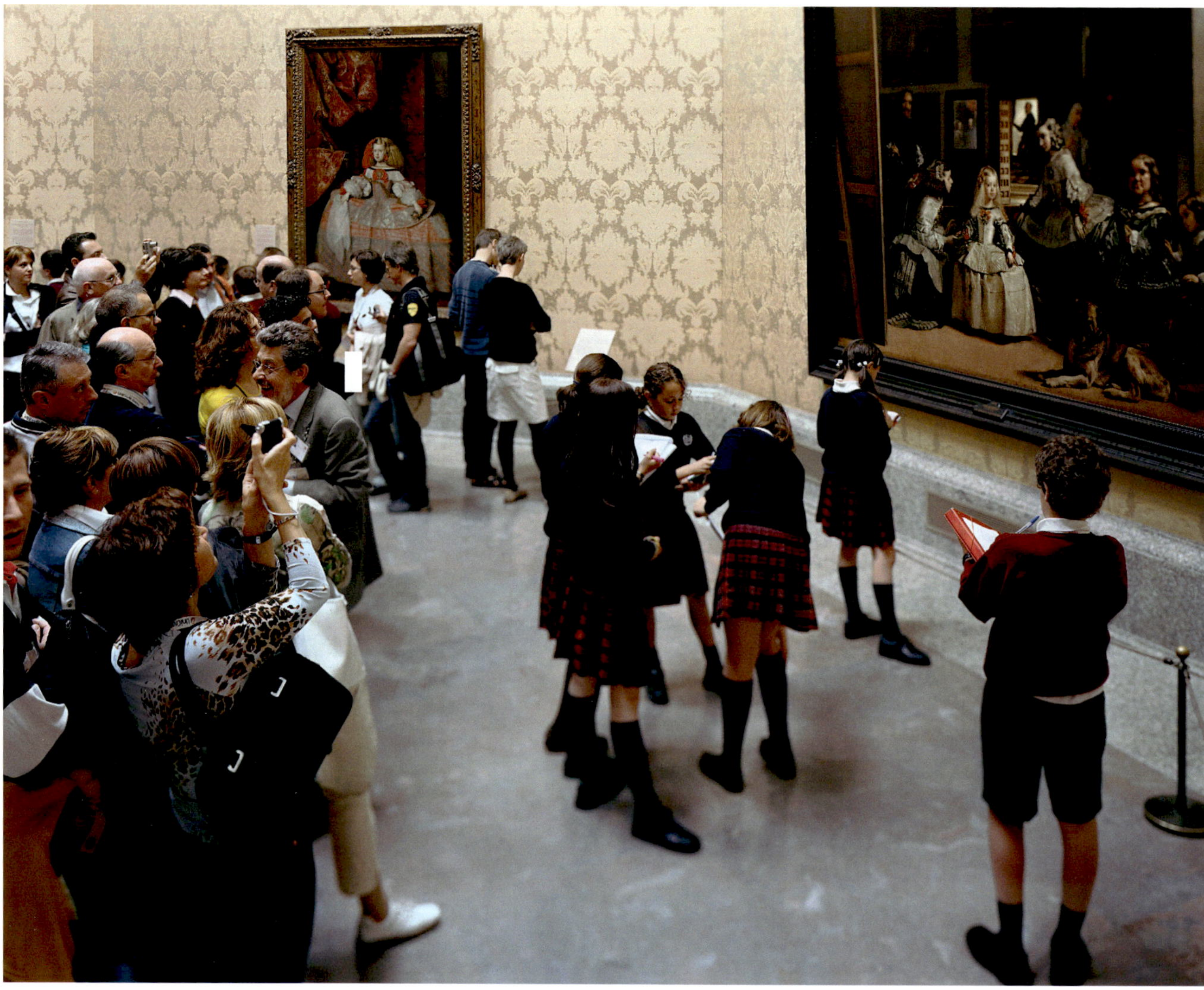

Tracey Moffatt's series *Something More* 1989 (fig.73) presents a fictionalised biographical account of a young Aboriginal woman's desire to leave her rural life for the city. The backdrop is clearly painted, conferring a theatricality onto the scene of a rough shack inhabited by equally rugged figures, with others in the background. They all stare at a woman in the foreground, who seems indifferent to them. Her urbane elegance and dress mark her apart, and she appears to be thoughtful, perhaps pondering her future. This is not a Cinderella rags-to-riches fantasy though, as the subsequent pictures show: the disturbing story ends in violation and a miserable death. Moffatt's early work often takes the form of fictionalised re-enactments of personal memories, such strategies seeking to supplement known histories with other narratives not usually represented in cultural archives. The National Gallery of Australia in Canberra, the country's capital city, now owns this work, so by finding

Figure 72
Thomas Struth,
Museo del Prado 7, Madrid 2005 2005,
Chromogenic print,
177.5 × 218.6
© Thomas Struth

Figure 73
Tracey Moffatt,
Something More 1989
type C photographs

Moffatt's photographic series stages an implied narrative: a young woman dreams to leave an isolated Australian home for the big city, but never arrives.

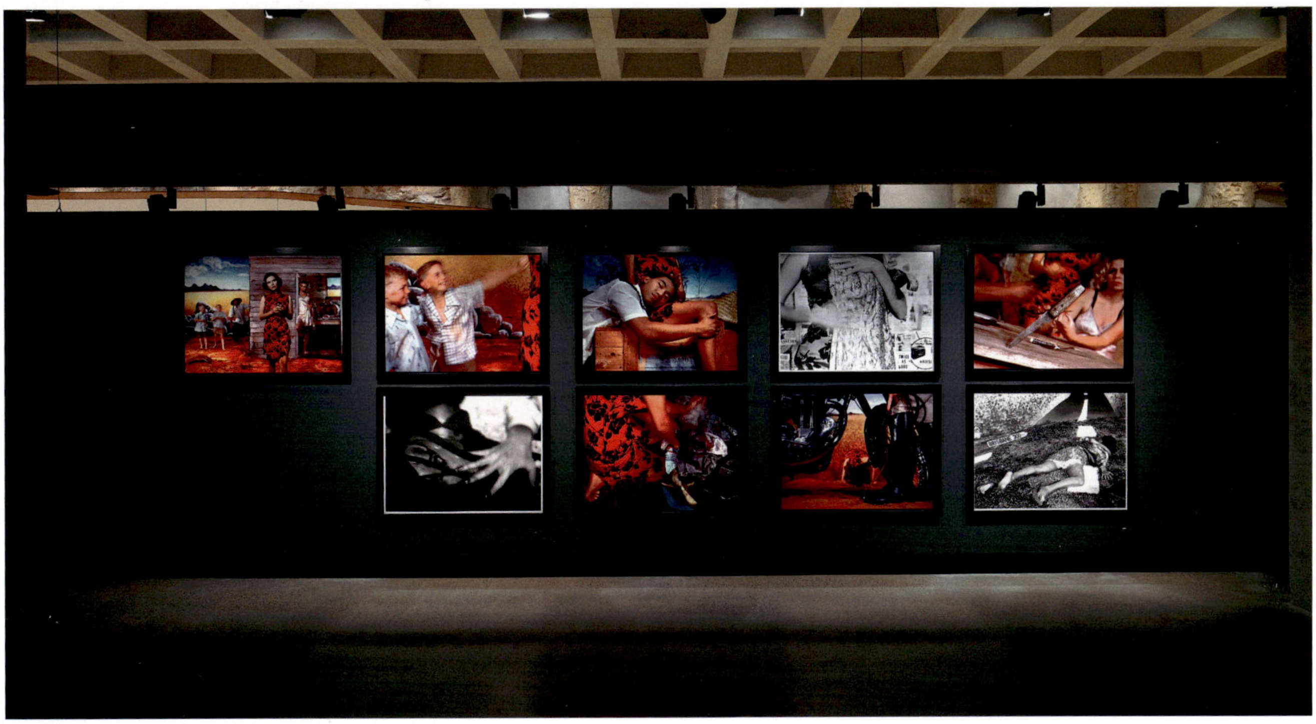

its way into a national archive, this Aboriginal story of desire and social violence helps re-figure an understanding of the past within the present, which also fosters and hopes to anticipate a different future.

Susan Hiller's *Dedicated to the Unknown Artists* 1972–6 (fig.74) is a collection of some three hundred postcards, all of the coast around Britain. Each postcard presents an image, variously black-and-white or hand-tinted photography, several of them paintings; all are of waves crashing over different parts of the coastline. Arranged on fourteen panels in grids, the pictures become part of an archival display of how a culture sees itself, repeated over an iconographic trope – the postcard seascape. A map on one panel plots the location of each image. Together, the scenes create a kind of musical rhythm, with the seas rolling lyrically against the shores of the British Isles. Postcards are usually seen as ephemeral, as folk art or popular culture that usually circulates outside high-art institutions (even if they can be bought inside them). By bringing together these postcards, Hiller begins to show something more: the imaginary belonging that is at work across them. The pictures create an image of Britain as relentlessly besieged by the sea, its coastal edge repeatedly battered by the elements. The sea's accumulating natural force begins to suggest a very powerful energy (as also featured in Turner's famous paintings), which stands in metaphorically for an imagined or actual invasive force or power. This effect might also be linked to some emotional threat by a hostile person or idea, against which one must create defences. In what seems to be an adoption of the attitude and methods of an anthropologist or cultural archivist, Hiller suggests that these images are worthy of a level of attention beyond that which they would usually

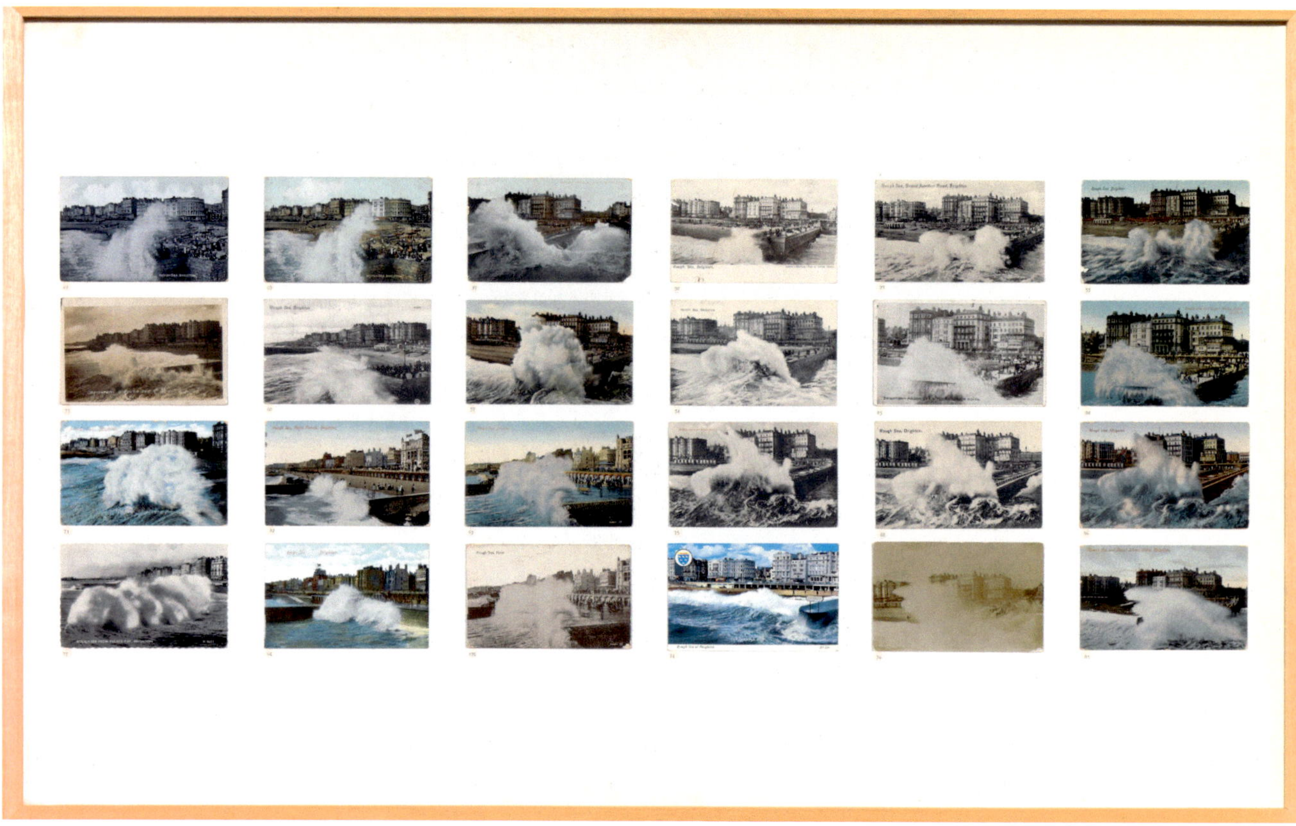

Figure 74 Susan Hiller, *Dedicated to the Unknown Artists* 1972–6 305 postcards, sea charts and map mounted on 14 panels, each panel 66 × 104.8 Tate

The postcards depict waves crashing onto shores around Britain. A large map annotated with each of the locations featured in the postcards is included in the first panel. The title refers to the overlooked and forgotten artists who painted, photographed or hand-tinted the seaside images, elevating them to art through memory and as a memorial.

receive as mere postcards. Yet by turning them into an archival artwork she does something else to them too.

Hiller celebrates the authors of the postcards as 'unknown artists' – a term that resonates with the 'unknown soldier' of war memorials. The anonymous artists who made these images are recognised as belonging to a whole group of 'unknown artists', which by simply installing the postcards in the gallery raises the question of their status within culture and social memory. Why is the coast such a considered and repeated scene in postcard imagery? Is the violence of the sea a symptom of what people identify as important? In effect, this is what Hiller's work asks: do these humble, anonymous postcard images not tell us something about a particular popular concept of the British Isles? Are these anonymous artists speaking to some collective idea or ideal through the

7 Foster 2004; also extract reprinted in Merewether 2006, p.145.

repeated iconography of the sea and coastline, imagining some abstract fear signified with the edge of the island? Do these pictures not dramatise and allegorise in a popular form the imagined community of an island under siege by external forces?

Postcards often inhabit people's homes in places that art does not: on the front of a fridge, propped on a shelf or mantelpiece, stuck on the wall or a door, and so on. Made in the 1970s, Hiller's work offers a counter-memory, an alternative to the sometimes-bombastic history of art told through galleries or a nation's trophy war-chest of paintings and sculptures, which frequently belong to the 'official histories' of a nation or population. Contemporary artists and photographers bring new types of imagery to the archives of museums and walls of galleries, contributing different types of images, narratives and aspects of culture to them, as seen in Hiller's work.

In the aftermath of historical events, archives can become a resource through which to rethink 'what happened?' Archive materials can be used to generate unofficial accounts, which may well conflict with official stories. The retelling of stories helps to situate conflicting accounts of official and unofficial histories, but differently. Photography can play a huge role in this cultural issue. Photographic collections promise (or threaten) to overwhelm museums with masses of archives, as people have taken photographs all their lives, from commercial photographers to amateurs, with a list of themes that is potentially endless. Some such archives and practices have found their way into art, or are mobilised explicitly to make it. The particularly strong emotional effect of photographs and their sense of specific historical presence are often key elements in this type of archive practice. By implicating the viewer in fragments of different stories in a very direct way, photographic images help to make possible new or other stories, other versions of what happened. So while we tend to think of museums as orientated towards collecting the past, they are in fact as orientated towards the present and future too.

Remembering and Forgetting

Today the internet and the wide availability of mobile phone cameras have begun to transform the speed and quantity of visual recording and archiving of experience. Within reasonable economic means, it is easy to select and distribute pictures and have access to modes of representation. Anyone can send pictures and texts to others online to relate their social or personal experience. As the internet has begun to show, 'archive fever' is a prevalent aspect of human behaviour, with everyone collecting something or other, either as objects or via photographs. Photography enables anyone to collect anything - food, clothes, found objects, pets, people, places, scenes, events, activities and processes - as part of a personal online collection. We can increasingly see that, while any archive makes present the past, it is always produced according to the particular interests of those involved, and in this way develops a conditional presence for its future use. Thus, cultural memory becomes a problem of whose memories and perspectives are stored and retrieved and whose are forgotten.

In a polemical essay, the US critic Hal Foster contrasts the archival impulse to an allegorical impulse and the ruin of meaning, which had been so central to postmodernism.[7] Although they both appear to have similar strategies of sampling, quotation and reframing of popular images and stories, the archival impulse is different. The tactic enables archive artists to construct new, fragmentary stories that are associative and partial, related to history. The allegorical impulse in postmodernism was associated with a critique of established systems of signification by mixing them up to ruin historical meaning. This differs from the aim of archive-based art, which seeks to relate different realities in new ways, presenting effective elements as triggers for potential narratives, which can be completed by the spectator.

Just as museums intentionally construct archives, so an archival drive sets out to capture or create a new field of knowledge through documents, objects, images and texts. The meanings organised for these archive materials shift from one to another, depending on the institutional location and the discipline or discourse of one institution, whose context is being reconsidered from within another's.

Mike Mandel and Larry Sultan's exhibition and photobook *Evidence* 1977 (fig.75) brought together photographs from government agencies,

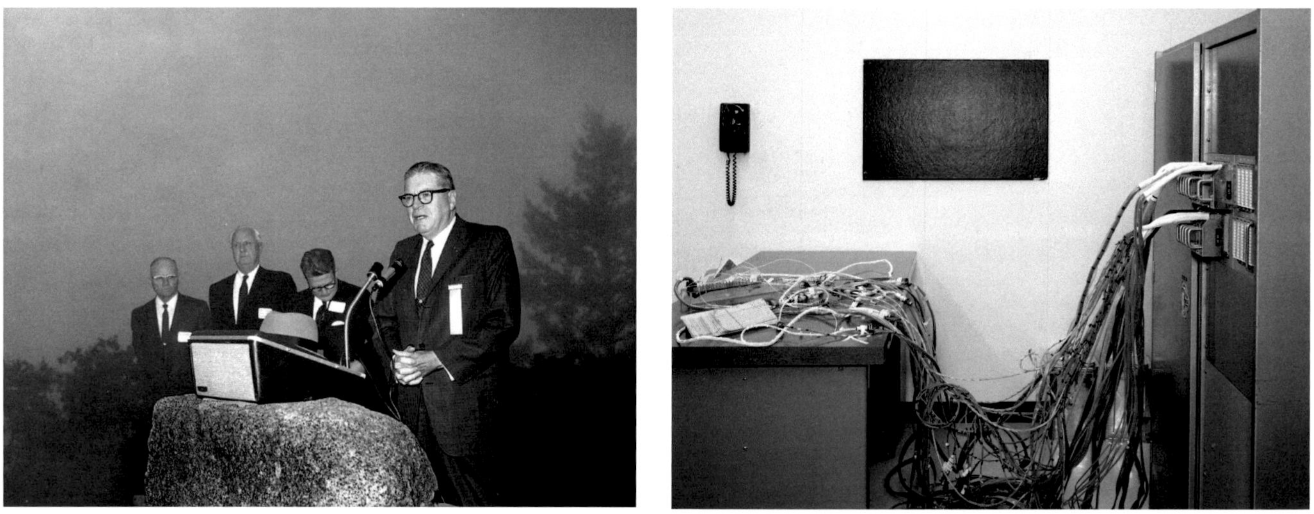

Figure 75
Larry Sultan and Mike Mandel, *Untitled* from the book *Evidence* 1977
Gelatin silver print, 25.4 × 20.3

corporations, research and educational institutions. Being granted access and reproduction rights by such organisations' archives is no mean feat.[8] The monochrome photographs document a variety of scientific and other experiments, but since the artists' selections remain uncaptioned, there are few or no clues as to the context of their original purpose beyond the fact they are documenting something. Each image could as readily be a science-fiction scene as a document of scientific research. These types of presentation replicate a bystander's outsider view – outside the institutions' specialist knowledge. The photographs' often bizarre scenarios foreground our lack of actual knowledge as to their purpose, and force us to consider the evidence of meanings and events to which there is otherwise little or no access. The limits of the popular belief that photographs speak for themselves become only too apparent when the discourse to which they belong is withheld.

Anonymous pictures culled from archives or found in attics are a recurring theme, attractive to artists for their enigma, the riddles they pose and the uncertainty of meaning in their aesthetic values. Never originally

8 Mandel and Sultan 1977/2003.

9 There are many such examples, see the exhibition and book by Hunt 2011.

10 The standard essay on this topic is Allan Sekula, 'The Body and the Archive', in Bolton 1992. See also Tagg 2012.

intended as art, these pictures from other spheres often bring strange visual values, with what might otherwise be regarded as mistakes or incorrect pictorial values. Inadvertently, these different aesthetics renew interest in what can be done with a camera.[9] Eventually, though, the unfamiliar has become familiar, as many albums and archives of photographs are uncovered or rediscovered. The forgotten is made visible. In this sense, photography has been responsible for a much wider set of transformations towards a visual knowledge, with the massive use of photographic images as documents and records across a wide range of many, if not all, institutions and practices. Today almost every organisation uses photographs to archive events, document its staff and display its values to others.

There is a strong surrealist legacy to these practices of disrupting conventional social signification systems. Although the use of archives is often identified with conceptual art, the revaluation of the outmoded or discarded was a key component in the surrealist toolkit. Surrealist publications often included found images, postcards and other anonymous pictures. Browsing in street markets and elsewhere, junk was retrieved, photographed and given new significance through a kind of re-archival method. The discarded became the regarded. Compiled into a new archival space, the photographs served to critique existing culture and its histories.

Images and their objects were used to signify 'thing presentations', to reveal unconscious or repressed thoughts. The surrealists created deviant archives, opposed in structure and form to the criminal or medical photographic archives found in organisations maintained by the state.[10] The criminal archive developed by the police was designed to form a rational picture of criminal identity. The 'criminal body' was photographed in ways that was often informed by medical or quasi-scientific theories of physiognomy and anthropometric measuring systems. The values of medical and police photography were intertwined to serve as disciplinary images, aimed to exert power of the state over the individual subject.

Salvador Dalí's *The Phenomenon of Ecstasy* 1933 (fig.76) intentionally undoes this power structure by mixing up medical and criminal photography alongside other types of image. As a mini-archive, this picture is thoroughly eclectic and anti-scientific. Dalí's montage jumbles male and female, medical and criminal genres, sculptures and real humans, ears and hair all together in elements of irregular size and shape. Dalí appears to adopt the logic of the archive, to produce not a stable scientific record but a jouissance, a kind of ecstasy and deathly pleasure. Hysteria and ecstasy are not easily distinguished from one another, as was argued at the time by medical theory. Subverting the dominant medical theory that hysteria was only feminine and never masculine, Dalí reuses photographs from such classification systems to insinuate that, just as hair and ears are found across both sexes, so is the state of ecstasy. No state-sanctioned scientific values can constrain these bodily experiences.

French artist Sophie Calle has regularly used the construction of a photographic evidenced-based archive as the model for her artworks. She creates chronicles of daily events, for example, using a diary mode with photographs, mimicking official records of a scientific process. In *Hotel Room 28* 1981 (fig.77), evidential-type monochrome photographs of a hotel room in one panel are juxtaposed with a singular colour photograph

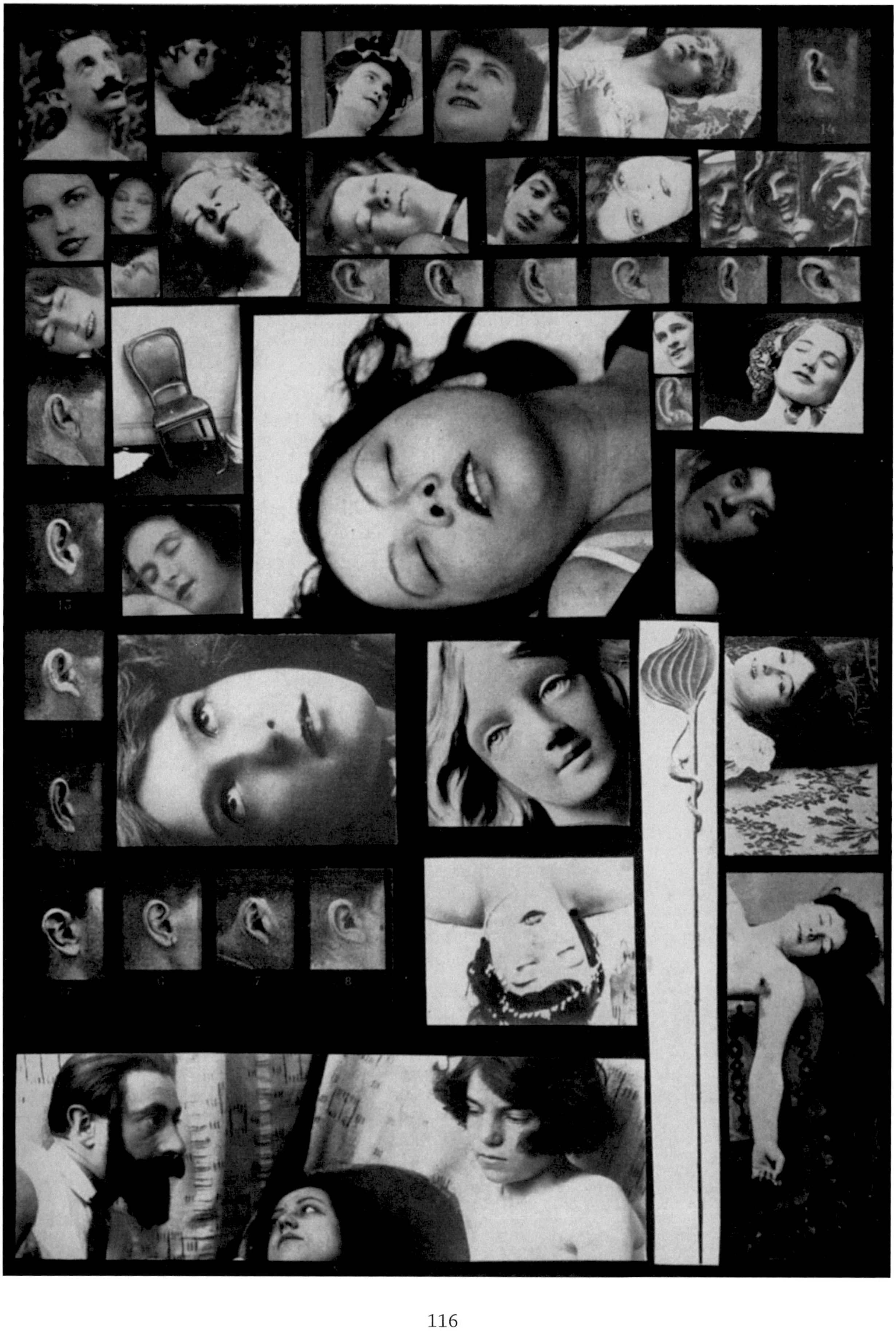

of a hotel bed and fine-printed text in another. The text describes in the neutral manner of a detective report what was found or seen in the room on specific days. The accompanying introduction to the work informs us that Calle had been temporarily employed as a chambermaid in a Venetian hotel for three weeks, during which time she had taken these photographs and made the notes that accompany them.

Figure 76
Salvador Dalí,
The Phenomenon of Ecstasy 1933
Photomontage, colour original, 27 × 18.5
Published in *Minotaure* journal, nos.3–4 (December 1933)

The apparatus of the archive provides a ready-made structure for the work and the viewer's understanding of how to read it. Calle gives an authorial voice to the images via the texts, which hint that some sort of surveillance operation has been engaged in. The artwork implicates the viewer in this process, making one feel complicit in investigating these people's lives. Like a detective report by Sherlock Holmes, or the many fictional detectives in stories that have updated the genre ever since, the viewer is given a set of 'facts' from which a mystery is to be solved. Only here, there is no crime apparent in these images; there is only the evidence provided by the unwitting hotel customers, whose belongings are disclosed as *if* they are part of a crime scene. We are tricked into suspicion.

The enigma of the story is in fact Calle's curiosity, not the actions of the room's occupants. Her report, made through subterfuge and spying, mobilises the apparatus of the archive to introduce us to Calle's (and presumably our own) fascination with what goes on in hotel rooms, their residents and what can be read into their possessions. We too are implicated in the creation of a mystery. But what is this mystery? What is the story to be disclosed by these photographs and texts? What we find out about these people is perhaps less interesting than the artist's methods and our own prurient activity as voyeurs. Of course, the hotel is a notorious location for illicit affairs and dubious deals, as well as for innocent visits. Calle's voyeurism, and our own, no doubt trades on these ambiguities: the work induces a guilt in looking into people's private lives, yet this also seems justifiable, in that perhaps, as in the movies, we are observing people who are guilty of something. But this in turn begs the question of whether, if they are not innocent, this justifies the scrutiny of their affairs. The viewer is certainly left to consider the ethical implications of the position in which they have been put. We may admire Calle's audacity, or feel quite uncomfortable about her furtive intrusion into privacy, but the interest in her work thrives on the uncertainty of these attitudes and values.

Yet Calle's work does come close to the sense that something disturbing has happened here, some sort of mystery, a primal scene or hidden plot or story that it would seem to be too embarrassing to mention directly. The archive is thus often associated with trouble, as a scene of trauma: distant memories, either repressed or partially forgotten, returning to haunt the archive investigator or the viewer. Detective stories set out to dispel mystery, to reveal the 'truth' of the story, but we only scratch the surface of the drama here. Calle manages to balance the work elegantly on a fine line between the question of public knowledge and private intimacy. The surface knowledge given by the pictures and the texts constructs an archival presence but gives no depth to any interpretation, nor to any real intimate knowledge of the goings-on in the hotel. In this way, the work frustrates the true voyeur, dissatisfied with what they see,

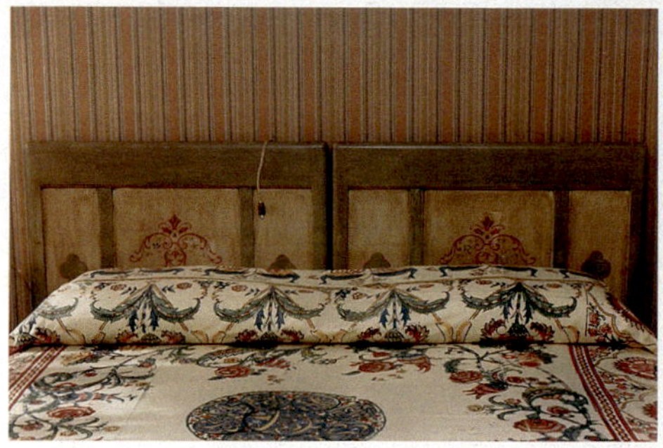

ROOM 28

Monday February 16, 1981. *9:30a.m. I go into room 28. Only one bed has been slept in. I find an impressive pile of luggage on the right along the wall. Four Vuitton suitcases stacked on top of each other, three travelling bags, a row of shoes: eight pairs for the woman (size 38) and five pairs for the man (size 42). I open the wardrobes. On the right, some men's clothes including three new pairs of shoes in felt covers, a hat, two pairs of white underpants and one pair of pants with big suspenders. All of them of a fine quality. I imagine some older well-off people. In the bathroom, nothing special except a pink flannelette nightgown. I put on some of the Chanel No.5 perfume. I hastily open one of their suitcases. I catch a glimpse of* The Economist *magazine, some bananas in a plastic bag. Once the room is made up, I leave.*

Tuesday 17. *9:10a.m. The twin beds have been slept in. In the wastebasket, the banana peels, a bottle of water and a pair of hardly worn black flat heels (they fit me, I take them). On the chair, a thick white cotton pajama bottom. To the left, some mints, a crossword grid on a bedside table and some pink slippers within reach. On the right bedside table, an alarm clock, a flashlight, a roll of scotch tape, three pairs of glasses, a book* Games with Love and Death *by Arthur Schnitzler. In the chest upper drawer, I find two handbags, some pearl necklaces in a plastic bag and ten small identical boxes full of white pills wrapped in a Fitzgerald shoe cover. The two lower drawers contain some women's clothes, silk blouses, pastel color scarves.*

Wednesday 18. *9a.m. The two beds have been slept in. There is some progress on the crossword grid started yesterday. The pajama bottom is still in the same place. I lift the suitcases: three of them seem to be full. I open them. In the first one I find a toilet kit, in the second a set of identical Brooks Brothers shirts with blue and white stripes. In the third one, a book* Artists in Crime *by Marsh, a Minox camera, a denture (lower jaw), a 7" x 9 ½" photograph of a sailing boat on the sea, a reservation at the Milano Carlton for February 19, a portrait of the Pope, an envelope addressed to Mrs. H., Baltimore...with the following notations on the back: Jean-Paul Belmondo, rue de la Paix, Paris 5e (the street number is not mentioned, the arrondissement number is wrong, the post-office cancellation has been written over with a ball-point), a series of index cards with columns of numbers (stock exchange quotations?).... I hear some noise, hastily close the suitcase and make the bed.*

Thursday 19. *Noon. They have gone. They have left nothing behind. I take a last photograph of the unmade beds. The memory I will keep of them is the obscene image of the pajama bottom, stupidly lying on the chair.*

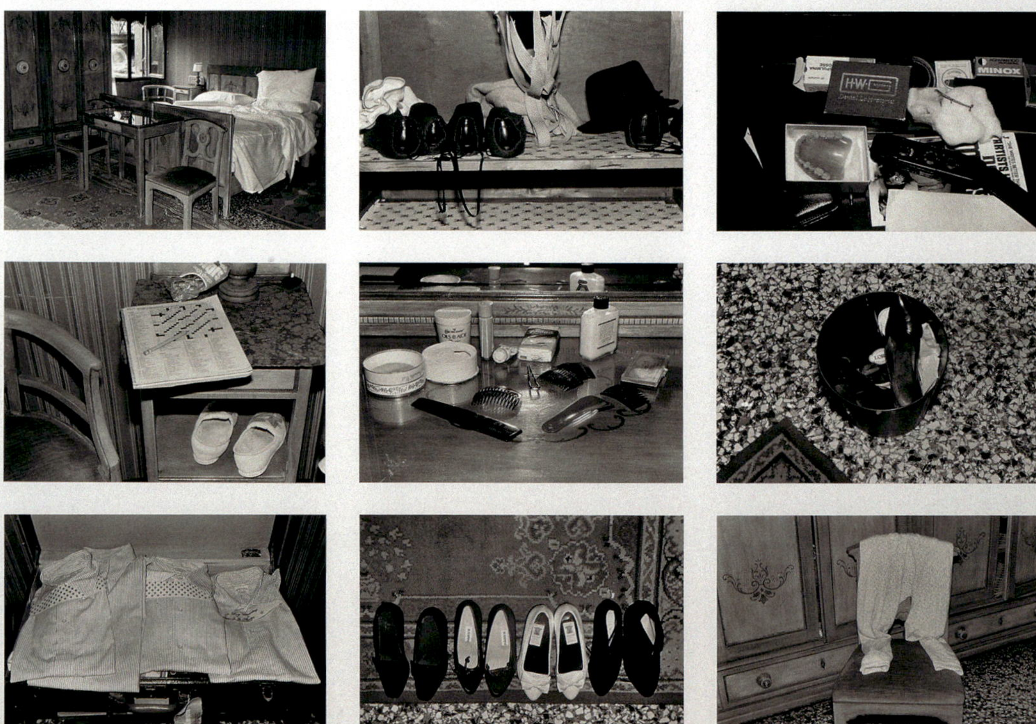

11 Derrida 1996, p.19.

12 See examples in Schaaf 2000.

13 William Henry Fox Talbot, cited in Schaaf 2000, p.179.

because they always want to see more. The archive impulse in Calle's work invokes a narrative drive in the viewer, which ultimately is never resolved and remains elusive. This desire to know belongs to what can be called 'archive fever'.

Figure 77
Sophie Calle, *The Hotel, Room 28* 1981
Two works on paper, photographs and ink, 214 × 142
Tate

Archive Fever

As long ago as 1995 French philosopher Jacques Derrida described 'archive fever' as a contradiction at the heart of the idea of conservation.[11] Conservation is driven, paradoxically, by the possibility of forgetting. Since human memory is limited and not infinite, the retention and registration of impressions within photographs has come to be associated with the idea of remembering and the desire to return to something beyond the capacity of spontaneous conscious memory. The anxiety of remembering is thus that which we will forget. It is also true, on the other hand, that we may wish to forget something that has already happened. We can see all this as the paradoxical drive of archive fever, which is at work right from the beginning of photography and other forms of memory inscription.

William Henry Fox Talbot anticipated the idea of photography as an archival practice, useful as a 'museum' in itself. The prospective applications and purposes of this would turn out to be, to understate the case, both multiple and considerable. Photography is now clearly a pervasive means to register information and to record impressions, from the banality of ordinary insurance records and parking offences to family events, friends and many other social experiences. Photographic data files remain a vital tool across diverse fields of state and scientific knowledge, used to document geographical, military, police and political activities and processes, alongside their massive use in personal, social and popular-culture industries.

Talbot's *Articles of China* (fig.78) is one of several photographs he produced of collections of objects: glassware, books, hats, set dining tables, vases, jars and plant leaves.[12] Writing on the *Articles of China* picture in *The Pencil of Nature*, Talbot notes that 'the whole cabinet' of a collector 'might be depicted on paper in little more time than it would take him to make a written inventory'.[13] Today it would be a little quicker. Talbot speculates that the photograph might be a novel kind of evidence used in testimony against a thief caught with purloined objects, to show the true ownership of the treasure. Talbot's archive desire already anticipates a future violence – in the theft of his possessions. Although this is merely one future meaning that might be anticipated by the collector, it demonstrates how the archival drive is also wedded to a future significance, as much as to the present or the past.

In practice, human memory is a complex and unstable matter, not easily reducible to simple binary oppositions like past and present, true and false, reality and fiction. Memory can conflate or compress separate moments together, and confuse different times entirely. By consigning memory to documents, texts, images and objects, this relieves the human brain of the burden of recording or remembering things accurately, yet seems to pass on the capacity for uncertainty to these prosthetic substitutes too.

We know, for instance, that this depiction of china by Talbot is an invented archive. The realism of the photographic image denies its constructed nature. We cannot tell from the photograph that these shelves

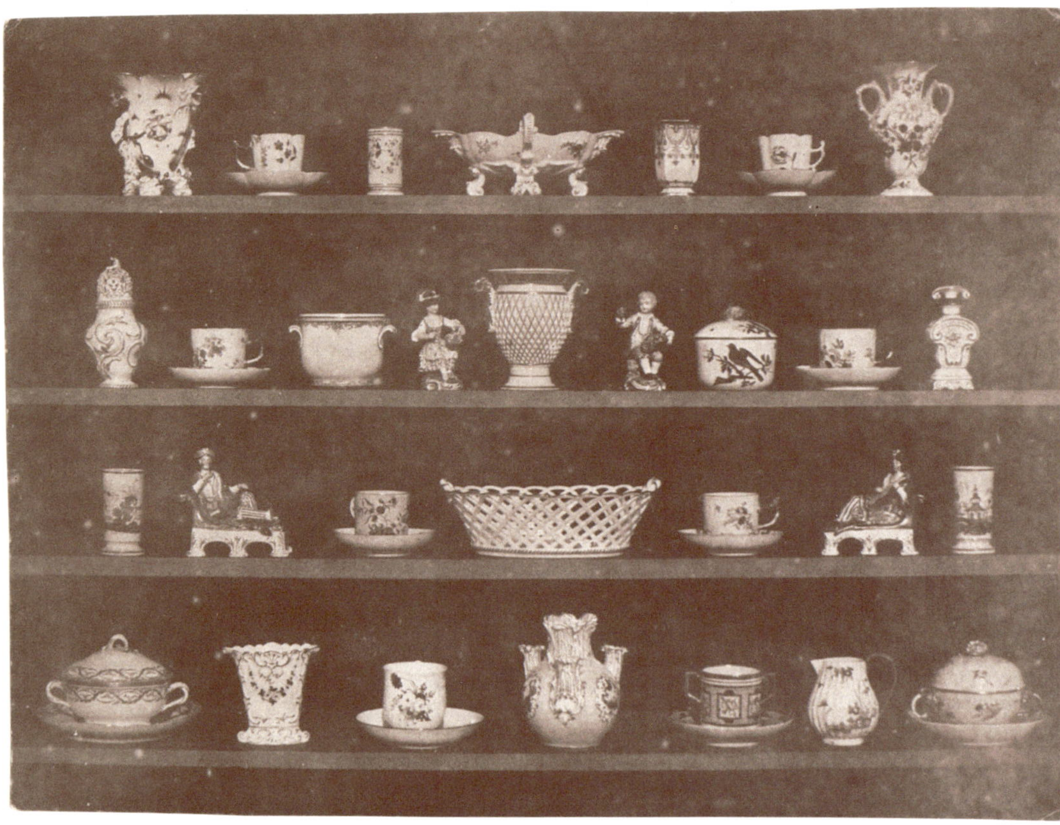

14 Barthes 1984.

15 Proust 2003.

were hastily erected in Talbot's garden (rather than in his house, which would have had insufficient light for the process). Nor can we really tell very much about the china either, since although the denotative information of a photograph proposes a fact, we have little evidence as to the verity of its status without reference to other sources of information. Often the back of a photographic print can give more indications of its story - a date or a name, for example - just as digital files have metadata that can be mined for information too. Only in this sense are photographs part-archives, components of a larger body of knowledge, which belong to and are situated within a narrative context or discourse. In the case of Talbot, this is his archive of negatives, diaries, letters, notes, and so on.

Despite the scepticism that may be felt towards the truth-value of any photographic resource, the photographic image itself nevertheless creates a real positivity, which is affective as much as it is logical. In this way, the significance of the photographic archive lies not merely in designating what is true or false, but also in constituting a dimension of knowledge. Whether divisive or distinct, the photographic image represents a statement for interaction with human memory and culture. The question to ask - in art, at least - is not so much 'is it true?' as 'what does it do?' 'What is the effect of the story or fragments of insight that a work relates?'

Figure 78
William Henry Fox Talbot, *Articles of China* c.1843/4
Plate III from *The Pencil of Nature* (1844-5)
Calotype salt print, 18.89 × 22.7

Return of Repression

Some students of photography may expect a dutiful reference here to *Camera Lucida*,[14] Roland Barthes's last book on photography, for its work on memory and the 'return of meaning' in a photograph that the book eventually addresses via a family archive. *Camera Lucida* meditates on the role of memory in photography and establishes a duality of meaning in photographs, as social and personal. Barthes makes this distinction in Latin terms: the social meaning of a photograph being its *studium*, where a social message is read via cultural codes derived from a particular society; and the *punctum* betrays a highly personal meaning, something private and purely individual, which affects only a particular viewer. Barthes's thesis on memory is prefigured by one of his references, Marcel Proust's literary epic *In Search of Lost Time*.[15] Proust deals with the accumulation of memories during a lifetime and makes a distinction between voluntary and involuntary memory - distinctions that resemble Barthes's photographic categories of *studium* and *punctum*. Like Barthes's *punctum*, Proust's involuntary memory is also activated by some detail, like the treasured madeleine cake in his novel, which in turn sparks an associative chain of mental images and forgotten memories. The past is conjured up, recovered and associated with the thing that triggered it. Photographs also have this capacity to trigger and generate memories, just as an object or smell can, and can even be used to reinvent their meaning. The mechanism of involuntary memory may explain the fascination for anonymous photographs encountered in an archive, where an image suddenly sparks an associative chain of other images in the mind of the viewer. The photograph has involuntarily triggered obtuse emotional feelings, beyond any obvious logic, not easily rationalised by the *studium* or social meaning of the picture.

As Proust had noted, voluntary or conscious perceptions are surface perceptions without depth, and he likens them to the instantaneous glance at photographs in an exhibition. Involuntary memory, by contrast, refers us to something already identified as significant and embedded in our memory, even or especially if we are not actually conscious of it at the time. Proust's 'madeleine moment', when the odour of the cake envelops the whole of the protagonist in a memory, is the classic example of this type of involuntary memory as effect, which introduces memory as a problem to the photographic archive. The meaning of Talbot's photograph of china, then, despite his own assertions about its future social function, may well end up being subject to involuntary associations generated by other viewers. In this duality of voluntary and involuntary meanings, fantasies about history and the subject's own relation to these antiquities can intertwine, activating new meanings, steering the photographic image into domains of thought that are far from Talbot's original description. Such is the slippage of meaning to which all historical images may be subject.

Proust's distinction between voluntary and involuntary memory shows that the effect of engaging with archive images is far from guaranteed, the outcome is far from certain and indeed, for that matter, not necessarily as pleasant as the 'madeleine moment'. The memory trace can evoke not only an uncanny disorientation, but also an involuntary pain. Barthes developed in *Camera Lucida* an understanding of this negative dimension of effect. In such cases, the terror of the sign is not in the material image archive, but in its interaction by those who encounter it, located within hidden memories. Here is the idea of the traumatic 'return of the repressed', as Freud understood it, for example in soldiers returning from the First World War. In the return of the repressed, Freud argued, an experience that is not quite registered at the time returns later to haunt the subject in other life experiences.[16] Involuntary memory, whether positive or negative, pleasurable or painful, leads to associative tracks in human memory that extend beyond the literal image.

Archives, then, in the formulation and methods explored here, are never passive entities simply waiting to be found or discovered, but the result of someone in the construction of some discourse or other. No matter how ramshackle, eclectic, disorganised or rational an archive appears, it will have been mobilised, narrated and organised for a number of purposes or means. Curiously, Proust was himself an iconophile, obsessed with photography. He would purportedly demand a portrait photograph from any new person he met who especially interested him. Those who promised to send one but failed to do so were besieged with letters complaining they had not met their promise and requiring them to do so – a refrain he would continue until they complied.[17] We find here the same archive fever at stake as in Talbot's image, whose wish to collect objects together is for a future anticipated meaning, although we do not really know what this was in Proust's case. What we can say, though, is that archive and memory are obverse terms to one another, mirror images held apart by the photographic impression and its potential for life stories. These archives are the narratives we tell ourselves about who we are, will be, or were. Collecting things is an activity of memory, perhaps in anticipation of its dissolution. This might even be, as Derrida has hinted, like Freud, an anxiety about death, even, paradoxically, in archive images of war and conflict.[18] Such are the negative and positive dynamics

16 Freud 1984.

17 Bernard 2002.

18 Derrida 2010.

orchestrated by artists who use archives in the formulation of an artwork, whether it is pronounced as a cultural, social, political or individually orientated work. The internet provides a new way to consider links between archives, and to create different networks and narratives. However, it is the space of culture and memory that gives narrative space to these forms. The photograph, with its pensive form, lends a certain visibility to these anonymous narratives. A photographic archive enables the construction of a bridge between art and non-art, to reformulate who we are and the temporal space in which to conceive the images of where we live.

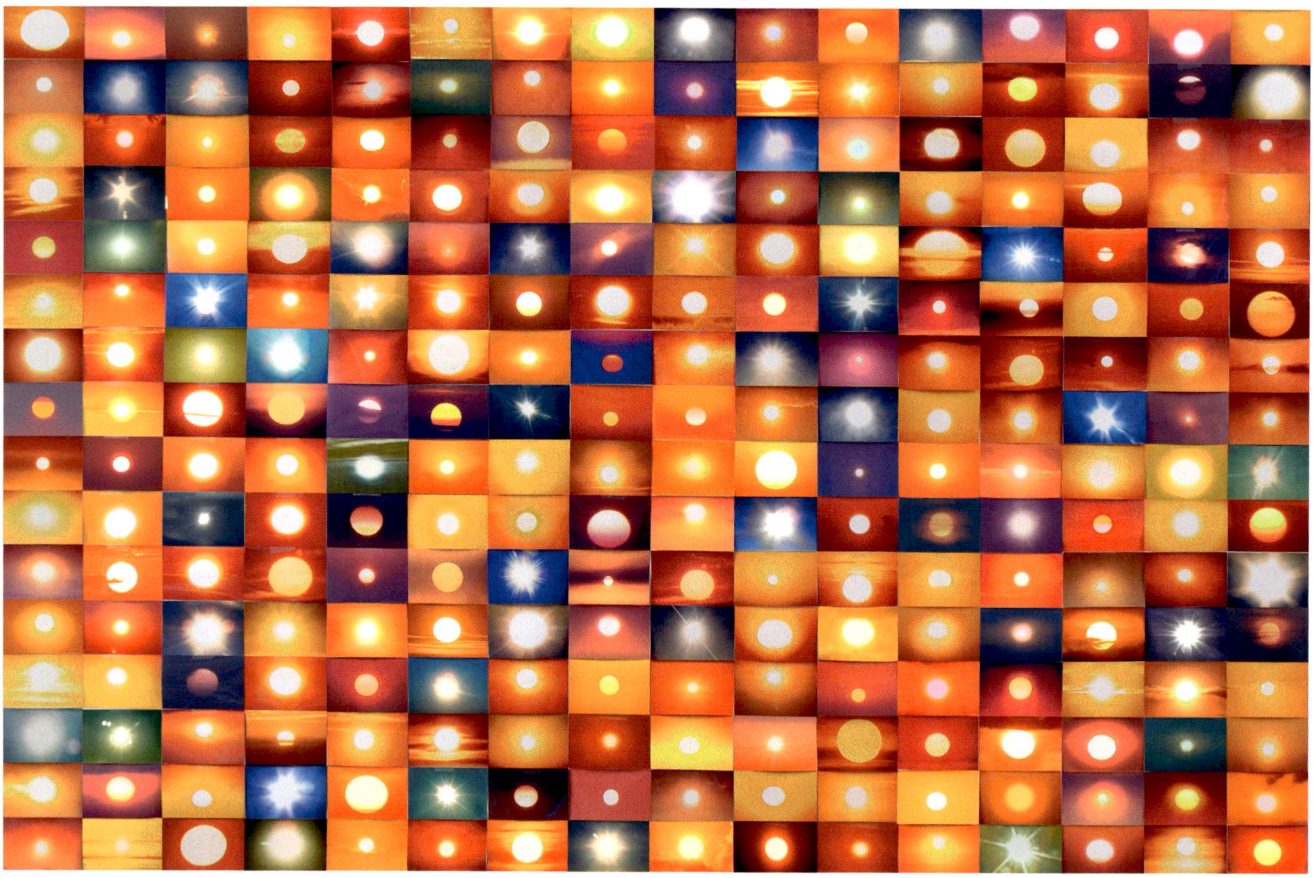

GEOGRAPHY AS INHABITED SPACE

1 Title: "541,795 Suns from Sunsets from Flickr (Partial) 1/26/06", Date: 2006 Medium and size: detail, 2000 4in x 6in machine c-prints Credits: courtesy Penelope Umbrico and Mark Moore Gallery, LA

'Inhabited space transcends geometrical space,' says Gaston Bachelard in *The Poetics of Space*.[1] Bachelard's sentence reminds us of the distinction, and what may be an implicit conflict, between geometrical space and the habitation of it by the human imagination. This distinction is highlighted in photographic images because space is codified by the camera and lens into geometrical space. This space is always constructed, for example, as 'normal' or wide-angle perspective, as long-focal lens, in colour or monochrome, with pixelated, grainy, sharp or soft effects, and so on. Whether the space pictured is real or fabricated, the photograph's different coding precisely links geometry to the viewer's different imaginings of space. Whatever the photographic coding and composition, its effect - if it succeeds as an image - is to absorb the spectator into the scene of the visual image, to invite inhabitation of its space.

Penelope Umbrico's massive grid of photographs, *541,795 Suns from Sunsets from Flickr* 2006 (fig.79), takes this a step further by demonstrating the universal appeal of the sunset photograph. The ubiquity of these amateur sunset snapshots emphasises how a space can be inhabited by the imagination more than any geometry of place. The geometrical consciousness of place as an actual location in the world, for which photography is so renowned, is replaced by a luminary psychological effect, replete with all the imagination of human feeling. The sunsets, repeated as a variation on a theme, are used to enhance a set of emotive feelings, which are only tangentially grasped by aesthetic theories of the beautiful and the sublime. Put simply, a beautiful scene pacifies the spectator, whereas the sublime excites their desire. In the case of the sunset, it can usually do both at once, invoking the sun with feelings of melancholic passion. The sunset photograph is a classic example of how a psychological image can be imposed onto geometrical space: the effect exceeds the information provided about geographic place.

Geography in pictorial space is thus not merely geometrical, it is also an imaginary space. Bachelard gives the example of an attic, which in reality may have been cold in winter and hot in summer, but in a daydream or memory becomes a place laden with comforting thoughts, indifferent to real experience. More than mere metaphor, the image of an attic or a sunset is haunted with fantasy. This is why such images can be both irritating and satisfying, plunging the viewer into a reverie that conflicts with personal memories of the real space. A sunset photograph for example, occurring as it does at the end of the day, makes for an image that creates an idealised space, a photographic place that wipes away any stains of the day, giving closure to images of actual life.

Space and place are thus linked in photography to a psychological topography too. Sigmund Freud used the term 'psychical reality' to designate a distinction between what inhabits the mind of a person and actual

Figure 79
Penelope Umbrico, *541,795 Suns from Sunsets from Flickr (Partial) 1/26/06* 2006
C-prints, each 10.2 × 15.2

Penelope Umbrico began the series *Sunsets from Flickr* in 2006, when she searched the image-hosting website Flickr and found 541,795 pictures tagged 'sunset'. She cropped the pictures to include just the suns and uploaded them into 10.2 × 15.2 cm machine prints. For each installation the title is reconfigured to reflect the number of images found on the day the prints were made. The later title, *5,377,183 Suns from Flickr (Partial) 4/28/09*, becomes a comment on the ever-increasing use of web-based photo communities and a reflection of the ubiquity and stereotypical nature of online content.

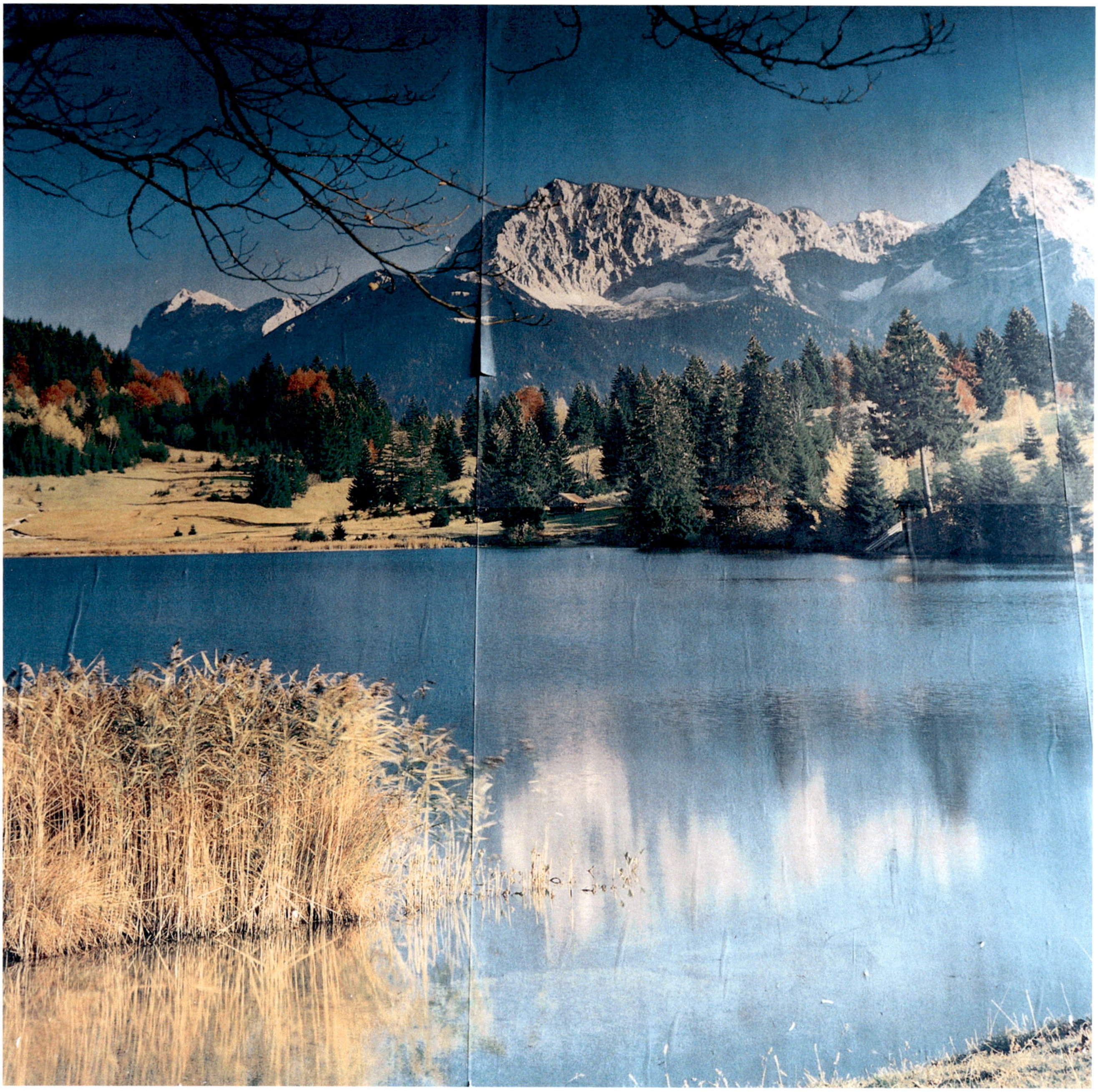

material reality.[2] Psychical reality, in which unconscious fantasy plays a part, may not take account of or correspond exactly to material reality. Photography and art offer precisely one means of overlaying or infusing geometrical space and place with psychological images and the pleasures or terrors of the imagination.

One has only to consider, for instance, how a house can have a character in its own right – something on which horror films frequently capitalise. A house may be haunted, not only by people, but also as if it were a being invested with feelings (usually hostile) towards its inhabitants and the world around it. We project our own, sometimes irrational, feelings into a space. Bachelard's study does not deal with such hostile spaces but, by his own admission, only considers images that attract.[3] The house for Bachelard is 'our corner of the world', which he likens to a daydream, relived as the past, present and future.[4] We may, however, extend Bachelard's attributes of the house image to other expressions of belonging to or alienation from geographic territories and dream spaces.

Yto Barrada's *A Life Full of Holes: The Strait Project* 2001 meditates on the border space between North Africa and Europe.[5] The torn corner in *Papier Peint [Wallpaper] – Tangier* 2001 (fig.80) indicates that this is a photograph of a photomural, a representation of a representation. The photomural image, an idyllic forest landscape, is a bit worn out, literally an 'old image' presence within another space, as signified by the torn corner. The location of Barrada's photograph, captioned as being situated in Tangier, the port city across the Mediterranean Sea from Spain, is where many migrants have gathered, departed from and been returned to. One might imagine this photomural to be in a passport office, where a promised future represented by this picturesque landscape is, quite literally, a faded ideal. The dream image of another place looks a little tired, rubbed away, and belongs in fact to the past. Barrada produces conflicting temporal dynamics, the photomural once signifying a future, but now the past, in the present tense of her photograph. Even though the picture has all the coordinates of a geometrical scene, it is inhabited with dreams, loss, hope and fantasy. Such spaces are what Michel Foucault calls 'heterotopias'.

Heterotopias

In his short but brilliant essay 'Different Spaces' 1967, Foucault opens up a way of thinking about geography and space that is not limited to traditional fields of study. Foucault argues that the modern era, and its anxiety, is defined by space more than time, and that the simultaneous and scattered have overcome the hierarchical ordering of space.[6] Time is still significant, but we are more likely to experience it through space: 'We are in an era of the simultaneous, of juxtaposition, of the near and the far, of the side-by-side, of the scattered.'[7] In this era of networks, as Foucault called it long before the internet, different points or elements are connected together. Space is a set of relations to place: a place of transit, for example, comprises spatial relations between roads, trains, bus and metro. The place of rest and repose is formed by the house, the room, the bed, and so on.[8] Our relationship to space is organised through bundles of relations that are simultaneously linked, juxtaposed and opposed. Although such places are diverse and plural, they bear common features that make description of them possible.

2 For a summary of this concept see Pontalis and Laplanche 1988, pp.363–4.

3 Bachelard 1969, p.xxxvi.

4 Ibid., p.6.

5 Barrada 2005.

6 Foucault 2000, p.177.

7 Ibid., p.177.

8 Ibid., p.178.

Figure 80
Yto Barrada, *Papier Peint [Wallpaper] – Tangier* 2001
From the series *A Life Full of Holes: The Strait Project* 2001
C-print, 60 × 60

Foucault is interested in two particular types of place: utopias and heterotopias. Utopias are essentially unreal places, even if they are based on real ones; heterotopias are places that contest or are in conflict with themselves, and which reverse the space in which we live. Foucault gives examples of crisis heterotopias, what have become 'deviant behaviour' heterotopias: psychiatric hospitals, prisons or the more benign care centres for the infirm or elderly. We might recognise immediately a sort of visual topography of these spaces, represented across cinema, art and photography in many different ways, by films such as *One Flew Over the Cuckoo's Nest* 1975 or social documentary projects that feature these institutions, or exhibitions of art made within them. We can extend such topographies to other types of heterotopia, including the seeming disparate places of theatre, cinema and garden, which are in fact blissful places. For Foucault such heterotopias are characterised by the ability to represent different spaces or locations, incompatible with themselves. Hiroshi Sugimoto's series of photographs in cinemas, for example, tends to highlight this aspect of the cinematic space and draw out the internal conflict in this heterotopic arena. The cinema, essentially a dark box full of anonymous people watching a sequence of images and sounds, creates an illusion of the elsewhere. This illusion of the elsewhere is threatened at any instant by the disruptive spectator, who reminds the viewer of the place they are in, in conflict with the space in which they immerse themselves, in their individual ways, which is the illusion of the cinema.

Sugimoto's photographs of old cinema auditoriums (fig.81) and drive-in movie theatres have a haunting effect about them. The cinema space is illuminated by the projection of a film image, the duration of which dictates the exposure of the photograph. The white rectangle of light on the screen is created by this projection, and this overexposure, a surfeit of images projected onto the screen, spills across the whole cinema and illuminates it, the light falling off further away from the screen. The photograph reverses the spectator's experience of the cinema, since it makes strangely absent the filmic images that we habitually watch in such places, instead using this light to reflect on the cinema space itself, emptied of cinematic illusion but illuminated by the excessive presence of the filmic image. No doubt the work involves time in the duration of the exposure, but its function is to change the relation to space that we normally adopt in the cinema. Instead of the cinema becoming the place for an 'elsewhere' - the space created by the film - this cinematic light is used to illuminate the cinema as a type of fantasy space. In the redistribution of light, from screen to cinema, the cinema is dissembled: the servile function of the building to house illusions is itself reversed to show the illusion that the space itself already fosters. The cinema, now perhaps a fading institution, is a heterotopic space, offering a real place for illusory images, incompatible with itself, both real and unreal in the virtual images that it serves up. Like the mirror image, which Foucault also invokes in his essay on heterotopias, the cinema offers a place where 'I am not'. Designed for the representations of utopia and dystopia, the images on the screen offer a 'placeless place', one that oddly locates the viewer in a place other than that occupied by their bodies.

The cinema has fascinated a number of photographic artists in recent years, perhaps because it has been outmoded by mobile digital screens, which are again affecting our assumed relations of space to place. Looking back, we can see that television played a similar heterotopic role to cinema, altering the spatial relations of domestic space, as well as social and public places such as airports and waiting rooms. The effect of these television screens on the public and private aspect of cultural spaces is still underestimated, even today. It is artists and photographers who have frequently been quick to note such factors of changing technology on life, and it is no coincidence that the television was featured in Robert Frank's 1950s ground-breaking work *The Americans*.

Figure 81
Hiroshi Sugimoto,
Akron Civic, Ohio, 1980
Gelatin silver print,
50.8 × 61

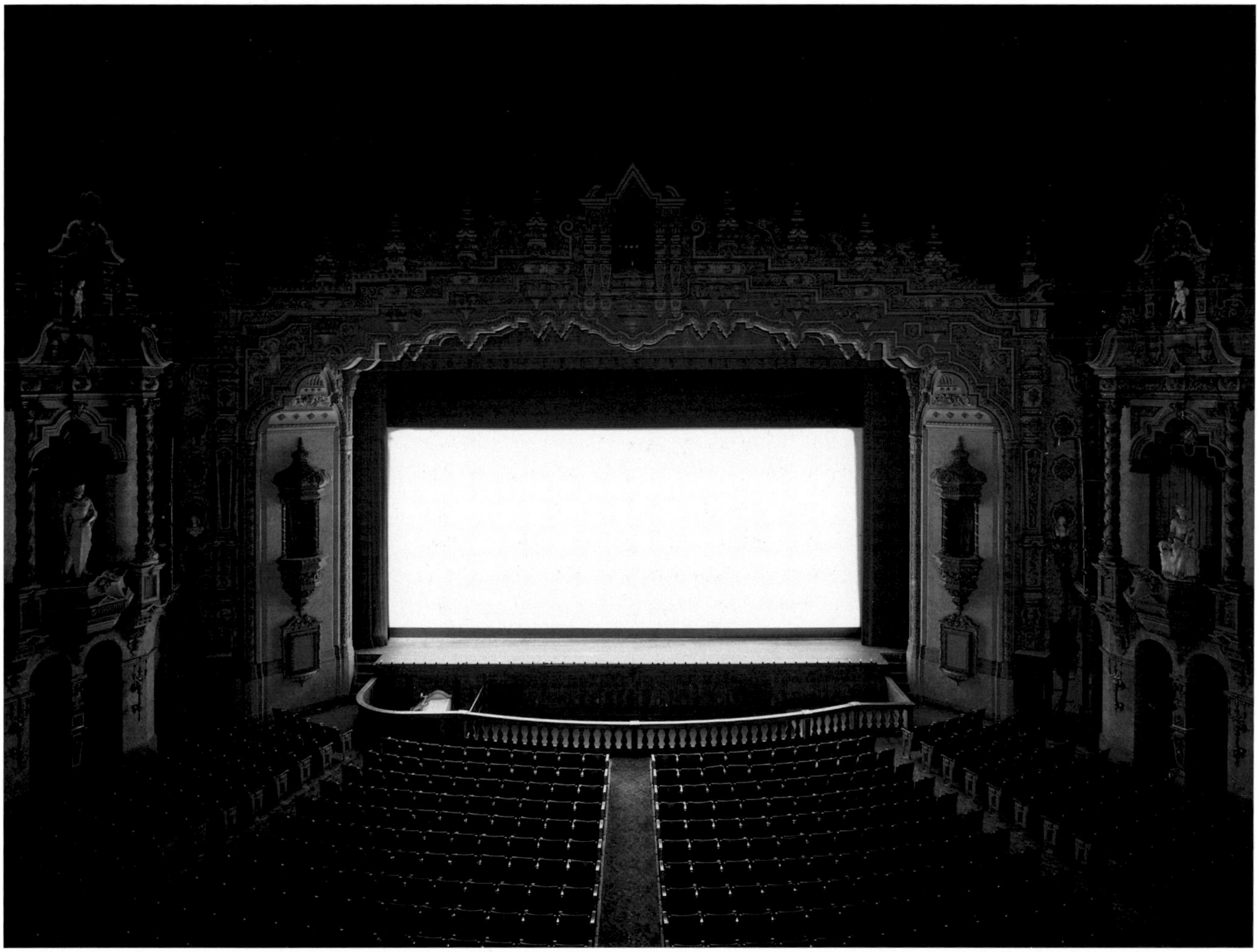

The television in Robert Frank's *Restaurant – U.S. 1 Leaving Columbia, South Carolina* 1955 (fig.82), from *The Americans*, heightens the emptiness of this social space. Light from the outside window bleaches a white highlight spot onto the table and chair, while the television set plays to an apparently empty room; the onscreen character, too, is looking elsewhere (as indeed are most of the people in Frank's pictures). The photograph, perhaps inadvertently, registers the effect of a television, once it is turned on, to transport any place to an elsewhere. Indeed, in Frank's photograph it is as though everyone has gone elsewhere. It suggests the fracturing of space that a television creates, which is now amplified by the myriad

Using a 5 × 4-inch camera Sugimoto opens the shutter for the duration of the film. The 'overexposed' screen shows the entire film in one *frame, making it 'blank', but also illuminating the cinema with the light emitted by the film projector.*

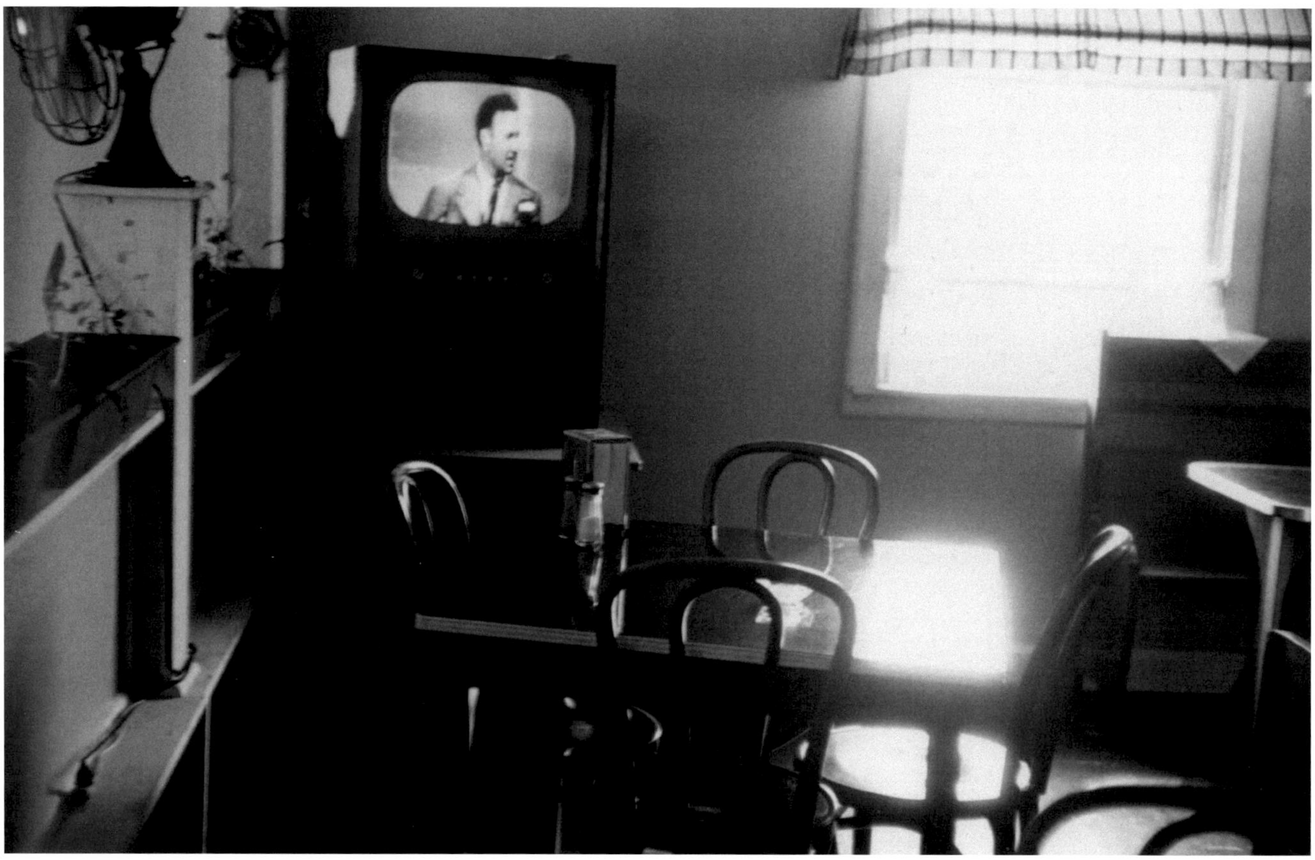

9 Augé 1995, p.78.

10 Foucault 2000, pp.185–6.

11 There is an extensive literature and visual history of this field. On Charles Baudelaire's *flâneur*, see Benjamin 1989.

Figure 82
Robert Frank,
Restaurant – U.S.1 Leaving Columbia, South Carolina, 1955
1955

digital data screens that occupy almost all social spaces. Whereas we may look back to a time when a television set supposedly unified attention towards a homogenised elsewhere, today the plurality of screens multiplies or fragments the idea of a singular elsewhere into endlessly different elsewheres. In a sense, the division between psychical space and material space, which was once noted by the surrealists and other avant-garde artists as something to be eradicated by bringing these spaces together, has now has been supplanted by a media reality.

The surrealists were early pioneers in rejecting the hierarchy of place over space. They moved freely from one place to another through their beloved Paris. Cinemas, restaurants, bars, offices and homes were all woven together into one psychical reality, a surrealist city, a latticework of modern space. This reconfiguration of space constituted the radical dimension of the surrealists' work and informed the images made by them. They were probably the first group to draw on psychoanalysis in their conscious attempt to combine psychical and material reality. As an explicit strategy, both in life and in their many literary, visual and sculptural works, the surrealists redistributed the different elements of place in their visual explorations of life-dream objects. Geometry and geography were linked to imagination and desire, as a way to deconstruct the oppositions between them and to inform a new surrealist unity of internal and external space. Surrealist photography, on the one hand, often disrupted the usually coherent coordinates of geometrical space and, on the other, used this very space to challenge, interfere or disrupt the way we 'see' the relations between things within it. These ideas often continue to reverberate within art today. In photography there are many links, both direct and obtuse, to these histories, even if the works are informed by a very different impetus.

What such images frequently have in common is a contestation or critique of the spaces in which we live, although social spaces have changed since the time of the surrealists. Anthropologist Marc Augé, for example, already identified newer types of space, such as motorways and other intermediary links like airports and gasoline, bus and train stations as 'non-places': 'a dense network of means of transport which are also inhabited spaces is developing; where the habitué of supermarkets, slot machines and credit cards communicates wordlessly, through gestures, with an abstract unmediated commerce; a world thus surrendered to solitary individuality, to the fleeting, the temporary and ephemeral'.[9]

Augé's non-spaces are redolent of heterotopias that are based on exclusion. For Foucault, writing in the 1960s, the American motel is the exemplary space of exclusion, a private yet public place, which we may liken to the interior of the ubiquitous automobile.[10] This idea of the road or landscape as a psychical space is emphatically explored in the work of John Stezaker (fig.83), the outside space being a signifier for the interior or human psyche.

One of the most emphatic spaces to be explored within art photography has been the street. As already discussed (see p.70), Charles Baudelaire's figure of the *flâneur*, the lone stroller, usually male, who observes as a non-participant the activities of those on the street, was taken up by European painters in the late nineteenth century and redeveloped by photographers ever since.[11] The street photographers' view of this

Figure 83
John Stezaker,
Mask XCI 2009
Collage, 24.5 × 18.5

ready-made world is an environment in which the camera represents these fleeting encounters in different ways. Some of these encounters are bruising, others are poetic, critical, sarcastic, ironic, unpleasant, sad or exciting. The street photography encounter is as global as the streets that offer them their politically, socially and legally liberal space in which to happen.

These spaces or non-places through which one comes and goes, and the transitory and fleeting ephemeral encounters with them, can be contrasted with those places charged with accumulating time: libraries, museums, archives and machines for data storage, such as the internet. These are all heterotopias of time, which accrue historical materials. As Foucault puts it, these places represent 'the desire to contain all times, all ages, all forms, all tastes in one place, the idea of constituting a place of all times that is itself outside time and protected from its erosion'.[12] (Photography might well be included in this list too, as seen on p.199,

12 Foucault 2000, p.182.

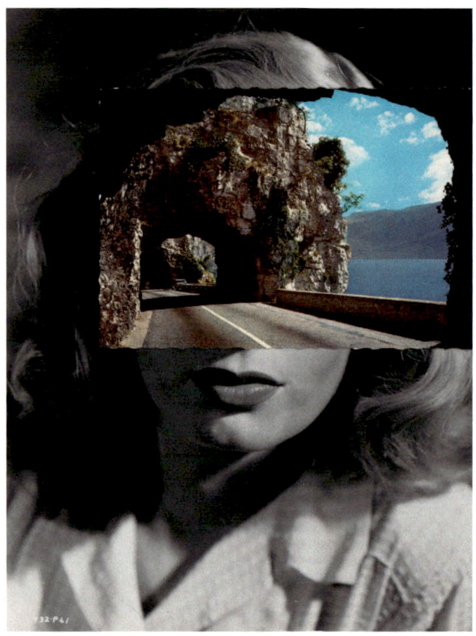

but I will not deal with this here.) So when art photographers like Thomas Struth, Candida Höfer, Louise Lawler, Lewis Baltz and others train their cameras on these places, they prompt a contemplation of the functions of collected time. The photographs are not themselves timeless, but quite specific in time.

The primary colours in Candida Höfer's photograph of the Düsseldorf Museum (fig.84) – the yellow of the hallway on the left, the separate red, yellow and blue volumes distributed on the bookcases – provide a focus in the otherwise flat geometry of the furniture. The strong rectilinear bookcases create associations with Mondrian's universalist abstract paintings. The different volumes of books prompt a contemplation of knowledge held within them: encyclopaedias of artists, exhibitions, catalogues and art history. Books embody the remnants of systems of thought, and the basis of historical knowledge. The various bound books behind glass are visible, yet closed; what is in them remains invisible. The books represent archives, both tangible and forgotten, residues of the past that remind us of who we are and perhaps how a culture has become what it is now.

Foucault describes festivals, both ancient and modern, holidays and fairs as 'chronic heterotopias' because of the way they abolish time for the duration of the event. All such festivities, carnivals, parties and equivalent celebrations generate an imagined, exoticised space that breaks away from workaday life, disrupting social norms, if not overturning, reversing or abandoning them altogether. These spaces are often geographically located elsewhere, and include those spaces for initiation or rites of passage that necessitate a removal from ordinary life, such as the honeymoon or youthful vacation. It is clear that vast numbers of photographers have also extensively explored these types of spaces and the activities they encompass in multiple ways, and across many different geographical locations. Perhaps it is indeed the fleeting transience of these heterotopias that, like street photography, makes them so attractive to photographers.

Figure 84
Candida Höfer,
Museum Kunstpalast, Düsseldorf VII 2011 2011
C-print, 160 × 293.3

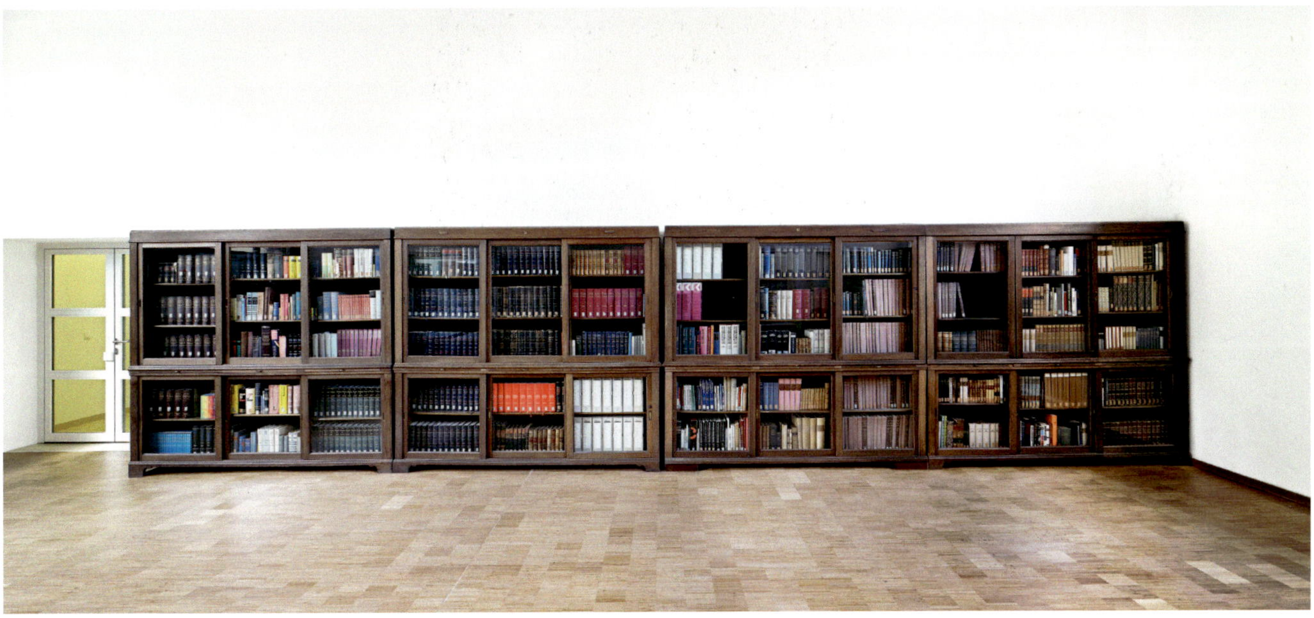

There is a dual attraction, not only in the fleetingness of the events, but also the potential capacity of photography to record or to 'capture' them. The beach or holiday resort, the 'leisure destination', is a prime example of this fascination. Putting together some of the different work from this theme can enable us to glimpse some of the different approaches taken or pursued. In a more extensive study, we would also begin to grasp the cultural and global discrepancies of different geographical imaginations of these heterotopias in different parts of the world.

Beach Image

The beach is certainly a popular theme among European photographers, who have explored its space in very different ways. Rineke Dijkstra's portraits of teenagers on resort beaches make a study of the uncertainty of their transitional age. Youthful bodies wearing only swimwear are seen on the cusp of adolescence, all in slightly awkward poses with the sea functioning as a backdrop. As in classical myth, it is a symbolic site

Figure 85
Rineke Dijkstra, *Kolobrzeg, Poland, 26 July 1992* 1992
Chromogenic print, 121 × 101
From the series *Beach Portraits*
Tate

Dijkstra created the series of twenty *Beach Portraits* (formerly known as *Bathers*) between 1992 and 1998.

of birth or rebirth, and indeed, reviewers often refer to Botticelli's painting of Venus rising from the sea and note the same posture in Dijkstra's Polish model seen here (fig.85). However, whereas Botticelli's Venus emerges on a shell, Dijkstra's figures stand on the beach, located firmly between sea and land, literally a marginal space of transition between one place and another. The figures remain at the edge, in a space of uncertainty that can be identified with the precariousness of adolescent social and sexual maturity. The sea is also one of the great signifiers of the voyage, of exotic adventure and piracy, social transgressions, romance and encounters with strange creatures and mythical islands. The beach is a reality that, on the edge of a land, invites real and imaginary departure from the everyday world and its rules. At the beach there is a breeze of freedom. Change is in the air, at least for as long as the holiday lasts.

The Italian photographer Massimo Vitali's high-resolution photographs give an elevated view of the beach, in which the details of all the people

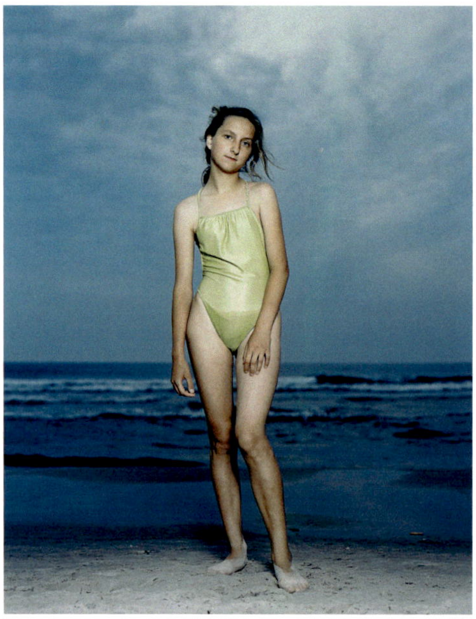

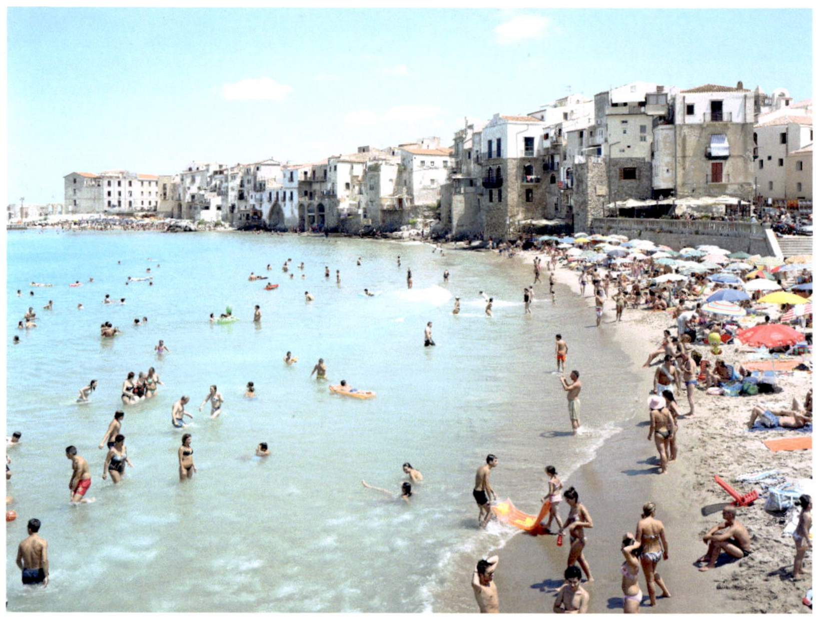

Figure 86
Massimo Vitali, *Cefalù Nonna* 2008
Chromogenic photographic print with Diasec mount, 180 × 220

and their activities are just discernible (fig.86). The light tones of the photograph are resonant of that moment when your eyes are suddenly opened in bright sunlight – everything is overexposed. This vivid illumination of the photographic scene adds to the imagined impression of being at the beach. Vitali's photograph, and the others in the series, makes us conscious of the multitude of individuals, couples, families and friends, and the spatial dynamics between social groups on the beach. The sea and surrounding land are part of the spatial environment too, a space shared in most bathing destinations. With the sociological gaze that this type of picture encourages us to adopt, we may well become all too conscious of our own looking, aware that we are tourists too. Whether we look at individual people, their bodies, clothes, faces, postures, gestures or their interactions with others, we can nevertheless identify with them on many levels. We might also become aware of the ritualistic habits of the beach, and its community of people in various states of undress. We might even feel embarrassed as we catch ourselves lingering

13 Ibid., p.183.

14 David Lynch's popular TV series *Twin Peaks* (1990–1), and dozens of other dramas in cinema, literature and television, begin with the finding of a corpse of a young woman, often on the beach. See Anikka von Hausswolff 2004, p.19.

over some figures longer than others. Vitali's picture reflects this chronos or time scene back to us as we stand before his large photographic prints in a gallery, or browse them in a book, perhaps at home. The work makes us conscious of the disjunction between the space shown and the location in which we are viewing them. There is also something of the spectacle about these general scenes too, their large scale offering us abundant information.

Descriptive photography like this throws the task of interpretation back onto the viewer. Such pictures ask: why are we looking at this scene? What do you want to *see*? At a safe distance, far from the beach, and through the behest of the photographer, we are offered a picture that gives no answers; it may even seem baffling as to why we should look at it. Foucault describes vacation villages as offering 'three short weeks of a primitive and eternal nudity to city dwellers'.[13] The notion can be extended to beach holidays, and Vitali's work exploits this situation. The partial nudity of beaches enables him and us to look at these bodies at a safe distance from them. The experience of the photograph itself offers up a kind of heterotopic space, one that we can occupy from afar. Today the

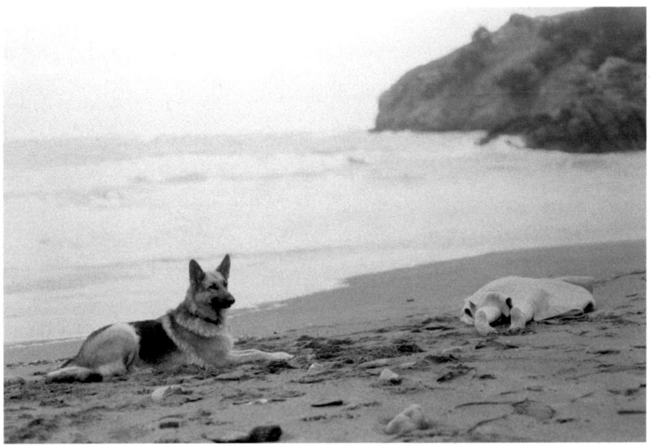

Figure 87
Annika von Hausswolff, *Hey Buster! What do you know about Desire?* 1995
C-type print on MDF-board, 180 × 240

notion of 'getting away' signified by these photographs is precisely the desire to reach a heterotopia – no matter how geographically proximate to 'home'.

The beach figures as a liminal space in the Swedish artist Annika von Hausswolff's *Hey Buster! What do you know about Desire?* 1995 (fig.87). The German shepherd dog is attentive and alert. A woman's dead body is under a blanket or towel and the disturbed sand suggests a struggle. The corpse in this cold-looking scene is the reverse of the idealised image of Venus, the allegorical figure for love emerging freshly from the sea. Here, the woman is dead, undesired. The attentive guard dog is looking at something or someone out of frame, but we do not know what or who. The title of the work asks directly: what is desire for you? While the dog may know, we neither know what happened, nor why.

As the artist notes, an image of a woman's corpse is 'such an incredibly potent and telling symptom of our culture and the image of women within it.'[14] Here it plays part of an allegory, which, like a crime story, requires us to piece together clues to construct meanings as metaphorical propositions, rather than any literal narration of events. The picture asks the spectator questions not only about the meaning of the picture itself, but our own assumptions as to what it means. The troublesome woman, the hapless victim, the discarded wife are negative values that may typically converge in such an image – which is part of its point. In allegory, it is left to the spectator to figure out what to do with the elements of a picture or text, like pieces of an incomplete jigsaw puzzle. As in a crime story, the action has already happened, its outcome equally tragic and melancholic. The picture functions as a series of clues, and the dog, too, can be subject to such readings. This type of dog, for example, is often associated with police or guard duties, a signification connected to authority and power. In art history, dogs often signify fidelity, although here we do not know to what or whom. Buster, do you know what your desire is here? It is as though the picture asks the question: the ruin of woman is at the cost of whose desire? Hausswolff purposely leads us towards these issues, but we must interrogate them ourselves as author via the heterogeneous elements of the picture, which do not add up simply to any final verifiable or resolved meaning.

Allan Sekula's late photographic works take us in and on the sea itself as a space of work: of global shipping and the manual labour associated with sea work. Sekula's photographs observe the vast industry of international freight, and track its social and environmental consequences. Oceans and docks, as sites of labour and capital, tell a partial story of the sea. Sekula's metonymical realist art remains allegorical, using fragmentary images to achieve their effect, opening up a space for the imagination that is as uncharted as the ordinary person's view of the sea. As a type of heterotopia, nautical geography remains invisible even if a catastrophe makes the news. Sekula writes of the history of the sea and its representation as fading from the imaginary of modernity.[15] The iconography of ocean liners and holiday cruises, so popular in the early twentieth century, have all but faded in the wake of the aeronautical ideal of flight as the dominant mode of contemporary escape. The romance of the sea is now consigned to history, but Sekula shows its massive importance still as a global transport system. Foucault, of whose work Sekula was very aware and which he references, notes that: 'the ship is a piece of floating space, a placeless place, that lives by its own devices, that is self-enclosed and, at the same time delivered over to the boundless expanse of the ocean, and that goes from port to port, from watch to watch ... you see why for our civilization ... the ship has been at the same time not only the greatest instrument of economic development, of course ... but the greatest reservoir of imagination.'[16]

We may gauge the power of this reservoir of nautical imagination by simply noting the name of the royal yacht that used to carry Queen Victoria around the British Empire: it was called *Fairy*. Today the historical imagery of the ship has been usurped by other iconographies, which are perhaps equally transient and unstable, and a greater modern 'reservoir of imagination'.

Homely and Unhomely

The idea of inhabited space, with which this chapter began, finds its quintessence in the idea of home. Home is the space of the intimate. This identification of life with dwellings suffuses our language, which

15 See Sekula 1995.

16 Foucault 2000, pp.184–5.

17 Bachelard 1969, p.5.

is why when a loved one dies or a relationship ends we might say we feel 'derelict'. Buildings and people can both be condemned or given a new look. The home and its components provide very strong psychological images: the functions and furnishings of rooms, chairs, tables, sofas, wardrobes, carpets, beds, mats, floors, cellars, garages, spare rooms and hallways lend themselves to psychological usage. An empty chair can signify an absent person, a carpet is rolled out to denote a welcome, the cellar can become a hellish place of terror, and so on. We know our home before we know other places, and so it is coded individually as well as

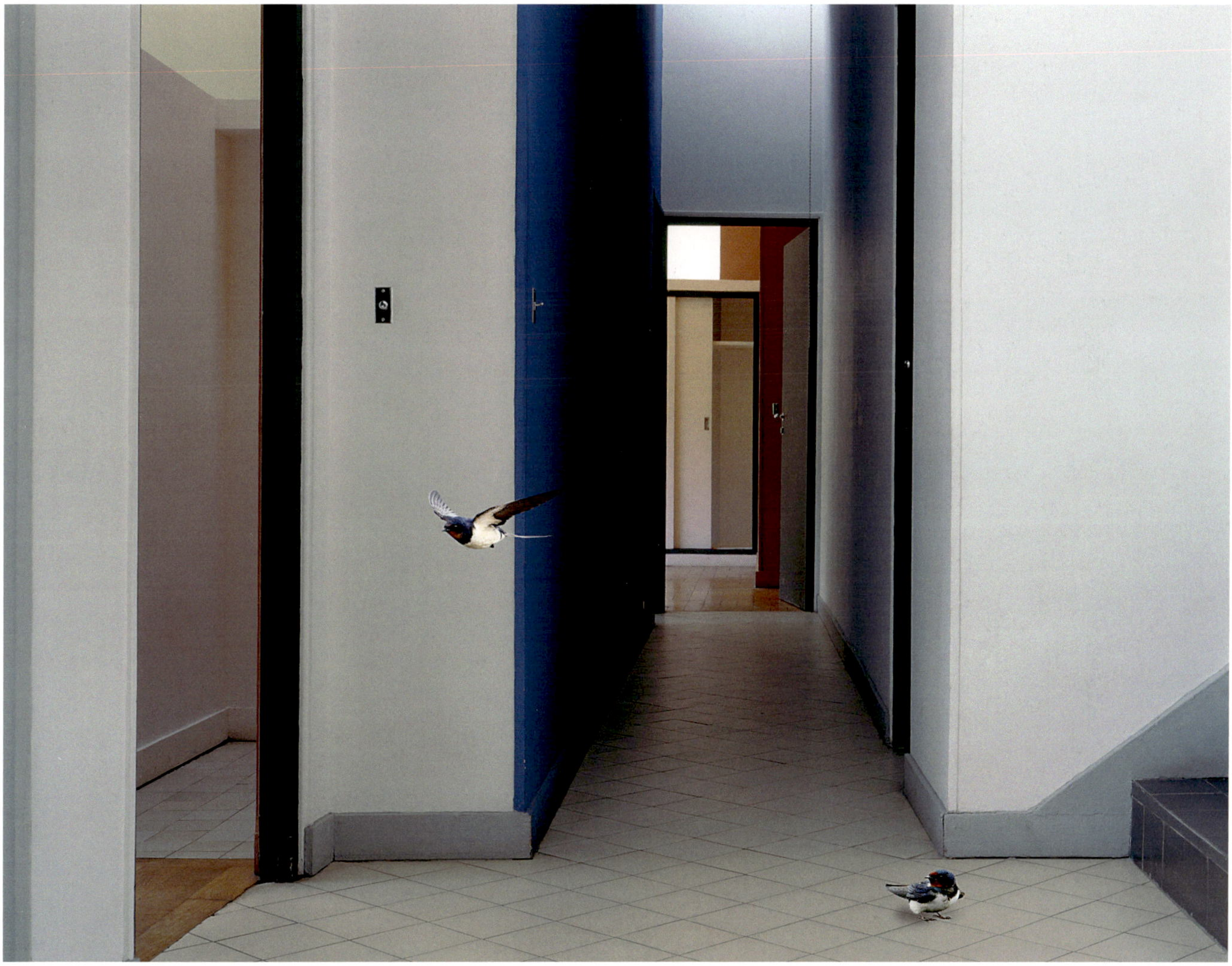

Figure 88
Karen Knorr,
The Passage (Villa Savoye) 2004–8
Lambda c-photograph, Fuji Cristal Archive print, 70 × 90 and 122 × 152

culturally, although as Bachelard noted, 'all really inhabited space bears the essence of the notion of home'.[17] Home is where we find shelter, an intimacy, which may not be in the dwelling actually called 'home'. As cinema, novels and many artists and photographers have shown, homes can become unhomely, with parts of them totally unfriendly. In fact these unfriendly components may not be hidden at all, but visible in the full glare of daylight.

Modern architecture, like much avant-garde culture of the early twentieth century, sought to exorcise these ghosts. Glass walls and transparent screens opened up domestic spaces and offices to eradicate the nooks

Figure 89
Thomas Demand,
Büro /Office 1995
C-print on Diasec
mount, 183.5 × 240

Like all of Demand's images, this is based on an existing location and photographs of it.

and crannies where evil spirits, as much as dust and dirt, were conceived as hiding. Transparency and the obliteration of shadowy areas, however, can lead to agoraphobia, or at least to the desire to recede within a translucent or more opaque space.[18] Any space without frontiers throws into question the idea of place or, for the human subject of modernity, troubles the idea of intimacy within it.

18 See, for example, Beatriz Colomina, 'The Split Wall: Domestic Voyeurism', in Colomina 1992.

When Karen Knorr photomontages birds into the rooms of Le Corbusier's 1929 Villa Savoye (fig.88), she investigates this symptom of anxiety that modernist space produces. The birds situate geometrical points within the photographic space of the home. As a fable of stability,

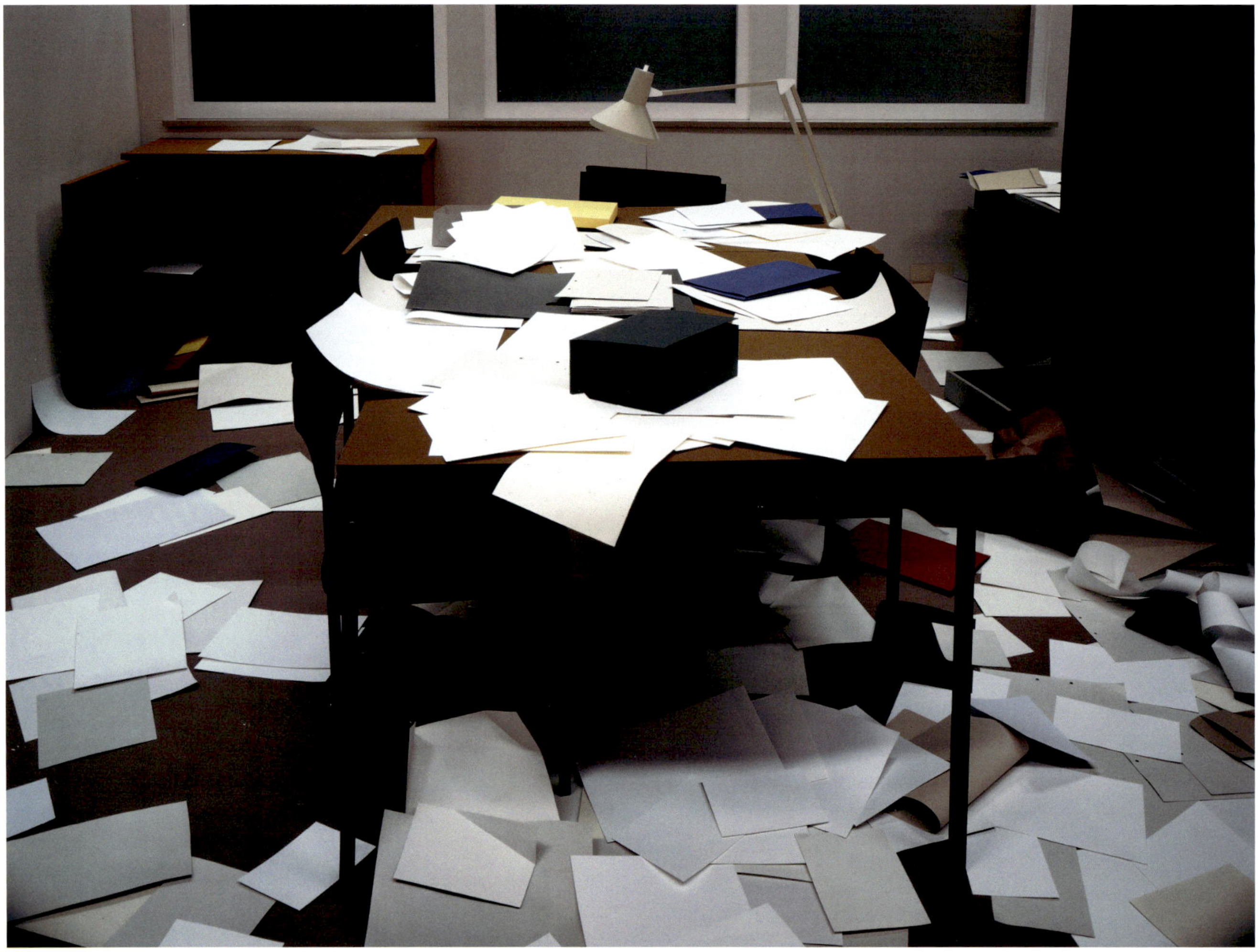

This looted Stasi office, after the collapse of East Germany, is a reinterpretation of the original as a life-size paper model, which Demand then photographed. The model is destroyed, leaving the photograph as an original image.

nature traditionally offers an image of certainty, which perhaps can exist only as a dream-image now, given our consciousness of human-caused environmental disasters. Filling the emptiness of the modern home space is a way of living in it, turning it into an inhabited place, and not an abstract space. (Hence showroom houses do not seem lived in.) Clutter belongs to the everyday pathology of life, which some may love, others merely tolerate or hate.

Thomas Demand's *Office* 1995 (fig.90), a photograph of a meticulous 1:1 scaled model made entirely of paper (which was destroyed after photographing), replicates the unhomely chaos of a ransacked office. It is

19 Bachelard 1969, p.37.

based on an image of the East German Ministry of State Security, or Stasi, headquarters in Berlin after it was stormed by protestors in January 1990. The picture's artifice resonates with the blankness of bureaucracy and the disorder that came with the regime's demise. The chaos is also symptomatic, through allegory, of the private lives that were disturbed by the collection of secrets by Stasi spies, active and disguised throughout the populace. We would hope to be able to consider the home a retreat from such abusive interferences in intimate lives.

Helen Sear's photographic image of a hut, *Unnamed* 2000 (fig.89), offers an even more remote retreat. This intimate, anonymous refuge in a tangle of woods is different in dynamic from the sort of place we tend to imagine as 'home'. The hut stands alone, a private space amidst the woods – a place for solitude, not loneliness. The home or hut is singular, the house is plural, or as Bachelard puts it, the house is 'a world in itself.'[19] Here the hut is like a bastion of the self, a space enclosed by wildness, which is excluded, expelled as not-the-self. In contrast, the plurality of the house extends to its different components, where even

Figure 90
Helen Sear,
Unnamed 2000
Lambda print, 74 × 77

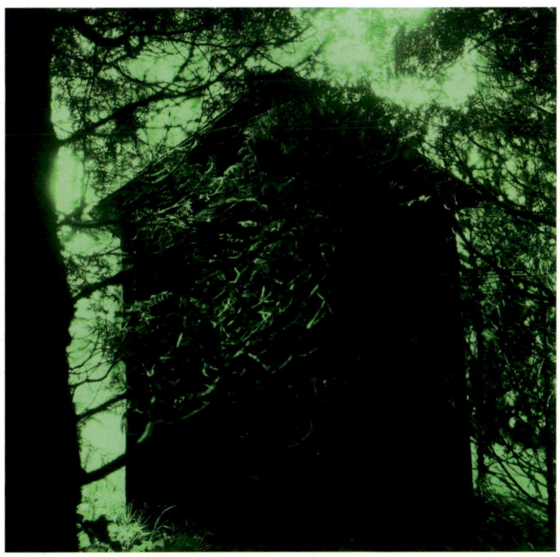

the idea of a bed, whether in a home, hospital or hotel, gives rise to many psychological images of inhabitation, relating to different aspects of our lives: birth, death, illness, sex, love, marriage, sexual politics, and even the simple everyday routines and rituals of life. Similarly, in Carrie Mae Weems's photograph from her *Kitchen Table* series (fig.91), the kitchen is a space of community and friendship, but also of dispute, conflict and fear. A character plays solitaire, biding her time as we watch and she waits. The kitchen remains a social space par excellence, a focus for the family and friends alike. We are accustomed to seeing the kitchen in advertising, cinema, television and literature as the site of harmony, intimacy, engaging conversation, arguments or even violence. It is hard not to read such images in relation to this repertoire of emotional states. The camera remains in the same position throughout Weems's series, and the subjects seem oblivious to it. In this way, the viewer is definitively stationary and a passive observer – no participation is implied here.

This outsider viewpoint is quite unlike Jo Spence's snapshot colour photographs, which insinuate the viewer into a direct and intimate encounter. As a photographer who looked at intimate questions of the body, the proximity and direct address of the picture to the camera and audience may still make some viewers uncomfortable, since it implicates them in a 'me-other' relationship. Her pictures depict aspects of Spence's life within a hospital setting, and focus on her desires and fears as a patient.

Spence's work about her experience of treatment for cancer takes the body as the site of 'home', of 'who I am'. Throwing off the cloak of decency, or in this case her medical gown, Spence exposes the sense of disunity and fragmentation she experienced (fig.92). Ostensively, through a form of phototherapy, she enacts anger and pain at the camera. The geometric space of the human body itself comes under assault, not only from the medical gaze to which this picture was addressed, but also to the psychical image of her body.

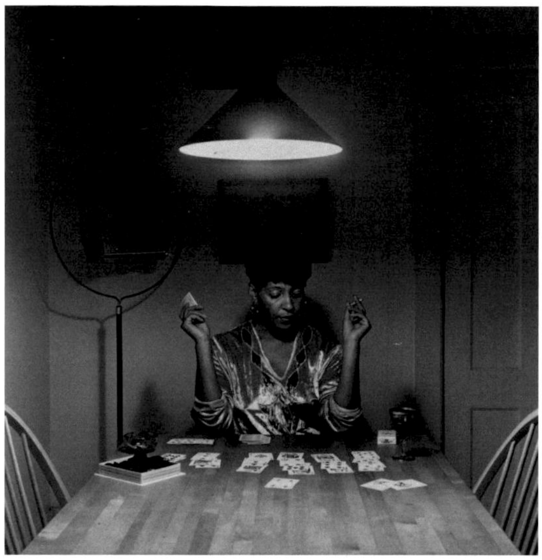

Figure 91
Carrie Mae Weems, *Untitled (Woman Playing Solitaire)* from the Kitchen Table Series 1990
Silver gelatin print, 69.2 × 69.2
Art Institute of Chicago

It has long been noted that the coherence of the body as a spatial image is not bound by geometrical space, even if photography tries to fit us back into it, via images.[20] If the mirror is the heterotopic space of our idealised selves, photography has become its mobile equivalent, not least in the new genre of the selfie. Notwithstanding that photographic images have a very powerful impact on how we see others, they now even more clearly inform how we see ourselves. The fragmented body or dis-membered corpse in a photograph has an effect, reminding us of the fragility of our own psychological image of our bodies too. This is true not only in specifically traumatic practices, like war photography, but also in ordinary images of bodies, which are expected to be perfect and judged against other images.

Formally, the conventional harmony expected between figure and background of any photograph, and the geometrical space that it generates, offers a space to be 'inhabited' by the viewer. But historical avant-garde strategies, upon which Spence and other contemporary photographers draw, undo the normative relations of geometrical space. No doubt any landscape – a term that fuses geographic space and pictorial framing

20 See, for example, the discussion by Victor Burgin in Burgin 1996.

– involves a sense of place located in space. This location of the viewer at a stable point is why photography has remained so central as a technology even in its digitised forms. The photograph is a scenographic space in which a whole set of activities, whether human or otherwise, fictive or real, can occur.

The early twentieth-century proliferation of collage and montage – 'the completely free combination of "fragments of reality",' as Franz Roh called it in 1930[21] – introduced a fragmentation of classical geometrical space, which had been so centrally established as the technological norm of photographic representation. Although photography has come to epitomise spaces describable by Euclidean geometry, these montage practices, like cubism before them, were an attempt to break with this classical mode, and to reformulate visual space in radically different ways.[22]

21 Franz Roh, 'The Value of Photography', 1930, in Phillips 1989, p.162.

22 For a summary of these visual issues relating to photography, see David Bate, 'The Automatic Image', in Bate 2004.

We can see how the avant-gardes initiated new ideas, then how post-war conceptual art and certain strands of 1980s postmodernist art and

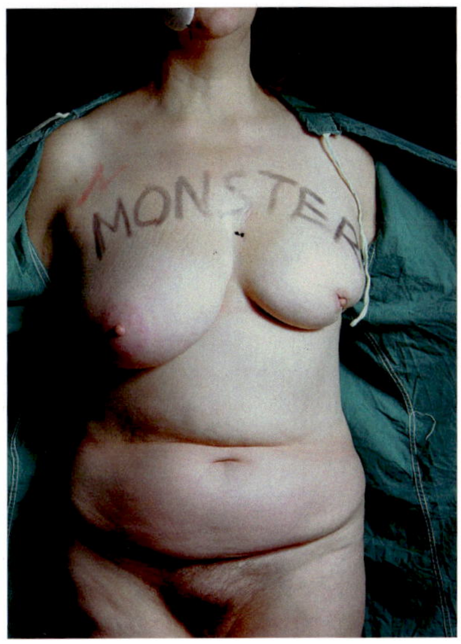

Figure 92
Jo Spence (in collaboration with Tim SHEARD), *Exiled: Narratives of Dis-ease* 1990
C-print, 42 × 60

photography began to revive them through the use of montage, text, quotation and overtly constructed and theatrical spaces. All these tactics aim in different ways to construct or deconstruct a new and different space for culture. In idealised visions, the different cultural place provided by photography offers an innovative technological world of virtual space. However, in the dissensual aftermath of 'new technologies' we may again find an interest in avant-garde tactics.

Analog-Digital Space

Computers have not, on the whole, led us outside geometrical space, but back into it, re-confirming Euclidian geometry through computer simulations, albeit now multiplied across transient screens. The new-old digital image of inhabited place and geography is dispersed across different photographic and computer spaces. The computer is perhaps the ultimate modern heterotopia: contradictory, real and unreal at the same time. Perhaps this spatial dispersal is simply a more accurate or appropriate way of representing the psychological aesthetics of contemporary human space. Infinity, in spatial terms, is no longer a singular abstract and

Figure 93
Amy Stein, *Groceries*
2007. From the
Domesticated series
Chromogenic print,

homogeneous geometrical point in space, a vista, but of multiple and heterogeneous spaces, as Foucault had insisted. Yet, this comes suspiciously close to the idea of a utopia, where power structures lurk in wait for us. We would do well to consider the other work of Foucault, in which power is installed precisely through the operations of space.

One response to the new computer heterotopia was to declare the digital photograph as 'post-photographic' and merely a form of 'data space'. As a computer code in a set of algorithms, the classical aesthetics of pictorial space is rejected, converted back into the digital primary code from which it was constructed. Like the structuralist films of the 1970s, artists are called to return to the specificity of the medium, to consider computer images as form, as data within what is, in effect, a new techno-modernist paradigm of discourse about digital photography. Digital abstraction becomes another universal language, like Mondrian's desire for a universalist picture. The effect is to also return the viewer to 'pure' data code, whose legibility requires specialist knowledge. The idea of accessibility that drove the agenda and manifestos of avant-garde photography is lost to a post-visual domain of metadata, of viral tags and algorithmic computing structures. In an echo of the dematerialisation of the object in conceptual art, the new techno-modernism dematerialises the representational image into abstraction. So it is no coincidence that art photography in this field begins to resemble abstract paintings. Photographic space is purified of its capacity for social reference and retreats into a technological space.[23] No longer a geometrical space in the classical sense of a pictorial image, it is nevertheless a space we can inhabit. In a very different way, we are returned to the issue raised by Bachelard earlier in this chapter: 'inhabited space transcends geometrical space'. Just as the sunset seeks to replace geometrical experience of geography with psychological effect, so too did many of the early avant-garde and their descendants in art, albeit with very different ambitions. These ambitions were often political or social and seen as ways to change the social world.

The return of attention to *visual* space in digital photography recalls these almost forgotten histories of analogue photographic experimentation, which aimed to produce new forms of photographic image space. From the material photograms of William Henry Fox Talbot to Hannah Höch's layering, abstracting, erasing and adding of elements, from the psychical photograms of Man Ray to Lazlo Moholy-Nagy's spatial dynamics, photo-experimentation is linked with new models of vision. It remains to be seen on what terms new forms will emerge from the digital spaces that now occupy the contemporary human imagination. The dream of clearing out the old spaces begins again.

23 See, for example, Squiers 2014.

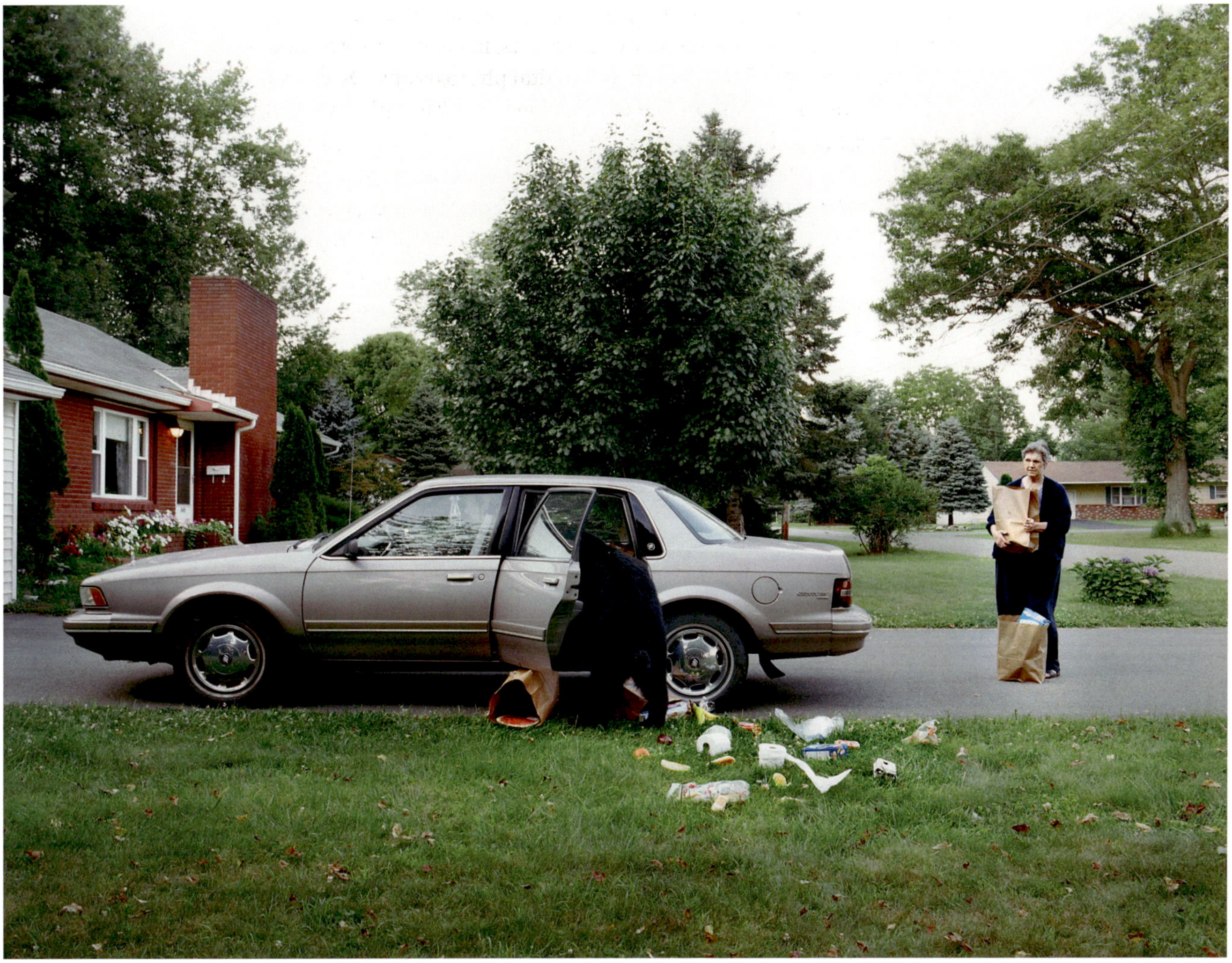

SELECT BIBLIOGRAPHY

Svetlana Alpers, *The Vexations of Art: Velàsquez and Others*, London 2005

Eugène Atget, *Photographe de Paris*, New York 1930

Marc Augé, *Non-Places: An Introduction to SuperModernity*, London 1992

J.L. Austin, *How To Do Things With Words*, Cambridge 1975

Gaston Bachelard, *The Poetics of Space*, trans. M. Jolas, Boston, MA 1969

Gerry Badger and Martin Parr, *The Photobook: A History*, vol.1, London 2004

George Baldwin *et al.* (eds.), *All the Mighty World: The Photographs of Roger Fenton, 1852–1860*, London 2004

Stephen Bann, *Parallel Lines: Printmakers, Painters and Photographers in Nineteenth-Century France*, London 2001

Yto Barrada, *A Life Full of Holes: The Strait Project*, London 2005

Roland Barthes, 'Death of the Author', in *Image-Music-Text*, London 1981

Roland Barthes, *Camera Lucida: Reflections on Photography*, London 1984

Roland Barthes, 'The Reality Effect', in *The Rustle of Language*, Oxford 1986

Roland Barthes, *The Responsibility of Forms*, London 1991

Roland Barthes, 'The World as Object', in *A Roland Barthes Reader*, London 2000

David Bate, *Photography and Surrealism*, London 2004

Charles Baudelaire, *Art in Paris, 1845–1862: Salons and Other Exhibitions Reviewed*, London 1965

Charles Baudelaire, 'The Salon of 1859', in *Modern Art and Modernism: A Critical Anthology*, eds. F. Frascina and C. Harrison, London 1982

Charles Baudelaire, *The Painter of Modern Life and Other Essays*, trans. J. Mayne, London 2012

Walter Benjamin, 'The Short History of Photography', in *Classic Essays on Photography*, ed. A. Trachtenberg, New Haven 1980

Walter Benjamin, *One Way Street and Other Writings*, London 1985

Walter Benjamin, 'The flâneur', in *Charles Baudelaire*, London 1989, pp.00–00

John Berger, *Ways of Seeing*, London 1972

Anne-Marie Bernard, *The World of Proust, as seen by Paul Nadar*, London 2002

Benjamin Buchloch, 'Conceptual art 1962–1969: from the aesthetic of administration to the critique of institutions', *October: The Second Decade, 1986–1996*, Cambridge, MA 1997

Victor Burgin, 'Photography, Phantasy, Function', in *Thinking Photography*, London 1982

Victor Burgin, *The End of Art Theory: Criticism and Postmodernity*, Basingstoke 1986

Victor Burgin, 'Geometry and Abjection', in *In/Different Spaces*, California, 1996

Victor Burgin, *Situational Aesthetics: Selected Writings*, Leuven 2009

Luis Camnitzer, Jane Farver and Rachel Weiss (eds.), *Global Conceptualism: Points of Origin, 1950s–1980s*, New York 1999

Alejandro Chaskielberg, *La Creciente*, Portland 2011

Clément Chéroux (ed.), *Mémoire des camps: photographies des camps de concentration et d'extermination Nazis, 1933–1945*, Paris 2001

T.J. Clark, *The Painting of Modern Life: Paris in the Art of Manet and His Followers*, London 1990

Beatriz Colomina, *Sexuality and Space*, New York 1992

Wanda Corn, *The Great American Thing: Modern Art and National Identity, 1915–1935*, London 1999

Thomas Crow, *The Rise of the Sixties*, London 1996

T.J. Demos (ed.), *New Perspectives in Photography*, London 2006

Jacques Derrida, *Archive Fever: A Freudian Impression*, London 1996

Jacques Derrida, *Copy, Archive, Signature: A Conversation on Photography*, Stanford 2010

Robert Desnos, 'Spectacles of the Street – Eugène Atget', *Le Soir*, Paris, 11 September 1928, repr. Phillips 198.

Josef Maria Eder, *History of Photography*, trans. E. Epstean, New York 1978

Samuel Y. Edgerton, *The Renaissance Rediscovery of Linear Perspective*, London 1976

Samuel Y. Edgerton, *The Mirror, the Window and the Telescope*, London 2009

Douglas Eklund (ed.), *The Pictures Generation, 1974–1984*, London 2009

Peter Henry Emerson, *Naturalistic Photography*, New York 1890

Walker Evans, 'The reappearance of photography', *Hound and Horn*, 5, no.1, 1931

Walker Evans, interview, *Art in America*, 59, March–April 1971, p.87

Hal Foster, 'The archival impulse', *October*, 110, Cambridge, MA 2004

Hal Foster et al., *Art Since 1900*, London 2004

Michel Foucault, *The Order of Things*, London 1980

Michel Foucault, 'Different Spaces', in *Aesthetics: Works*, vol.2, London 2000

Sigmund Freud, 'Repression', in *Pelican Freud Library*, vol.11: *On Metapsychology*, Harmondsworth 1984

Michael Fried, *Why Photography Matters as Art as Never Before*, London 2008

Peter Galassi, *American Photography 1890–1965*, New York 1995

Helmut and Alison Gernsheim, *L.J.M Daguerre: The History of the Diorama and the Daguerreotype*, New York 1968

Helmut and Alison Gernsheim, *The History of Photography*, London 1969

Jean-Luc Godard and Anne-Marie Miéville, *The Old Place*, Munich 2006

Nicholas Green, *The Spectacle of Nature*, Manchester 1990

Clement Greenberg: The Collected Essays and Criticism, ed. J. O'Brian, vol.2, London 1986

John Hammond, *The Camera Obscura: A Chronicle*, Bristol 1981

Margaret F. Harker, *Henry Peach Robinson: Master of Photographic Art, 1830–1901*, Oxford 1988

Anikka von Hausswolff in dialogue with Sara Arrhenius, Lund 2004

Charles C. Hill, *John Vanderpant: Photographer*, Ottawa 1976

Eric Hobsbawm, *The Age of Revolution: 1789–1848*, London 1997

David Hockney, *Secret Knowledge: Rediscovering the Lost Techniques of the Old Masters*, London 2001

Katherine Hoffman, *Stieglitz: A Beginning Light*, London 2004

Robert Hooke, 'An instrument of use to take the draught or picture of any thing', in *Early Science in Oxford*, ed. R.T. Gunther, vol.7: *The Life and Work of Robert Hooke*, pt II, Oxford 1930, pp.753–6

W.M. Hunt, *The Unseen Eye: Photographs from the Unconscious*, exh. cat., London 2011

F. Jack Hurley, *Portrait of a Decade: Roy Stryker and the Development of Documentary Photography in the Thirties*, New York 1972

Ryuichi Kaneko and Ivan Vartanian (eds.), *Japanese Photobooks of the 1960s and '70s*, New York 2009

J. Kirk, T. Varnedoe and T.P. Lee, *Gustave Caillebotte: A Retrospective Exhibition*, Boston 1976

Joseph Kosuth, *Art After Philosophy and After*, London 1991

Liz Kotz, *Words to Be Looked At: Language in 1960s Art*, London 2007

Gotthold Lessing, *The Laocoön: An Essay on the Limits of Painting and Poetry*, London 1984

David C. Lindberg, *Theories of Vision from Al-Kindi to Kepler*, London 1976

Lucy R. Lippard, *Six Years*, London 1997

Lucy Lippard and John Chandler, 'The Dematerialization of Art', in *Conceptual Art: A Critical Anthology*, eds. A. Alberro and B. Stimson, London 2000

Mike Mandel and Larry Sultan, *Evidence*, New York (1977) 2003

Charles Merewether (ed.), *The Archive: Documents of Contemporary Art*, London 2006

Barbara L. Michaels, *Gertrude Käsebier: The Photographer and Her Photographs*, New York 1992

Catherine Morris and Vincent Bonin (eds.), *Materializing Six Years: Lucy R. Lippard and the Emergence of Conceptual Art*, London 2012

Laura Mulvey, 'Visual pleasure and narrative cinema', in *Art After Modernism: Rethinking Representation*, ed. B. Wallis, New York 1984

Molly Nesbit, *Atget's Seven Albums*, London 1992

Beaumont Newhall, *The Daguerreotype in America*, New York 1976

Linda Nochlin, 'Death in the Mid Nineteenth Century', in *Realism*, London 1978

Linda Nochlin, *Women, Art, And Power and Other Essays*, London 1989

Linda Nochlin, 'Mary Cassatt's Modernity', in *Representing Women*, London 1999

Thomas Padon and Alison Nordstrom (eds.), *Truth Beauty, Pictorialism and Photography as Art, 1845–1945*, Vancouver 2008

Erwin Panofsky, *Perspective as Symbolic Form*, New York 1997

Christopher Phillips (ed.), *Photography in the Modern Era: European Documents and Critical Writings, 1913–1940*, New York 1989

Christopher Phillips, 'The judgment seat of photography', in *The Contest of Meaning: Critical Histories of Photography*, ed. Richard Bolton, London 1996

Stephen Pinson, *Speculating Daguerre: Art and Enterprise in the Work of L.J.M. Daguerre*, London 2012

Griselda Pollock, *Vision and Difference*, London 1988

Jean-Bertrand Pontalis & Jean Laplanche, *The Language of Psychoanalysis*, London 1988

Marcel Proust, *In Search of Lost Time*, ed. C. Prendergast, London 2003

Kathleen Pyne, *Modernism and the Feminine Voice*, London 2007

Jacques Rancière, *The Future of the Image*, trans. G. Elliott, London 2007

Jacques Rancière, *Dissensus: On Politics and Aesthetics*, London 2010

Henry Peach Robinson, *Pictorial Effect in Photography: Being Hints on Composition and Chiaroscuro for Photographer*, London 1869

Henry Peach Robinson, *The Elements of a Pictorial Photograph*, London 1896

Henry Peach Robinson, *Picture-Making by Photography*, London 1902

Martha Rosler, *Decoys and Disruptions: Selected Writings 1975–2001*, London 2004

Martha A. Sandweiss, *Laura Gilpin: An Enduring Grace*, Fort Worth 1986

Larry J. Schaaf, *Tracings of Light: Sir John Herschel and the Camera Lucida*, San Francisco 1989

Larry J. Schaaf, *Out of the Shadows: Herschel, Talbot and the Invention of Photography*, London 1992

Larry J. Schaaf, *The Photographic Art of William Henry Fox Talbot*, Oxford 2000

Aaron Scharf, *Art and Photography*, Harmondsworth 1979

Allan Sekula, 'The body and the archive', in *The Contest of Meaning: Critical Histories of Photography*, ed. R. Bolton, Cambridge, MA 1992

Allan Sekula, *Fish Story*, Rotterdam 1995

Allan Sekula, *Performance Under Working Conditions*, Vienna 2003

Abigail Solomon-Godeau, 'Canon Fodder: Authoring Eugène Atget', *Photography at the Dock*, Minneapolis 1995

Lucy Soutter, *Why Art Photography?*, London 2013

Carol Squiers (ed.), *What is a Photograph?*, New York 2014

Phillip Steadman, *Vermeer's Camera*, Oxford 2001

Olga Sviblova, Elena Misalandi, *Quiet Resistance: Russian pictorial photography, 1900–1930s*, Moscow 2005

John Tagg, 'The archiving machine, or, the camera and the filing cabinet', in *Grey Room*, 47, Spring 2012

Alan Trachtenberg (ed.), *Classic Essays on Photography*, Leetes Island 1980

Ian Walker, *City Gorged with Dreams*, Manchester 2002

Jeff Wall, *Catalogue Raisonné, 1978–2004*, Göttingen 2005

Martin Warnke and Claudia Brink (eds.), *Der Bilderatlas Mnemosyne*, Berlin 2000

Terri Weissman, *The Realisms of Berenice Abbott*, London 2011

John White, 'The Development of Artificial Perspective', in *The Birth and Rebirth of Pictorial Space*, London 1987

John Willett (ed.), *Brecht on Theatre*, London 1964

Raymond Williams, *Culture and Society*, London 1979

Raymond Williams, 'Art', in *Keywords*, London 1983, p.42

Janet Wolf, 'The invisible *flâneuse*: women and the literature of modernity', *Feminine Sentences*, Cambridge 1990

Sylvia Wolf, *Ed Ruscha and Photography*, New York 2004

Elizabeth Wright, *Postmodern Brecht: A Re-Presentation*, London 1989

CREDITS

Copyright

© Vito Acconci p.85
© Keith Arnatt Estate. All rights reserved. DACS 2015 p. 90
© John Baldessari p.102
© Yto Barrada p.126
© Chris de Bode p.103
© Victor Burgin p.89, p.94
© Sophie Calle/ADAGP, Paris and DACS, London 2015 p.118
© Alejandro Chaskielberg p.52
© Gregory Crewdson p.51
© Salvador Dali, Fundació Gala-Salvador Dalí, DACS, 2015 p.116
© Thomas Demand, VG Bild-Kunst, Bonn / DACS, London p.138
© Raymond Depardon
© Riniki Dijkstra p.134 (fig.85)
© Succession Marcel Duchamp/ ADAGP, Paris and DACS, London p.91
© Robert Frank p.78
© Robert Frank from The Americans p.130
© Nan Goldin p.54
© 2015 David Goldblatt p.74
© Andreas Gursky. Courtesy: Sprüth Magers Berlin London/ DACS 2015 p.32
© Susan Hiller. All Rights Reserved, DACS 2015 p.112
© John Hilliard p.92, front cover
© 2015 Candida Höfer, VG Bild-Kunst, Bonn p.133
© Tom Hunter p. 16, back cover
© Georgia O'Keeffe Museum / DACS, 2015 p.40, p.91
© Yves Klein, ADAGP, Paris and DACS, London 2015 p.82
© Joseph Kosuth/ARS, NY and DACS, London 2015 p.86
© Louise Lawler p.108
© Richard Long/ DACS, 2015
© Carrie Mae Weems p.140
© Boris Mikhailov p.73
© Tracey Moffat p.111
© Abelardo Morell, courtesy of Edwynn Houk Gallery, New York p.15
© Zwelethu Mthethwa p.38
© Karen Knorr p.137
© Richard Prince p.96
© Doug Rickard, courtesy Yossi Milo Gallery, New York p.71
© Thomas Ruff/ DACS 2015 p.77
© Ed Ruscha p.98, p.100
© Die Photographische Sammlung/SK Stiftung Kultur - August Sander Archiv, Cologne; DACS, London, 2015
© Helen Sear p.139
© Cindy Sherman p.96
© Lorna Simpson p.95
© 2015 Succession Raghubir Singh p.69
© Jo Spence p.141
© Hannah Starkey p.49
© John Stezaker p.132
© Thomas Struth p.41, p.110
© Hiroshi Sugimoto p.129
© Larry Sultan and Mike Mandel p.114
© Penelope Umbrico p.124
© Massimo Vitali p.134 (fig.86)
©Annika von Hausswolff. Moderna Museet, Stockholm p.135
© Jeff Wall pp.42-43, p.45
© Gillian Wearing p.80

Image sources

Amon Carter Museum of American Art, Fort Worth, Texas p.48 (fig.29)
Courtesy of The Approach, London p.132
The Art Institute of Chicago p.58 (fig.38), p.140
Courtesy Ben Brown Fine Arts p.133
Bibliothèque Nationale de France p.6, p.22, p.58 (fig.39)
Boltin Picture Library/ Bridgeman Art Library p.28
© Centre Pompidou, MNAM-CCI, Dist. RMN-Grand Palais / Adam Rzepka p.57 (fig.37)
Photo: Rémi Chauvin Image Courtesy of Roslyn Oxley9 Gallery and MONA Museum of Old and New Art, Hobart, Tasmania, Australia p.111
Die Photographische Sammlung/ SK Stiftung Kultur - August Sander Archiv, Cologne p.64
Courtesy of the artist and Gagosian Gallery p.32, p.98, p.100
Courtesy of George Eastman House, International Museum of Photography and Film p.20
The Granger Collection, NY/Topfoto p.27
Solomon R. Guggenheim Museum, New York p.51
Photo: Teresa Healy, Vancouver Art Gallery p.46
Courtesy Jackson Fine Art p.61
Courtesy of the artist and Jack Shainman Gallery, New York p.38
Library of Congress, Washington pp.66-67
Magnum Photos p.104
Courtesy the artist and Marian Goodman Gallery, Johannesburg p.74
Courtesy of the artist and Marian Goodman, New York p.102
Courtesy of the artist and Mark Moore Gallery, LA p.124
Courtesy Maureen Paley, London p.49, p.80
Courtesy of the artist and Metro Pictures, New York p.96, p.108
©2015. Image copyright The Metropolitan Museum of Art/ Art Resource/Scala, Florence p.30, p.47, p.96
Photo by : Ellen Montelius p.34
© Museum of the City of New York p.59
© 2015. Digital image, The Museum of Modern Art, New York/Scala p.48 (fig.30)
© National Media Museum / Science & Society Picture Library - All rights reserved p.12, p.14 (fig.3), p.23, p.25, p.33, p.129
Courtesy Pace Gallery, London p.126
Courtesy Pace/MacGill Gallery, New York p.78, p.130
Panos Pictures p.103
Philadelphia Museum of Art, Pennsylvania, PA, USA / Bridgeman Images p.44
Private Collection p.91
RMN-Grand Palais (Musée du Louvre) / Gérard Blot p.57 (fig.36)
© RMN-Grand Palais (Musée d'Orsay) / Hervé Lewandowski p.36
© RMN-Grand Palais (Musée d'Orsay) / Jean Schormans p.35
© The Royal Photographic Society p.14 (fig.4)
Courtesy of the artist and Salon 94, p.95
Courtesy the artist and Richard Saulton Gallery p.141
Photo: Shunk-Kender © Roy Lichtenstein Foundation p.82
Staatliche Kunstsammlungen Dresden/ Bridgeman Art Library p.16 (fig.6)
Courtesy of the artist and Sprüth Magers Berlin London p.32, p.86, p.138
© Amy Stein p.143
© Tate Photography p.77, p.88, p.90, p.112, p.116, p.118, p.134 (fig.85)
Time Life Pictures/ Getty Images p.56
© The Trustees of the British Museum p.106
Courtesy Yossi Milo Gallery, New York p.71

Every effort has been made to contact the copyright holders. The publisher apologises for any errors or omissions and would be grateful to be notified of any corrections that should be in future reprints or editions of this book.

ACKNOWLEDGEMENTS

I am most grateful to the staff at Tate Publishing, in particular Nicola Bion, Project Editor; Juliette Dupire, Production Controller; and Miriam Perez, who worked tirelessly as Picture Researcher. Many thanks as well to Roger Thorp, who commissioned the book, and to Micha Weidmann Studio, who designed it.

I would also like to thank the CREAM Research Centre at the University of Westminster, whose valuable support made the publication of this volume possible.

David Bate

INDEX